EFE

Recent Titles in
Contributions to the Study of Mass Media and Communications

Freedom for the College Student Press: Court Cases and Related Decisions
Defining the Campus Fourth Estate Boundaries
Louis E. Ingelhart

The Press and the Decline of Democracy: The Democratic Socialist
Response in Public Policy
Robert G. Picard

Innovators and Preachers: The Role of the Editor in Victorian England
Joel H. Wiener, editor

Press Law and Press Freedom for High School Publications: Court Cases
and Related Decisions Discussing Free Expression Guarantees and
Limitations for High School Students and Journalists
Louis E. Ingelhart

Free Flow of Information: A New Paradigm
Achal Mehra

Shared Vulnerability: The Media and American Perceptions of the
Bhopal Disaster
Lee Wilkins

Communications and History: Theories of Media, Knowledge, and Civilization
Paul Heyer

Oratorical Encounters: Selected Studies and Sources of Twentieth-Century
Accusations and Apologies
Halford Ross Ryan, editor

Transnational Media and Third World Development: The Structure and
Impact of Imperialism
William H. Meyer

Predictions of Public Opinion from the Mass Media: Computer Content
Analysis and Mathematical Modeling
David P. Fan

Papers for the Millions: The New Journalism in Britain, 1850s to 1914
Joel H. Wiener, editor

EFE

Spain's World News Agency

Soon Jin Kim

Contributions to the Study of Mass Media and
Communications, Number 15

GREENWOOD PRESS
New York • Westport, Connecticut • London

Library of Congress Cataloging-in-Publication Data

Kim, Soon Jin.
  EFE : Spain's world news agency / Soon Jin Kim.
    p. cm. — (Contributions to the study of mass media and
communications, ISSN 0732-4456 ; no. 15)
  Bibliography: p.
  Includes index.
  ISBN 0-313-26774-X (lib. bdg. : alk. paper)
  1. Agencia Efe—History. 2. Press agencies—Spain—History.
I. Title. II. Series.
PN5311.A34 1989
070.4 ′35—dc20   89-7529

British Library Cataloging in Publication Data is available.

Library of Congress Catalog Card Number: 89-7529
ISBN: 0-313-26774-X
ISSN: 0732-4456

First published in 1989

Greenwood Press, Inc.
88 Post Road West, Westport, Connecticut 06881

Printed in the United States of America

The paper used in this book complies with the
Permanent Paper Standard issued by the National
Information Standards Organization (Z39.48-1984).

10 9 8 7 6 5 4 3 2 1

To my late father
and my aged mother

Contents

Tables and Figures

TABLES

FIGURES

Preface

The Spain of this book is not the land of carousing bullfighters and Bizet's *Carmen*. The Spain of this book is not the land of sun-drenched beaches for foreign tourists or the works of Velázquez and Picasso. The Spain this book depicts is "the fourth power of the Western world," as claimed by EFE news agency's president Ricardo Utrilla Carlón (1983 – 1986). And that is not a Quixotic romance or satire.

Spain occupies the number 4 Western position only after the United States, Great Britain, and France, for its news agency, EFE, is the fifth-largest after the "Big-4" news services: the Associated Press (AP), United Press International (UPI), Reuters, and Agence France-Presse (AFP).

Yet Spain's news agency is little heard of outside Hispanic countries. Unbeknownst even to press circles in the non-Hispanic world, EFE grew into an international communications giant by the mid-1980s, in the half-century since it was chartered in (1938 – 1939) during the Spanish civil war.

In its operational scope, this hidden world news complex, EFE, far outdistances West Germany's Deutsche Presse-Agentur (dpa), Italy's Agenzia Nazionale Stampa Associata (ANSA), or Japan's Kyodo.

Spain does not have to hark back to its glory days of the conquistadores of yesteryears to claim its place in the world. EFE is an earth-girdling communications empire, owing —to be sure— to Spain's American colonial heritage.

This book traces the Francoist origin, growth, democratic metamorphoses, and future potentials of Spain's world news agency. It is a definitive record of the hidden communications giant, "La Agencia EFE, S.A." (EFE Agency, Inc.). It traces the 50-year history of this state-owned agency's growth into the fifth largest Western news service. It analyzes EFE's shifting relationships with the successive Spanish governments —from the Francoist autocracy, through the post-Franco transition, to the present-day democracy. Particular attention is paid to EFE's roles in the democratizing process in Spain since 1975.

This book tries to prognosticate the proper role of a national news agency in the democratizing process of a nation once subjugated to the 40-year iron rule of a right-wing dictator. This is the only systematic study of the West's fifth-ranking news agency anywhere —in Spain, Europe North and Latin America. There is no known professional or scholarly analysis of the EFE news agency —not even a journal article.

In my 14-year (1961–1974) practice and teaching of journalism in Central America, I became familiar with the operations of the EFE news agency and its Isthmian subsidiary, ACAN (Agencia Centro Americana de Noticias). (The latter —a model for the formation of a regional news agency— is the only remaining vestige of the once prosperous Central American Common Market, now shattered by the political upheavals in those Isthmian republics.)

In addition to professional use of EFE and ACAN, I spent the year 1985 at EFE's Madrid headquarters, retrieving and organizing documents and data on EFE's history and operations. I conducted many interviews with former and current EFE executives, and with the old and new political and press personages of Spain. I exhausted the sources at the public and university libraries and archives in Spain. I visited many EFE bureaus in both Western and Eastern Europe, in the Americas, and in the Far East. I also paid visits to the central headquarters of the "Big 4" and ANSA for comparative perspectives.

That, then, is the genesis and meaning of this work.

NOTES ON STYLE

1. NON-ANGLICIZING. This book does not follow the common practice of Anglicizing many Spanish words, such as "Seville" for "Sevilla"; or Queen "Sophia" for "Sofía."

2. UNIVERSAL DATING. Dates are expressed in the more universal style of day-month-year (e.g., 18 July 1936) which eliminates 2 cumbersome commas as in "On July 18, 1936, Franco led. . . ."

3. NUMERALS. All cardinal numerals except one are uniformly expressed in Arabic figures. The only exceptions are: (1) when a cardinal number commences a sentence; (2) in citations of statements using spelled-out numbers; and (3) the words "million" and "billion." Ordinal numbers are spelled out below 20th. Percentage is expressed with the % sign.

4. *PESETA* (Spanish money). The letter *P* will represent *pesetas* in Spain's monetary units (e.g., P200 for 200 *pesetas*).

5. NAMES OF EFE UNITS. EFE's organizational units carry idiosyncratic Spanish titles, and their English version ofen does not convey the true sense. EFE has complicated the problem by its own haphazard Anglicizing with various awkward and misleading translations. This author retains his own English rendition of EFE's unit titles. (e.g., EFE administrative council, not EFE board of directors; publication control department, not editing department).

Acknowledgments

Many persons on both sides of the Atlantic contributed to the completion of this book. Only a few outstanding names can be acknowledged here besides a list of interviewees at the end of the book.

Dr. Angel Benito Jaen, dean of the Faculty of Information Sciences of Complutense University of Madrid, gave unstinting support during my sabbatical in 1985 in Madrid for the use of the university library and other facilities, and in obtaining the help of journalism students for content analyses of EFE wires. One of those students, Gonzalo de Salazar (and his father and his aunt, herself an EFE journalist) gave sincerely of their time and efforts in frequent vain searches for unobtainable documents. Professor José Altabella Hernández, an erudite Spanish press historian and ardent guardian of forgotten historical records, supplied me with invaluable documents from the 1940s on EFE.

EFE's top management of 1985 accorded me all-out assistance in my research for this book, although our purposes were at odds by nature. EFE president Utrilla had given blessing to the initiative of executive editor Manuel Velasco to give me office space with a computer in EFE's Madrid headquarters, (obviously a promotion effort). When an "official" EFE history did not result, "Manolo" Velasco was froced to resign in 1986. It was a sad, unavoidable story.

During the writing stage of this book (1986–1987) back in the United States, 2 intellectuals made this work possible. Edward J. Levenson, a former student of mine and now a professional friend working at the Pennsylvania daily *The Intelligencer*, edited my original 600-page manuscript. A capable and detached editor, he kept me in proper perspective when I tended to get mired in a sea of data.

Howard H. Frederick, formerly of Ohio University and now at the California State University – San Bernardino, a sincere friend and ideological colleague, helped during the spring months of 1988 in paring the manuscript to 350 pages. This I could not have carried out, for I was too infatuated with the original version.

The book also enjoyed intellectual encouragement from some distinguished writers on Spain in the United States, including Stanley Payne of the University of Wisconsin at Madison, Robert Whealey of Ohio University, and James Cortada of IBM at Madison.

The research activities for this book in Spain, Europe, and Latin America would not have been possible without a $20,000 grant from the Tinker Foundation of New York and understanding help from its chairman and president, Martha Twitchell Muse.

Towson State University at Baltimore, where I have toiled since 1975, has accorded me with research, time-release, and sabbatical grants for my work on EFE since 1983. Towson State's reference librarians have all been helpful. Robert E. Shouse has opened up new library resource fields to me, while Marcella Fultz came up miraculously with rare Spanish books that I could not find even in Spain. Printing Center's Larry Dernetz also greatly helped.

This book has been a family endeavor. My wife, Aie Love, accompanied me on my Madrid sojourn and my research treks all over Western and Eastern Europe. My U.S. college–educated daughters —raised earlier in Central America— also pitched in: Sori Azalea Meredith helped with expert computer production of the manuscript; Mari Eco read every single word and held a tight rein over her "father's flowery English"; Kari assisted with graphic works; and Yuri Crystal kept order in the endless sheaves of manuscript pages.

Dr. James T. Sabin, executive vice president of Greenwood Press, lived up to his reputation for his creativity and care for scholarly works. Greenwood's Maria E. Bulgarella demonstrated her superior intellectual versatility in copyediting the manuscript. Production vice president Susan Baker and production editor William Neenan moved the book efficiently through the final production stage.

Soon Jin (Jim) Kim

Abbreviations and Names

ABBREVIATIONS

DGP: Director General of Press at the Directorate General of Press, the feared press czar of the Franco regime.

MIT: Ministry (or Minister) of Information and Tourism established in 1951 to exercise press control.

LPI: The 1966 Law [on] Press and Printing (*Ley de Prensa e Imprenta*) —with "voluntary consultation"— that "liberalized" the 1938 Press Law.

PSOE: Partido Socialista Obrero Español (Spanish Socialist Workers Party), in power since 1982 under Premier Felipe González Márquez.

FREQUENTLY APPEARING NAMES

ANSON OLIART, Luis María: EFE president, 1976–1982.

FRAGA IRIBARNE, Manuel: minister of information and tourism, 1962–1969.

GÁLLEGO CASTRO, Vicente: EFE founding director, 1938–1944.

GÓMEZ APARICIO, Pedro: First EFE subdirector; director, 1944–1957.

MENDO BAOS, Carlos: EFE director, 1966–1969, "took" EFE to Latin America.

SERRANO SÚÑER, Ramón: EFE's "godfather"; Franco's brother-in-law, nicknamed *"Cuñadísimo"*; interior and foreign minister, 1937–1942.

UTRILLA CARLÓN, Ricardo: EFE president, 1983–1986.

VELASCO LÓPEZ, Manuel: EFE executive editor, 1983–1985.

Hispanic names can be confusing. Full names usually consist of 2 given names and paternal and maternal surnames or family names. Under normal circumstances, only the paternal surnames are used. When either or both surnames are compounded with a hyphen, complexity ensues. Also, when a surname consists of more than a word, for example, De Leon or De la Serna, the problem is compounded. A married woman's name has *de* (of) before her husband's name. Take, for example, the name, *MARÍA DEL CARMEN JOSÉ ARIAS-SALGADO DE LA SERNA DE GIMÉNEZ-ARNAU*. In this case, *María del Carmen* and *José* are the 2 given names, *Arias-Salgado* and *De la Serna* are paternal and maternal family names, respectively, and María is the wife "of" (*de*) a man whose name is compounded with a hyphen, *Giménez-Arnau*. This woman's second given name, *José*, is another complication. Not infrequently, Spaniards are given a second name of the opposite gender in deference to a family ancestor or for other reasons. *José María* is very common among men. As if rejoicing in the confusion of foreigners, some Spaniards and Latin Americans prefer their maternal surnames to the paternal, like in the case of *Pablo (Ruiz y) Picasso* and the current EFE president, *Alfonso (Sobrado) Palomares*. Some "maternal-namers" even use their paternal names in abbreviation, like the English middle initial.

EFE'S HALF CENTURY
SHIFTS IN GOVERNMENT & EFE MANAGEMENT (1936–1989)

Year	Nation Government — Epoch	Premier	Other	CHAPTER	EFE Agency — President	Director
	AUTOCRACY					
	Civil War (3 years)			P		
1936		Franco 7.18		T		
1937			Serrano 4.19 (cuñadísimo)	E R		
				1	Foundation Era	
1938	Press Law 4.22				EFE Group	
1939						
	World War II (6 years)			2	Nazi Era	
1939					Noriega 1.3	Gállego 1.3
1940					Pabón 1.1	
1941			Arias 5.20			
1944						Gómez 7.13
1945						
	Isolation (6 years)			3	Isolation Era	
1945						
1950						
	Peace (15 years)			4	Peace Era	
1951			MIT 7.20			
1957						De Mier 1.1
1958						Aznar 2.5
1960						-Vacant-5.1
1962						Sentís 2.1
1965					Sentís 6.10	Mendo 6.10
	Moderation (4 years)			5	Mendo Era (Latin America)	
1966	New LPI 3.18				Toledo 10.1	
1967					Mateu 2.23	
1968					Aznar 9.24	
1969			Sánchez 10.30		Armesto 12.1	
	Regression (6 years)			6	Armesto Era (Central America)	
1970						
1975		Arias 12.10	Fraga 12.10			
	DEMOCRACY					
	Transition (7 years)			7	Anson Era (World)	
1976			MCSE		Alfaro 2.12	Mendo 2.12
--76		Suárez 7.3			Anson 9.30	Anson 10.12
1981		Calvo 2.25				
1982		González 12.2				
	PSOE Rule (4 years)			8	Utrilla Era (U.S.A.)	
1983					Utrilla 1.25	Utrilla
1986						
	PSOE Rule II (3 years)				Palomares Era	
--86					Palomares 11.1	Palomares
1989						

(Numbers after action or name show **month.date** of action or each man's appointment.)
(**CHAPTER #** in the book discusses the respective national "epoch" and EFE "era")

FIGURE 1: The past half century of Spanish history marked 8 distinct EPOCHs, in which the premiers/ministers in charge held tight rein over EFE's development in 8 ERAs parallel to the goverment changes.

EFE

Prologue

The Spanish Were Coming (1936–1986)

Five computer printers were quietly busy as usual. But there was an unusual tension in the air just outside of the third-floor suite of executive editor Manuel "Manolo" Velasco López in the Madrid headquarters of Spain's news agency, EFE. All principal wire services were spewing out thousands upon thousands of words about the 10 May 1985 return to Washington of U.S. president, Ronald Reagan, after a 10-day European swing. For the past fortnight, the news of the world had been dominated by his controversial visits to a Bitburg cemetery, to Bonn for a 7-nation summit, to Madrid, Spain, to the Parliament of Europe at Strasbourg, and to Portugal.

Velasco's attention, however, was anxiously fixed on obscure short items from Washington unrelated to the big news. Earlier that spring, the EFE news agency had offered to buy all operations in Spanish of the United Press International (UPI), and the EFE management was still waiting for a formal response from the Western world's second-largest news agency. Sitting in his presidential suite 2 rooms away, EFE president Ricardo Utrilla constantly talked on the phone with his Washington bureau chief without getting any satisfactory information, even though the correspondent was working out of the EFE bureau on the ninth floor of the UPI building itself.

Two weeks earlier (28 April), a $45-million deficit had forced the UPI management to file for protection from its creditors under the U.S. Federal Bankruptcy Act. Then, EFE's president had made an offer to buy all the Spanish operations of UPI to owners William Geissler and Douglas Ruhe in New York, and also to president Nogales in Washington. Relations between the 2 factions had been ugly; both were interviewing prospective UPI buyers separately. But all 3 UPI executives had received EFE's offer "with the greatest interest."

That Saturday morning, 11 May 1985, the European edition of *USA Today* circulated in Madrid with a cover story about the UPI crisis in its economic section. That piece revealed to the world public, including the Spanish, UPI's economic straits, already well publicized among the international press circles. EFE president Utrilla and executive editor Velasco could not wait anymore. They made a decision to go public with the EFE bid for part of the second-biggest world news agency, as if that would make the UPI–EFE deal a fait accompli.

On Saturday afternoon, all EFE circuits including its English service transmitted an 8-paragraph news wire datelined MADRID, in which Utrilla announced the EFE offer to purchase "all the Spanish-language operations of United Press International (UPI)."[1] This item was carried in the Sunday editions of all Spanish papers. The Spaniards thus learned that EFE, their government news agency, had joined a multinational bidding war for UPI. Throughout the rest of the year 1985, EFE was in the UPI fray rubbing shoulders with such world communications giants as the British Reuters and the Financial News Network (FNN), a partner of Merrill Lynch & Co., Inc.

By June 1985 Reuters, which had purchased the UPI international picture service 3 years previously, was the first to drop out of the competition for UPI ownership. Press accounts had named as many as a dozen individuals and companies that at one time or another expressed interest in buying UPI.[2]

SPANISH – UPI CONNECTIONS

Since 1983, EFE had played a role in relation to UPI, unbeknownst even to the U.S. press circles. As will be described in chapter 8, EFE and UPI had collaborated in a joint Spanish-language radio news program entitled "Nuestras Noticias" ("Our News"), which aired 17 times daily throughout the United States and Canada from the studios in the ninth-floor suite of EFE in the UPI headquarters in Washington, D.C. But until the 1985 UPI bidding contest, the Spanish news agency EFE had been very little known outside of the Hispanic communities of the world.

Formally chartered during the waning days of the Spanish civil war on 3 January 1939, EFE had grown into a hidden world communications giant by the mid-1980s. The EFE agency now staffs 73 bureaus and offices on 5 continents with 1,640 employees worldwide. EFE serves about 620 Spanish and 1,600 foreign subscribers. In its operations, EFE definitely is the top Spanish-language service: it transmits daily more than 500,000 words worldwide and dispatches about 125,000 words each day to its clients in Latin America by 17 circuits, utilizing the INTELSAT satellite over the Atlantic Ocean. EFE maintains exchange agreements with 33 major international and national news agencies of the West, East, and the Third World.

EFE's relationship with UPI (formerly UP) dates back to April 1945. Then, EFE contracted the services of the United Press with exclusive national distribution rights, given by the neutralist Franco regime, in an opening gesture toward the United States, which was emerging as the victorious world leader from World War II. In the 40 years since then and 10 years from the demise on 20 November 1975 of the dictator Francisco Franco, Spain and its news service EFE had come a long way. Now in 1985, the Spanish news agency was bidding for the ownership of its former provider. *The Spanish were coming, the Spanish were coming!*

By November 1985, the ownership war for UPI was turning in favor of a joint bidding by Mario Vázquez Raña and Joseph Russo. UPI president Nogales and Washington bankruptcy court judge George Bason both expressed favorable consideration for a $40-million-plus offer for UPI from Vázquez, owner of 70 Mexican newspapers, and Russo, a Houston land developer, with 90 and 10% shares, respectively. The Financial News Network (FNN) quickly countered this Vázquez–Russo bid by forming a consortium with several other contenders and presenting an improved proposal to the 2 principal UPI shareholders —Geissler and Ruhe. These 2 UPI owners requested permission from creditors and the bankruptcy court to study the "better offer by FNN" on 12 December 1985.

High-ranking FNN executives and lawyers traveled to Madrid to court their Spanish colleagues for EFE's participation in the FNN consortium. With the FNN representative frequenting the EFE hallways, an excited EFE executive editor Velasco discounted the press accounts from the United States over the pending Vázquez-Russo victory, and confided that "you haven't heard the last of UPI yet." Velasco mouthed one of the obvious FNN arguments that "U.S. subscribers will resist a 'Mexican take-over' of UPI" and he fondled with a possible future dateline of "FNN–EFE" news.[3] To the Spanish, it was a heady elating idea to own —or at least partially own— the world's No. 2 news service. *Definitely, the Spanish were coming!*

THE FEAR OF EVERYTHING

Up until Franco's death in November 1975— only a decade before EFE's UPI bid— Spain had been in the backwaters of Europe, somnolently underdeveloped in defiant isolation behind the Pyrenees ranges. Spain under Franco had been a pariah state and the Spanish had withdrawn from European affairs. How could the same Spaniards, in 10 short years, gather up the valor to partake in this multinational contest for the ownership of the West's second-largest press association, the United Press International?

Juan Luis Cebrián, editor of *El País* (*The Country*), the new leading Madrid daily, told a U.S. journalist in 1985 that Spaniards' loss of fear was "the most important" change that had occurred in Spain during the decade since the demise of Franco. The Spaniards had lost the "fear of speaking, fear of writing, fear of traveling, the fear of everything, . . . "[4]

Spain under Franco

How had this pervasive fear of everything been formed in Spanish society? How had it been instilled into the minds of the Spaniards, the proud descendants of the Conquistadores of the New World of yesteryears? And, how had the same fear dissipated in 10 short years? To put the development of EFE in a historical perspective, a brief synopsis is called for on the events of the past 53 years in Spain since 1936, with special attention focused on its press. During that half-century, Spain lived through —in 8 distinct political EPOCHs— the civil war, 40-year dictatorship, post-Franco transition, and democratic growing pain. (Reference to Figure 1 on p. xix will facilitate the tracing of these 8 political EPOCHs of Spain. [The chapter numbers in Figure 1 correspond to the paragraph numbers below.])

1. Civil War (1936–1939). On 18 July 1936, General Franco led the military rebellion against the Second Republic founded in 1931.[5] The rebels were supported by the conservative business class and the Catholic Church. In the ensuing civil war, the Republican Loyalists and the rebelling Nationalists both sought help from abroad. The rebelling Nationalists immediately appealed to, and received air force and land troops, tanks, and artillery from Nazi Germany and fascist Italy. The Western countries simply protested while doing nothing. Only the Soviet Union countered the Nazi violation of "nonintervention," by giving arms to the Republicans who also had domestic and foreign backing from socialists and various liberal sympathizers. And the Communist International took the initiative in recruiting the International Brigades. Thousands of volunteers from many countries responded, including the United States' "Abraham Lincoln Brigade."

The bloody civil war ended on 28 March 1939 when the Nationalists entered the starving capital city of Madrid. The war left about 1 million Spaniards dead or displaced in Spain or exiled abroad. Upon winning the civil war, the Nationalists installed the harshest and longest-lasting autocracy in Spanish history with Generalissimo Franco as the chief of state, (*El*

Caudillo [The Leader]). It ended only upon his demise in late November 1975.

2. World War II (1939–1945). The Second World War erupted barely 6 months after the Spanish civil war, which was called the prelude to the world conflagration. Having been aided by Nazi Germany and Italy in his domestic war, Francisco Franco maintained a "prudent neutrality," clearly in favor of the Axis during most of the 6 years of World War II. It was not until the waning days of the Third Reich that Franco converted his "nonbelligerence" to a real, not only "formal," neutrality. Throughout World War II, the Spanish press was totally subjugated to the Nazi propaganda machine both in Spain and in the German efforts in Latin America.

3. International Isolation (1945–1950). For his pro-Axis neutrality, Franco suffered an open hostility of the Allies after World War II and exclusion from the United Nations. Most countries withdrew their ambassadors from Madrid. The Franco regime skillfully used this international ostracism to rally the Spaniards to unity under the Falange movement. Franco had confidence that with the East–West cold war going on, the United States soon would enlist Spain in military alliance. It occurred after the U.S. assistance to Greece and Turkey in 1948 and its intervention in the Korean War of 1950. The international isolation of Franco was short-lived.

During the late 1940s, the Spanish press came under complete censorship, controlled by the ministry of national education through the feared "Dirección General de Prensa" (DGP). The DGP established an elaborate press control apparatus denominated *consignas* (secret orders), as described in detail in chapters 3 and 5. The director general of press (also DGP) became an omnipotent press czar.

4. Fifteen–Year Peace (1951–1965). The United States led the Western rapprochement with Spain by returning its ambassador to Spain on 1 March 1951. Only 2.5 years later the U.S. signed a 5-year military and economic assistance treaty with Spain. Franco now received hundreds of millions of dollars of economic assistance in exchange for U.S. utilization of military bases in Spain. In Spanish domestic politics, the Opus Dei ("God's Work," a lay Catholic organization) steadily gained Franco's favor. The technocratic segment of the church replaced the state corporatism of the Falange with a capitalist system of market mechanism. The new policies were successeful in promoting the fast growth of international tourism and investment, which resulted in a spectacular economic expansion (a growth rate of 7% from 1962 through 1965). The Franco regime boasted of "25 years of peace" from 1939 through 1964, during which it "kept Spain out of the perils of wars."

In 1951, the ministry of information and tourism (MIT) was created to assume press control from the national education ministry. The idea was to mobilize the press as a means of national image-making for promotion of international tourism. Under that concept, a stringent press censorship was not only maintained, but upgraded into a more sophisticated operation under the iron grip of Gabriel Arias-Salgado de Cubas, who was promoted from the DGP to minister of information and tourism (also abbreviated MIT).

5. Penurious Moderation (1966–1969). During the final 10 years of his life, Franco saw Spanish society in growing ferment for political changes, a natural result of a 30-year dictatorship. He loosened up on his tight autocratic rules in all aspects of Spanish life. The "reformist" Law of Press and Printing (Ley de Prensa e Imprenta, LPI) was passed in 1966, to replace the wartime Press Law of 1938. But LPI only replaced prior censorship with "voluntary consultation." The Spanish press found the "consultation" much less comfortable to deal with than outright control. But MIT Manuel Fraga Iribarne touted the 1966 LPI as a "symbol of progress." The *Caudillo* provided slowly for transfer of powers after his departure. In July 1969, Franco nominated Prince Juan Carlos as his future successor.

6. Abrupt Regression (1970–1975). In the final years of the Franco rule, Spain oscillated between openess and regression. Fraga's "reformed" LPI, for example, was rapidly countered. A 1967 reform made the penal code more punitive and the 1968 Official Secret Law was enacted. In June 1973 Franco relinquished the premier's post to Admiral Luis Carrero Blanco though he still remained chief of state. Upon the assassination in 1973 of Carrero Blanco by the Basque separatists, interior minister Carlos Arias Navarro took over as premier. In December 1974, Arias Navarro allowed limited rights to form political associations (except for a Communist party). During these final years, the MIT post was occupied by no fewer than revolving-door ministers who were faulted for their "degenerrating" press control. On 20 November 1975, the 83-year-old dictator died.

Franco had allowed no freedom of expression, and the Spanish press was subjected to licensing, censorship, confiscations, and closures. In addition, the Falange operated the journalistic complex "Prensa del Movimiento"

(Movement Press), the most important in Spain and one of the biggest in Europe, with about 40 dailies, 2 national magazines, 2 weekly newspapers, and a news agency, PYRESA (la Prensa y Revistas, S.A., Press and Magazines, Inc.).[6]

LOSING THE FEAR

Carlos Saura, Spanish filmmaker, told a former U.S. correspondent that all Spaniards had kept a bottle of champagne in their home refrigerators. Upon Franco's death on 20 November 1975, "tremendous noises went up all over Spain, not from gunshots, but from popping of the champagne bottles."[7] With joyous toasts of relief, Spaniards bubbled to a vibrant post-Franco renaissance. In the momentous decade of 1976–1985, Spain went through eventful demoestic democratization. On the foreign front, Spain joined as a full-fledged member many international organizations such as the European Communities (EC) and the North Atlantic Treaty Organization. Metamorphoses from the "fear of everything" occurred in 2 distinct stages.

7. Transition (1976–1982). Spain became a constitutional monarchy on 22 November 1975 under King Juan Carlos. Premier Arias Navarro lifted bans on political activity but the country became extremely impatient with the slow progress of the reforms. Widespread demonstrations were staged and Arias Navarro resigned in July 1976 at the king's request. New premier Adolfo Suárez González instituted political reform quickly. The Political Reform Law was approved by a 94% vote in a referendum on 15 December 1976. A new electoral law was adopted on 15 March 1977. The numerous political parties —recently legalized— took part in the general elections for the Cortes held on 15 June 1977. The Suárez coalition, the Union de Centro Democrático (UCD), won a majority. The new bicameral Cortes legislated a new constitution, and had it endorsed in another national referendum on 6 December 1978, "Día de la Constitución" (Constitution Day).

But the UCD coalition suffered a gradual disintegration. Suárez resigned on 29 January 1981. Vice premier Leopoldo Calvo Sotelo was the nominee to succeed Suárez. As the second vote was being taken on 23 February for the Calvo nomination, a group of armed civil guards under Lt. Col. Antonio Tejero stormed into the Cortes floor, taking 350 deputies hostage. Lt. Gen. Jaime Milans del Bosch, the Valencia military commander, declared a state of emergency in his Valencia district and sent tanks to the streets. King Juan Carlos immediately secured the loyalty of other military commanders.

Some 30 military officers were tried and the coup leaders received long prison terms. The new Calvo Sotelo government was faced with many contentious issues in 1981: the passage in June of a thorny divorce law and the decision to take country into NATO.

The 28 October 1982 general elections gave a landslide victory for the Partido Socialista Obrero Español (PSOE, Spanish Socialist Workers Party), led by Felipe González Márquez, who formed a new cabinet on 2 December 1982. In these elections, Fraga Iribarne's party, Alianza Popular (AP), with 25% of the vote emerged as the main opposition party to the governing PSOE. Ever since 1982, Spanish politics has seen 2 figures vying for the leadership: PSOE's Felipe González Márquez and AP's Manuel Fraga Iribarne.

8. Democracy (1983–1989). The new parliamentary politics was played out in a new Spanish nation, in which the economy and terrorism posed a constant menace to the fragile democracy. The national unemployment kept rising from 5% in 1976 to 22% by 1985. This fermented labor unrest, and widespread strikes occurred. Francoist Spain had achieved the position of the eleventh leading industrial nation in the world, but it slipped back down to 22nd or 23rd by 1985. Despite these economic woes, Spain gained long-awaited accession to the European Communities (EC) as of 1 January 1986.

Salient also in the post-Franco era was the issue of regional autonomy —how to institute local autonomy without damaging national unity. The PSOE government forged on with the autonomy process. By May 1983, the process was completed and Spain had 17 functioning regional autonomies. But the process was fraught with many intractable problems in the Basque region, where Basque national separatists had been fighting for decades to attain an independent ETA (Euzkadi ta Azkatasuna, or "Basque Homeland and Liberty") for some 750,000 Basque people. The ETA had been notorious for the violent means it employed even under Franco's iron rule. Since 1975, the ETA had killed more than 500 persons, including 150 civil guards. The ETA claimed to be waging a "war of national liberation." However, all Spanish parties saw the ETA as "terrorists" who had to be harshly dealt with.

On the diplomatic front, democratic Spain gained accession to another international organization, NATO, in March of 1986. The PSOE had originally been opposed to Spanish membership in NATO. On assuming power, however, the PSOE gradually shifted its position and advocated NATO membership in exchange for reduction in U.S. armed forces stationed in Spain. The PSOE administration kept postponing the promised NATO referendum time after time until it built up sufficient support for its new pro-NATO position. Upsetting negative polls and prediction, the PSOE won the NATO referendum on 12 March 1986. González quickly capitalized on the referendum victory, and called an election for 22 June 1986, 4 months early. His party won an absolute majority.

In November 1986 the PSOE restructured the armed forces, appointing civilians to head the notorious civil guards and the paramilitary national police. It was the very first time in 150 years that Spanish civilians had held these military positions. The armed services' acceptance of the changes indicated how much the political climate had changed, since the death of Franco.

EFE AGENCY's PLACE

This, then, is a synopsis of 50 years of Spanish history. In that half-century, how did the Spanish agency EFE grow to the point where it could aspire to part-ownership of the giant UPI? EFE has grown through many turns and twists since the 1936 outbreak of the civil war. EFE's history has closely paralleled the political history of the revolving-door governments which have ruled the country since 1936, for EFE has always had to serve the governing administrations faithfully.

Desspite the vehement claims by all its partisan promoters and managers, EFE has always been the loyal mouthpiece of the Spanish government throughout its half-century existence. Protestation by EFE executives that the new agency has served the national interests of Spain is an abstraction, not supported by the data to be presented in this book. However, that fact does not preclude the probability that EFE may have contributed to the promotion of Spain's image abroad. Each government utilized that promoted image of Spain for its own benefit, and EFE has been more than willing to serve those partisan interests.

The fact that EFE is supported by the Spanish government should not exclude it from scientific and historical studies. Only 4 world news agencies claim to be totally free of government influence. U.S. Associated Press (AP) and United Press International (UPI), Britain's Reuters, and the West German Deutsche Presse-Agentur (dpa). An overwhelming majority —95% plus— of world news agencies are either state-owned or -supported. The nation-states of the 20th century appear highly image-conscious and they all hang their national honor on 2 conspicuous enterprises: a national airline and a national news agency.

Falange's Propaganda Agency (1938–1975)

EFE's founders thought that the very survival of "Nationalist" Spain in the civil war was dependent on a national news agency. EFE was created by partisan interest of its founders, who believed that their Francoist interest coincided with the national interests of Spain. In the early stages of the civil war, the rebelling Nationalists felt that they confronted a hostile world. The Spanish military in revolt against the Second Republic were convinced that they were given "bad press" worldwide. They felt the Western press as well as the communist press were against them. They, indeed, accused the Western press of willing or unwitting connivance with the left. They perceived international conspiracies against their Nationalist cause.

The Spanish right-wing ideologues and journalists saw an urgent need to counter worldwide "anti-Spain propaganda." They sought a means to present their own agenda in the international discourse. They wanted to present their side of the war stories. The only way to accomplish that goal was to establish a news agency under their own control. They created the EFE news agency. Its creators believed that their rightist Falangist cause coincided with what they perceived to be Spanish sovereignty over news of the war. The EFE agency vehemently defended "information sovereignty" of the Falangist Spain.

During the remaining months of the civil war and also in the 6-year World War II period, EFE was taken over by the Nazi German propaganda apparatus set up in the Iberian peninsula. EFE's functions coincided with the pro-Axis "neutralist" posture of the Franco government. After the defeat of Germany and Italy, EFE served the Franco regime well in its international isolation from 1945 to 1950. In the 1940s, the Franco regime started utilizing the EFE "news" agency to distribute its secret orders (*consignas*) to the Spanish newspapers and magazines.

In the 15-year period from 1951, EFE's role as the conduit of press control continued, when the regime went through internal power consolidation. The 1966 Press and Print Law —which was supposed to signal in a "decade of moderation"— granted EFE an exclusive right on foreign news, de facto monopoly it had exercised before. In the 1966–1975 decade of "cosmetic moderation"[8] in the autocratic rule, EFE's legal monopoly on foreign news persisted until the very end, although somewhat less conspicuously than before.

Government News Agency (1976–1989)

Under Franco's 40-year dictatorship, it was to be expected that EFE could only exist and function as the mouthpiece of the regime. There was no other function assigned to the Spanish press as a whole except to serve the dictator. In the democratic Spain since 1976, however, EFE has not yet attempted to shake loose its servitude to governments in power. This sharply contrasts with the resilient renaissance of the free Spanish press in the post-Franco era. EFE executives try to draw fine lines between a "national" and "government" news agency, claiming that the EFE news agency is a "national" enterprise not a "government" organ. The facts, however, do not support the claim.

Because of its structure, EFE can not avoid being a government news agency. And the reluctance on the part of EFE's management, and the lack of political will on the part of the Spanish leaders —in politics as well as in press— have left the EFE structure relatively intact throughout its 50-year existence. Until that EFE structure is changed, EFE will not and could not live up to its full potential.

A HALF–CENTURY OF EFE

Spaniards of distinct stripes have nurtured EFE into its present number-5 position among Western press agencies through the civil war and 40-year dictatorship, the post-Franco transition, and recent democracy. EFE has grown through 8 distinct ERAs in its half-century existence. (Reference to figure 1 on p. xix will facilitate the tracing of these 8 EFE ERAs, which paralleled the 8 political EPOCHs of Spain in the past half century. [The chapter numbers in Figure 1 again correspond to the paragraph numbers below.])

1. The Foundation Era (1936–1939).

Upon eruption in July 1936 of military revolt, many a right-wing Spanish journalist fled Madrid away from real and perceived persecution by the Republican government, against all sympathizers of the Nationalist uprising. When the revolt progressed into war, these journalists banded together in the Nationalist bastion at Burgos, the northern city of the Burgos province. This band started spreading its version of the war stories —to combat what the group saw as international conspiracies of the "left" against the "Spanish cause." The ragtag group of journalists struck a sympathetic chord in the heart of Ramón Serrano Súñer, a youthful Falange lawyer who, as a "brother-in-law" of the rebel leader Franco, wielded power second only to Franco, as his wartime interior and foreign minister.

Serrano Súñer hustled up old and rich Spanish bankers for start-up money for a news service created in early 1938. It was named EFE taking the initial letter F (or Spanish $e\ f\ e$) of the "F-alange" and the initial letter of a Falange magazine, Fe (*Faith*). The name F-rancisco F-ranco also started with an F. The original EFE founders believed unabashedly in the Falange causes. As the civil war wound down to Nationalist victory in late 1938, Serrano Súñer expropriated an old news agency, Fabra, the Spanish subsidiary of the French Havas news service. EFE's formal incorporation took place on 3 January of 1939.

Led by Vicente Gállego Castro, its first director, EFE's journalists joined the ranks of the Nationalist army marching east to capture Barcelona, the Republican remnant city, where it established its first local bureau. But the EFE group did not march into Madrid when the capital city fell on 28 March 1939. EFE stayed in Burgos until after Franco moved his headquarters to Madrid in late 1939. When the fledgling EFE took up residence at the former Fabra building in Madrid, the Second World War was raging.

2. The Nazi Era (1939–1945)

Franco's civil war benefactors, Nazi Germany and Italy, strenuously wooed him to bring Spain into the Axis ranks. Hitler met Franco on 23 October 1940 at the French–Spanish border. Mussolini conferred with Franco on 12 February 1941 in Italy. Both meetings were covered with fanfare by the EFE agency. Urged by his fascist foreign minister, Franco walked the tight rope of "nonbelligerency" in favor of the Axis. Under the Schmidt–Tovar agreement signed in March 1941, German propaganda apparatus was set up in the Iberian peninsula, to take over EFE's functions both in Spain and in Nazi-occupied Europe. EFE director Gállego grew increasingly disgruntled at the German encroachment of his agency. He finally gave up EFE directorship in July 1944. It was taken over by a more docile subdirector, Pedro Gómez Aparicio, another member of the original EFE group at Burgos.

In the remaining World War II, press attaché Hans Lazar of the German embassy in Spain practically controlled EFE's news operation. He "suggested" the names of the Spaniards who were to be Berlin and Rome correspondents. All foreign news arriving in Spain distributed by EFE originated from the German Trans-Ocean agency. In silent protest, Gállego subscribed to the British Reuters news agency, because it then was the only non-German European news service. Pro-German news operations extended beyond Iberia, for the Schmidt – Tovar agreements provided for EFE to set up various branches in the Americas with the double mission of transmitting to Spain the news from the Americas, and receiving and distributing in the Americas the stories sent from Madrid. Germany was to furnish all material supplies.

3. The Isolation Era (1945 – 1950)

After World War II, EFE, led by director Gómez Aparicio, suffered a severe domestic isolation coincident with Spain's diplomatic ostracism. Despite its subscription to the United Press (UP) in April 1945, and the continuation of the Reuters service, EFE was seen as Franco's press control machine which it was. Contesting EFE's role was the powerful Falange movement press. With its own PYRESA news service, the Movement press menaced EFE's foreign news monopoly, entering into negotiations with another U.S. news agency, International News Service (INS). It was a typical power struggle within the Francoist regime. The EFE group had to fight for its life, issuing a series of "White Papers" on its legal and political status. Its "godfather" Serrano Súñer was no longer in power, having been replaced as foreign minister in September 1942. EFE was operating under the iron grip of the director general of press at the ministry of national education. DGP Gabriel Arias-Salgado had been hostile both to Serrano Súñer and EFE.

4. The Peace Era (1951 – 1965)

Franco's Spain was soon enlisted out of the diplomatic ostracism by the United States with the advent of the East – West cold war. So was EFE saved from its domestic isolation by the tactical need of its once despising master. It was an ironic coincidence. In July 1951 the Franco regime established the ministry of information and tourism (MIT) and promoted DGP Arias-Salgado to new minister. Now the new MIT, Arias-Salgado, had to consolidate his power base by bringing the EFE agency under his protective wing.

During the next 15 years, EFE prospered —along with the thriving Spain— into a legitimate domestic news agency, now that its hierarchy had clearly been established. Gómez Aparicio, who had risen to the EFE directorship in 1944, stayed in that position until February 1958, thus becoming the longest-serving director in EFE's half-century history. In an attempt to oust Gómez Aparicio, MIT Arias-Salgado appointed Waldo de Mier EFE subdirector in 1957. After Gómez Aparicio's departure in 1958, there followed the years of changes and vacancy at the EFE directorship, which De Mier filled as "acting" director. The instability ended with the naming in 1962 of the new MIT, Manuel Fraga Iribarne. A youthful technocrat, at age 39, Fraga was a harbinger to reforms in the Spanish press in general and metamorphosis in the EFE agency in particular.

Upon taking office in July 1962, Fraga boasted that he would have a new press law by the end of the year. Despite the prevailing air of moderation within the Franco regime, he ran into unexpected resistance, although he should have foreseen it. It took MIT Fraga till March 1966 to produce the new Press and Print Law (LPI) which, "in reform spirit," replaced prior censorship with "voluntary" consultation. The LPI gave EFE a legal monopoly right to foreign news in Spain, which it had previously held de facto. But the most significant change Fraga effected for EFE was the 1965 appointment of Carlos Mendo Baos, 32-year-old bureau manager of UPI in Madrid, as EFE director.

5. The Mendo Era (1966–1969)

Carlos Mendo took EFE to Latin America. It was a momentous step forward in EFE's history, as it was a quantum step outside of Spain —within which EFE had remained in the foregoing 3 decades of its existence. When he established the EFE bureau in Buenos Aires, Argentina, in December 1965, Mendo caused a metamorphosis in EFE. Until then, EFE had been a domestic news service, with the monopoly right to distribute foreign news received from UPI and Reuters in Spain. The "news" EFE distributed was not news as such. EFE served as the conduit for government-generated "news" and the MIT's *consignas* (secret orders) to Spanish newspapers. International news —from Reuters and UPI— was not distributed *in toto,* but EFE screened and rewrote it from a Francoist viewpoint. EFE had not been a news agency per se. It all changed with Mendo as its director.

After a short stint with the EFE agency upon graduation from the Official School of Journalism in Madrid, Mendo went to England to learn the English language and the British way of journalism. Returning to Spain, he was hired by UPI and sent to Rome as its Latin American news editor. UPI appointed him later as its Madrid bureau manager, a position he said had been always occupied by a U.S. journalist. By mid-1965, Fraga had practically completed the work on the new press law. He then turned his attention to the affairs of EFE, and found in Mendo a man of dynamism and a journalist with many a progressive idea. Fraga named Mendo EFE director and gave him a carte blanche to make the national agency an "Hispanic news service" in the style of other international news agencies to "exploit the community of millions of the Latin American people who speak the same language."

Fraga and Mendo thus became the "new conquistadores" of Latin America. Mendo opened EFE bureaus in Latin America and Europe, making EFE the preferred European news source for the Latin American papers and converting it into an "authority on Latin American information" for the European audience. Before Mendo, EFE had had only 2 bureaus in Spain. He doubled that number, and opened up 32 new foreign bureaus. Mendo —who professes to be an "old Liberal . . . convinced of the supremacy of the individual over the State"[9] —tried his "level best" to make EFE a newspaper cooperative like the Anglo-American news agencies. He sold one-third of EFE shares to Spanish papers, and once managed to have 8 newspaper representatives serve on the 15-member EFE board of directors. EFE's news wordage increased from 21 million in 1962 to 135 million in 1969, when Mendo was removed from EFE.

The Fraga–Mendo duo and other like-minded Spaniards did not succeed in turning the cosmetic moderation of the Franco regime of the mid-1960s into a fundamental reform. When Fraga lost his MIT post in a regressive political shakeup in October 1969, EFE director Mendo was summarily replaced by a protégé of the incoming MIT, Alfredo Sánchez Bella.

6. The Armesto Era (1970–1975)

Sánchez Bella was the Spanish ambassador to Italy when Mendo was working at UPI's Rome bureau. The conservative envoy developed an intense dislike for the dashing young journalist, whom he thought to be acting like a U.S. citizen instead of a compliant Spaniard. MIT Sánchez Bella promptly replaced Mendo with his former press attaché in Rome, Alejandro Armesto, who had been the editor of an obscure Spanish provincial sports daily.

During the Armesto era, EFE penetrated the Central American market to found in December 1972 a subsidiary news agency, ACAN (Central American News Agency), serving the 7-nation region. ACAN-EFE was a product of highly personal friendships typical in conservative Hispanic circles. During his long diplomatic peregrinations in Europe and the Americas, Sánchez Bella had nurtured friendship with many Central American generals and colonels, who served as military attachés. They later became presidents and ministers of Latin nations. It was largely due to these personal contacts that the MIT–EFE's Sánchez–Armesto duo could talk the Central American leaders into combining resources to begin a regional news agency with the financial and technical help of EFE from the "mother country" Spain.

ACAN-EFE has even achieved what EFE has not been able to do itself. ACAN-EFE is a news cooperative of the newspapers and broadcast stations of 7 Isthmian countries, (including Belize, formerly British Honduras). ACAN provides the regional news to its member media, and to the EFE Madrid Central, while EFE provides ACAN members with major Latin American and world news.

By all accounts ACAN-EFE is the best-functioning regional news agency of the world. With about 60 cooperative-member media, ACAN also is just about the only regional entity which is still successfully operating in war-torn countries where the once-booming Central American Common Market has now been shattered. Established during the waning months of the Franco era, ACAN not only has survived the Central American wars but has also endured the change which has accompanied the demise of Franco. The ACAN creators, the Sánchez–Armesto duo, did not. From 1973 to 1976, no fewer than 5 MITs succeeded Sánchez Bella and none of these revolving-door MITs stayed in office long enough to do anything to or for Armesto or his EFE news agency.

The Hispanic American successes of Fraga–Mendo duo and Sánchez–Armesto pair brought about an unexpected brawl to EFE in January 1976. *The Washington Post* accused EFE —among others— of involvements with the U.S. Central Intelligence Agency (CIA) in covert propaganda activities in 1970 against Salvador Allende Gossens, Marxist Chilean presidential candidate. Armesto denied the charges in a meek protest only in the Spanish papers but not to the *Post*. In February 1976 he was replaced now by Mendo. EFE did not pursue the CIA matter.

7. The Anson Era (1976–1982)

During the changes surrounding the demise of Franco on 20 November 1975, the old Fraga–Mendo team enjoyed an ephemeral ascendancy to power. Fraga Iribarne was named interior minister and also vice premier on domestic affairs in December 1975. Fraga, however, lasted in these posts for only 11 months. In that short tenure, he had Carlos Mendo called back to EFE as its director. Later, Fraga refused to serve in the second post-Franco administration led by Adolfo Suárez. In September 1976 Suárez named as EFE president Luis María Anson —the director of the prestigious Madrid daily *ABC*, which had been in circulation since 1905 and advocated a monarchist philosophy. Two weeks later Anson dismissed Mendo in a thrilling palace coup and put on the double hats of president and director-general. Until that time the EFE president was purely a ceremonial figurehead.

President/director-general Anson moved EFE headquarters to a 7-story edifice, inviting to its inaugural the entire high society —Spanish and international. Anson computerized the EFE communications system, replacing old typewriters and teletypes. Anson's EFE started using INTELSAT satellite, also replacing telephone and radio circuits. Anson instituted journalistic style manual. Having thus laid home groundwork, Anson took gargantuan jumps outward with EFE. He set out to make EFE "new conquistador" of the world, and launched out of Latin America toward the Pacific and beyond.

Anson took the EFE agency to the world. Mendo had taken EFE out of Spain to Europe and Latin America. In his 6-year tenure as EFE president/director-general, in a vibrating post-Franco Spain, Anson went to all 5 continents, propelling it up to the fifth position among Western agencies, rubbing shoulders with the "Big 4": AP, UPI, Reuters, and AFP. He increased EFE's domestic bureaus from Armesto's 5 to 13. And he boosted foreign bureaus from 33 to 76. Anson went to Asia, Oceania, the Middle East, Africa, and the socialist-bloc countries. He established news-exchange agreements with 31 foreign agencies, compared to Mendo's 7 and Armesto's 19. The EFE capital jumped to P800 million ($13.4 million) from Mendo's 20 million and Armesto's 50 million. The annual news wordage almost doubled to 265 million from Mendo–Armesto's 135 million.

Anson's EFE gave up an already inoperative formal monopoly on foreign news distribution, thus exposing EFE to open competition. Anson consolidated, under a single logo, the variegated services that had been offered under the confusing array of signatures of the CIFRA-National, EFE-International, CIFRA-Graphic, and ALFIL-Sports. Anson began television news service, and also created VIDEO–EFE, television screen display of news leads at public places. Anson started the French and English news services. To accommodate all the activities EFE undertook, Anson bought 15 houses —7 in Spain and 8 overseas— which some critics called "neo–classical palaces." Anson also ran up EFE deficits to an unprecedented P393 million ($6.58 million), compared to P6.6 million by Mendo. But it was not Anson's "reckless" extravaganzas that brought about his downfall at the end of 1982. Anson, indeed, was glorified for his brilliant feats. Even the editor-in-chief of *El País*, the new leading Madrid daily, acknowledged a "tremendous expansion and technological renovation" of EFE by his old competitor, Anson.

The government changed hands from the centrist alliance to the Spanish Socialist Workers' Party (PSOE) in December of 1972. Monarchist Anson was summarily dismissed as EFE president by the incoming administration. The specter of government hovered over EFE, as it had throughout its history. Anson, like Mendo, attempted to make EFE a newspaper cooperative independent of the government by bringing in a few press representatives to EFE's board of directors. But the government had the upper hand because of its hold on the purse strings.

8. The Utrilla Era (1983–1986)

Ricardo Utrilla Carlón maintained that he was appointed to the EFE presidency in January 1983 by none other than PSOE premier Felipe González himself, for he was "the best wire-service journalist in Spain."[10] Utrilla had been employed by AFP at its Paris headquarters and as Washington correspondent for a total of 13 years until 1972. Utrilla then returned to Madrid to participate in a press enerprise by 16 reform-minded Spaniards, "Grupo 16," who took advantage of impending political changes when old Franco fell ill. The group started with a weekly magazine, *Cambio 16 (Change 16)*, eventually to publish the second post-Franco era Spanish newspaper, *Diario 16 (Daily 16)*, whose editor was Utrilla.

Utrilla's management in his 4-year EFE tenure displayed contradictory nature. For one thing, Utrilla's EFE team acted as if it were a "transition" caretaker in the fully functioning Spanish democracy under a splurging socialist government. EFE under Utrilla reined in many of what he considered "excessive expansions" under the royalist Anson's reign. Utrilla cut EFE's Madrid payroll by 95 by the end of 1986 from 735 in Anson's days. This caused an uproar among the EFE staff, who felt that this was a betrayal of the socialist covenant. In a belt-tightening measure, Utrilla demoted to simple "chiefs" —with accompanying pay cuts— all EFE "directors" that Anson had created. This naturally turned some EFE managers against Utrilla. He also began to dispose of EFE's bureau buildings, which Anson had bought to save on rents EFE paid. Utrilla argued that the mortgages were more expensive than rents. Again, the Utrilla management had a short-range view of EFE's future. On everything else, Utrilla showed a "holding pattern," rather than striking out to new directions with his agency.

The only new direction Utrilla's EFE took came in tandem with the PSOE reversal of its mildly anti-U.S., anti-NATO position. Utrilla —who had worked for AFP which claims to present a non-U.S. worldview— moved EFE closer to the Anglo-American mode of operation. Utrilla placed increasingly stronger emphasis on the news coming out of Washington, D.C., and assigned higher-powered staff to its U.S. capital bureau. EFE had allegedly succeeded in the Hispanic American markets, "because it did not treat Latin America as did U.S. agencies, giving it news space only when there were coups, earthquakes, or other catastrophes,"[11] according to every EFE director since Mendo, including Utrilla.

But a 1985 study by this author demonstrated that EFE had originated 14.3% of news from Washington for its Latin American news circuits. Even Spain was the distant second with 6.4%, to be followed by 5.23% for Britain. None of the Latin American countries reached 5%. This pleased Utrilla and his executive editor Velasco as proof that the EFE news staff functioned on the same intellectual wavelength as journalists from other Western news agencies. That encouraged Utrilla to bid for partial ownership of UPI in the early spring of 1985, now confident that his news staff could well handle the entire Spanish operations of UPI.

This was a direct result of "professionalization" of EFE service, a proclaimed motto by Utrilla, as opposed to a "disorbited expansion" under Anson. While ostensibly acting as a newsman, Utrilla did everything against the press representation to the top EFE echelon. Utrilla fired all journalists on EFE's board of directors, and filled these vacancies with mid-level P.R. officials of the PSOE ministries and semigovernment entities, as if he did not want to see any journalistic rivals on his board. Thus, Utrilla made EFE completely government–dependent.

On the other hand, Utrilla demonstrated the biggest contradiction in his reaction to the requirement by Article 20.3 of the new democratic constitution of 1978, to bring all government-funded mass media operations under more representative parliamentary control. Utrilla was vehemently opposed to the efforts by the opposition groups to carry out the constitutional mandates and got the PSOE regime to frustrate these attempts. PSOE had persistently demanded the same thing when it was in the opposition. Utrilla argued that parliamentary control of EFE would fatally damage its overseas image. But he had completely filled the EFE board with government cronies.

Nobody in either Spain or Latin America believed the fiction that EFE was an "independent" news agency simply because it did not come under parliamentary control. The multiparty Congress represents the entire nation, while the shifting executive branch has always manipulated EFE for partisan advantages. The contradiction was utterly curious, because it came from an erstwhile AFP newsman who had first-hand experience with the French agency. AFP represents France as a nation, rather than the parties in power, precisely because the multiparty French National Assembly controls the AFP.

Therefore, it was not even ironic that the PSOE administration fired Utrilla without much ado in a PSOE reshuffle in late October 1986. Utrilla had now become another victim of the system he so ardently defended. In November 1986, the EFE agency started another era under the new president/director-general, Alfonso Sobrado Palomares, whom Utrilla had summarily removed from the EFE board in 1984.

Chapter 1

Casino de Burgos
(1936–1939)

Every afternoon in early spring of 1938, a handful of intense-looking Spaniards would gather at a casino in downtown Burgos, the capital city of the northern province of the same name. Now about 2 years into the Spanish civil war, Burgos had become the center of power and control in Nationalist Spain under the leadership of Francisco Franco.

The members of this *tertulia* —a Spanish informal social get-together— were Nationalist government press officials and Falange journalists engaged in a battle of news, "the deadly war of propaganda," as they would call their endeavors later. Leading the conversation was José Antonio Giménez-Arnau y Gran, age 26, director general of the press service of the ministry of interior. In that *tertulia*, Giménez-Arnau's assessments seemed to carry weight obviously because of his government position, although he would turn to the man sitting next to him, who appeared to be a little older than the rest of the party.

Vicente Gállego Castro was the man to whom the group showed deference. Gállego Castro, at age 42, had been a nationally known Madrid journalist before the civil war. He had been the editor of the Catholic morning paper *El Debate* (*The Debate*) and taught at its school of journalism —the first professional school in Spain. He had also directed a Catholic news service, Logos News Agency, and had some connections with the Madrid bureau of the Associated Press (AP)[1] of the United States. In January 1935 La Editorial Católica commissioned Gállego Castro to found an evening paper, *Ya* (*Already*), another Catholic organ to combat the "Red" Republican papers. In organizing the new daily *Ya* —which is still circulating as one of the leading Spanish papers after 54 years— he demonstrated his organizational skill by recruiting a "constellation of brilliant young journalists."[2] Upon the outbreak of the civil war, Gállego Castro had fled the Republican-held Madrid to the Nationalist zone, after a long and rough journey, whose last leg was through French territory.

Another regular at the Burgos Casino *tertulia* was Pedro Gómez Aparicio, 35-year-old chief of the National Press Service (Servicio Nacional de Prensa, SNP). A graduate of Gállego's *El Debate* school of journalism, Gómez Aparicio had reported for *El Debate*. He had also been the founding editor of the Granada daily *Ideal* in 1932, and returned to *El Debate* as its chief writer in 1934. In the first phase of the civil war, Gómez Aparicio served as war correspondent on the Nationalist side at the front of Guadalajara, Vizcaya, and Brunete. Working in 1938 for SNP, the former war correspondent played coordinating roles at the daily *tertulia*.

Among the young turks at the daily get-together was José Luis García Gallego. The 26-year-old García Gallego had also worked for *El Debate* as stenographer-reporter. When Gállego Castro began the evening daily *Ya*, he wanted García Gallego to join him, but the young reporter stayed on at the morning *El Debate*. When the civil war came, he joined the group of right-wing journalists at Burgos. Of the *tertulia* group, García Gallego was not only the youngest but also the most impatient about the slow progress of the project.

That "project" was to disseminate the Nationalist side of the news of the war and politics in Spain and abroad under the name of "EFE News Service." The news service had come into being with the blessing of the Nationalist interior minister, Ramón Serrano Súñer, "brother-in-law" of Generalissimo Francisco Franco. Serrano Súñer was given the nickname *"Cuñadísimo" cuñado* being the Spanish word for brother-in-law. The satirical superlative *cuñadísimo* implied his power base relative to *Generalísimo* Francisco Franco. The all-powerful interior minister had urged these journalists to fight the "Red" propaganda being spread in Spain and abroad against the Nationalist cause in the civil war.

The *tertulia* group was impatient because the only thing the news service had was a name. There was no organization, no fund, not even office space. The head of the EFE group, Gállego Castro, had to work out of a back room of a Burgos shop. All he had was an old wooden kitchen table and a rickety chair. Interior minister Serrano Súñer kept promising the *tertulia* journalists that he would soon give them a place, equipment, and funds.

THE PYRAMIDS OF EGYPT

On 1 October 1938,[3] Serrano Súñer at last convened a meeting of the EFE group at his office. As the EFE members filed into his attic office, they were introduced to solemn-aired old people sitting around the minister's desk. They were the presidents and directors of the leading Spanish banks: El Banco Español de Crédito, Banco de Vizcaya, Banco Hispano-

Americano, and others. Standing by the office walls (there being no more chairs), the group heard an impassioned speech from the interior minister. The 37-year-old *cuñadísimo* informed the old bankers that these young men were the "dedicated and self-sacrificing" people who were engaged in an international war of propaganda. The interior minister emphasized that he fully shared the group's "aspiration to have a certain independence in the news field, so as not to be 'colonized' as we are now colonized by the British Reuters, the French Havas, Associated Press, and United Press." The minister pointed out that it was the very first time he was approaching the bankers, for "we do not have money and we are soliciting you bankers to help us finance our efforts."

The young minister expounded his press philosophy:

> We are completely colonized. We do not even have the least amount of independence in the news field, to be able to give the news at least —if not with the tone completely suitable to us— to avoid that the news be given in a tone contrary to our interest, as is the case so often.[4]

Serrano Súñer now called the attention of that small, emotion-packed audience to 40,000-strong International Brigades, a "proof," he claimed, of worldwide communist, Masonic, and Jewish propaganda intent on polluting "the pure Spanish soul." He pointed to the men standing along the walls and said that they needed monetary support for their work against the international propaganda. They were confronted, Serrano Súñer emphasized, with not only "the left-leaning" foreign news agencies, but they had to combat the work of the Republican-financed news and propaganda services.[5] Serrano Súñer added that the Anglo-American-French news monopoly —aided by Spanish "traitors"— had caused an international uproar over the April 1937 Guernica bombing incident, painting the Nationalist forces as "barbaric," ignoring the Republicans' execution of hundreds of Catholic priests and the burning of age-old Spanish cathedrals. He urged the old bankers to come up with financial support for the efforts of "these young fighting Spanish journalists standing there."

The bankers promised that they would make financial donations for the cause, but they wanted to see the project spelled out in a formal proposal. Giménez-Arnau offered to write up a statute for the EFE news agency. It was proper for him to take up that task as the SNP director-general. Everyone in the group gave a nod to Giménez-Arnau's offer. Then and there, on 1 October 1938, in Burgos, a solemn promise was made to launch a Nationalist news service.

During October and November 1938, these 2 groups held several more meetings, the first few at the minister's office and most others at the customary *tertulia* locale, Casino de Burgos. When the old bankers showed up for meetings, the "impertinent" EFE group, all young, including the interior minister, would say to one another, "Now come the Pyramids of Egypt."[6]

The long-winded discussions were at times heated as plans were drawn and redrawn and figures calculated and recalculated. The old bankers would exasperate the journalist group with adamant demands for a legal and financial framework for the projected news agency. The bankers wanted to make sure that ownership of the new enterprise was clearly spelled out before they would cough up P10 million (equivalent to some US$1.1 million in 1938) they had offered for the project. The EFE journalists and the interior ministry officials insisted that the legal bases for the enterprise had amply been laid by the Press Law (*Ley de Prensa*) decreed only 6 months before, on 22 April 1938.

They insisted that the Press Law provided for government control of all publications and news agencies. But even Interior minister Serrano Súñer, good lawyer that he was, agreed with the old bankers that a formal statute had to be drawn up to implement those provisions of the law and give the EFE news agency "a certain legal status." In mid-November, Giménez-Arnau, who was drafting the statute, came up with an idea, a brilliant idea: The Nationalist government would take over an already existing private Spanish news agency, *"La Agencia Fabra."*

FABRA NEWS AGENCY

Nilo María Fabra y Deas, a Catalonian journalist, was born in 1843 in the village of Blanes on the Mediterranean coast in Spain's easternmost Gerona province bordering with France. In 1865 Fabra created his own "Centro de Correspondencia" to distribute articles and news to the provincial dailies, which lacked written materials to fill their pages in those days. In his journalistic travels to Paris,[7] Fabra had developed a friendship with the Spanish ambassador to France, Salustiano Olozaga, who introduced him to Charles Auguste Havas, the owner of the French Havas Agency (now the Agence France-Presse, AFP).

Havas offered Fabra financial and technical help to transform Fabra's "Centro de Correspondencia" into a telegraphic news agency, directly connected to the Havas. This would also accommodate Havas's plan to expand his news services to cover Europe. Thus, with French money and (instruction, the Fabra News Agency was born as a subsidiary service of the French Havas.

Young Nilo Fabra, then age 22, a genius avidly interested in novelty, knew how to introduce the innovative technology for rapid transmission of news. In 1868, Fabra installed, at Punta Tarifa in the Gibraltar Strait, a semaphore system, which utilized wooden-arm signals to flag news to and from the ships passing through the Mediterranean passage. In 1875 Fabra accompanied King Alfonso XII on his voyage from Marseilles to Barcelona aboard the frigate *Navas de Tolosa*. From the ship, Fabra used messenger pigeons to inform his newspaper, *Diario de Barcelona*, of the king's travel and the events on board the frigate, a day ahead of the 9 January arrival in Barcelona —an unprecedented reporting feat in Spain. Fabra had learned the use of messenger pigeons from the French Havas and the British Reuters. The most significant of Fabra's innovations was the establishment in 1880 of his "own" telegraphic station in the suburbs of Madrid.

Fabra sent reporters to the Spanish-French border town of Irún to receive, through the French telegraphic network, the Havas service. He then utilized the Spanish network to retransmit news to the Fabra station at Vallecas outside of Madrid. The longest dispatch sent through the Fabra system was over the 1919 Versailles Peace Treaty after World War I, which contained 10,000 words and took 11 hours to transmit completely. Fabra did not see this historic dispatch; he had died in 1903. On 1 April 1919, the Fabra agency was constituted legally as a Spanish company, with Havas owning 60% of its assets.

The legal constitution of Fabra as a Spanish company did not give it real independence from the French Havas. It continued only as the distributor of French news. Fabra still lacked a solid team of national correspondents, for the French Havas was not interested in detailed Spanish news. The Fabra agency was made a real Spanish company by military dictator Miguel Primo de Rivera, who ruled Spain from 1923 to 1931. General Primo de Rivera clearly understood the importance of a national news agency. In 1926 he called on bankers to help finance the nationalization of the Fabra News Agency, whose assets by then had gone up to P1 million. A few leading banks responded generously enough to buy off the Fabra stocks owned by the French Havas.

The Primo de Rivera regime fell in 1931. In the chaotic Second Republic of 1931–1936, the status of the Fabra agency was at best undefined. By 1933 the Fabra News Agency had obtained 5 radio transmitters, German-made "Hell"[8] long-wave equipment, and moved to the northern city of San Sebastián in the Nationalist zone.

Fabra To EFE

To the minds of Giménez-Arnau and his Nationalist comrades of the *tertulia* group, whatever ambiguous legal status given to the Fabra agency by the Second Republic was null and void. The nationalized status of Fabra could be revived. After all, the Nationalists were true successors to the Primo de Rivera regime. How come the old bankers —those "Pyramids"— had not remembered they themselves had put up P750,000 for the 1926 takeover of the Fabra News Agency?

The whole EFE group, interior minister Serrano Súñer, and the bankers rejoiced at the ideas of Giménez-Arnau. There was a legal base to the enterprise and the bankers thought that they could also recover that "lost" investment of 1926. Fabra director Luis Amato and its president, Marquis Noriega Ruíz, were called over to Burgos in late November 1938, and were "told" to transfer the Fabra assets and rights to the national enterprise, the EFE news agency. Only 2 months after that emotional meeting on 1 October 1938 at the interior minister's office, the *tertulia* group had turned the corner and could now formally constitute the news agency. (Marquis Noriega was named ceremonial president of the newly born EFE agency.)

EFE: A Political Symbol

A controversy over the history of EFE's origin flared up some 5 years after the demise of the Franco regime. The then president/director-general of EFE, Luis María Anson Oliart, triggered the uproar. In an 11 December 1982 article in the Madrid Catholic daily, *Ya*, Anson attempted to disassociate EFE under his command from the tarnished image of the now-extinct Franco dictatorship. Anson gave a very smart version to the etymology of the title *EFE*. It was a bit too smart for the Spanish public to believe.

> EFE received its name in 1939. The Agency's future structure was built on foundations that had existed in Spain for 20 years as Fabra Agency. EFE acquired this agency's assets and added technological, professional and human resources of the former agencies **FARO** and **FEBUS**. Oddly enough, all these agencies' names began with **F** which became an anecdote as well as a symbol. This **F** or **EFE** in Spanish, was adopted as the company logo. It became the *middle* letter in Agency's various services: **EFE** (foreign service), **CIFRA** (domestic service), **ALFIL** (sports service) and **GRAFICA** (photo service). EFE later acquired the **FIEL** Agency, whose name also begins with **F**. In

1978 the Agency centralized all its services under the international name **EFE**, while FIEL was kept for special services.[9]

Antonio Herrero Losada had been —and still is— the managing editor of the leading private news agency, Europa Press, since its 1960 founding. One of the heavyweights of Spanish journalism, Herrero Losada had earlier worked for EFE for 20 years. He wrote a letter to the editor of *Ya*, disputing the Anson version of the origin of the title *EFE*. A meticulous man knowing his contender, Herrero Losada accompanied his letter to *Ya* with a letter from former interior minister Serrano Súñer, the godfather of EFE. Serrano Súñer roundly rejected the Anson version. He said "proudly, without any hesitation" that the title *EFE* had originated from the letter *F* (*efe* in the Spanish alphabet) of the Falange and also from *FE* (short for the "Falange Español," which became a convenient acronym *FE*, the Spanish word for "faith"). *Fe* also was the name of the Falange publication. EFE, however, had not come from the initials of "Francisco Franco." "That would come later," he added. The public laundering of EFE's "dirty linen" continued over the 1982 Christmas season in letters to the editor.

Why is the meaning of "EFE" so important? Many Spaniards could not give an easy, quick reply to the simple question: What does EFE stand for? In the post-Franco period, Spaniards gradually gathered up enough courage to start questioning "everything" pertaining to the Franco rule, including the meaning of the title "EFE." Anson had tried to provide the Spanish public with his revisionist answer to the question, but he had not succeeded.

FASCIST PRESS PHILOSOPHERS

At Burgos in December 1938 a document enunciating a fascist press philosophy on the need for founding *"La Agencia EFE"* was published. No name(s) of author(s) appeared, as was customary in practically all Spanish papers, documents, and writings of this era, as if the writers attempted to hide their identities from unforeseen future political ramifications. This document is a study in a high-sounding totalitarian press philosophy. The chapter titles read:

      Forewords
I.   The Battle of the Propaganda
II.   The Domination of the News
III.   The World Network of News
IV.   The Agency, Political Instrument
V.   Spain, Territory Under Influence

A close analysis of the document —stripped of its declamatory harangue and glittering generalities— renders an insight into the Falange thinking behind the creation of the news agency EFE during the civil war. The EFE founding document expounded the ideas below:

Propaganda War

The nation-states have been historically engaged in the exercise of "spiritual influences" over others, and in that "spiritual war for imperialistic hegemony," the "strong nations colonize the weak ones." The efforts to disseminate "national conscience" become a "propaganda war." The best technique of propaganda is by means of the "news"; the news is much stronger as a propaganda tool than well-written editorials or signed articles. The news reflects fact and it accomplishes persuasion by subjecting fact "to different interpretations regarding its meaning, its importance and its occasion." Hence, the nations have been engaged in battles for "news domination." News wars are waged through national news agencies. The news agency, therefore, is no more or no less than a "national political tool."

The document avowed a modern history shows that great political leaders knew the importance of news war. They suppressed the hostile press and protected the docile press. They created, directed, appointed editors, and even wrote in the papers themselves. The document emphasized the importance of "propaganda wars" by citing the different governments' "true nationalization" of the news agencies. Czarist Russia and the Austro-Hungarian Empire constituted official news agencies. The Japanese government imposed the fusion of the Dentsu Agency and Rengo Agency into the Domei Tsushin Sha.

Even the "arch-democratic" United States passed a law requiring "at least 80% of the stocks of all businesses dedicated to the diffusion of news must be property of the North American 'subjects' [sic]." Another law promulgated in Brazil determines that "the participants in all news agency business should be born Brazilian."

The document then briefly described the founding of the French Havas News Agency by Portuguese-born Charles Havas in 1835; of the British

Reuters by Israel J. Beer —"a Havas employee and a German Jew"— who emigrated to England, changing his name to "Paul Julius Reuter" in 1851; of the German Wolff by Berlin editor, Dr. Bernhard Wolff, another former Havas worker in 1849; and that of the mighty Associated Press by the New York Associated Press (1848) whose member reporters rowed out to the ships arriving from Europe to obtain the news from the Old World.

Then came, the document said, the 1913 division of world news markets by the news cartel of the Big 4: Reuters, Havas, AP, and Wolff. The 1913 cartel divided the world. Reuters covered the British Empire, several Mediterranean countries, and most of Asia; Havas got the French Empire, Italy, Spain, Portugal, parts of the Balkans, South America, and parts of Africa; Associated Press received the 3 North, Central, and South Americas, though in South America it was to collaborate with Havas; and the German Wolff agency ended up with the worst deal out of this 1913 pact, reserving only Germany, Russia, and the northern Baltic states.

The nations now realized the importance of having their own national news agencies. The Soviets, "with their propagandistic experience of 20 years of tenacious efforts, have created around the Humanity an asphyxiating atmosphere, of whose fruits we Spaniards have seen too much damage." "The Nationalsozialist regime, more modern, more realist, more practical, and consequently, more conscious of the efficacy of the well conducted propaganda, rose —as soon as it could— against the 1913 convention, which, in the world concert, relegated the German influence to an unfair secondary level." The DNB agency (Deutsche Nachrichten-Buro) —created by the "Nationalsozialism" through the fusion of the Wolff Agency and Telegraphen-Union of Hugenberg— demanded, in 1934, the revision of the 1913 concert. After "laborious negotiations," it obtained a new pact effective 1 July.

Immediately after the triumphant revolution, Italian fascism paid attention to emancipate the Stefani agency from its bond to French Havas agency, and placed it under state service. Mussolini gave frequent personal attention to its economic, political, and technical development. Through Stefani, Italy let loose a violent anti-British propaganda campaign in its dealings with England on the problems of Ethiopia and the British Middle East mandates, especially Palestine.

Even in the countries of ultrademocratic traditions, the importance of propaganda is realized. Great Britain had to defend its interests by signing the Anglo-Italian Convention of 16 April 1938, by which she obtained Italian commitment to desist from the campaign of propaganda among the Moslems. In France, the Popular Front government of Leon Blum created a subsecretary of propaganda, attached to the presidency of the state council.

SPANISH FAILURE

The EFE document sounded most vehement and grandiose in regards to "Spain's failure" to engage in the war of propaganda: "Spain's internal vitality must be given exit to the outside world to excite and obtain external benevolences and sympathies." Spain must diffuse "the reason for the Nationalist Uprising and explain the real truth of the [Falangist] Movement to the world." But Spain remained "defenseless." Spain had suffered "a defeat in propaganda war in spite of its military victory," because of the "news inferiority." Spain must wage an efficient news battle in order to bring together the divided fatherland and must return to the unity of all, in fervent longing for the "Fatherland, Bread, and Justice" [Falange slogan].

The foundational document counted various cases of the Spanish "failures in the news war." From its founding in 1860–1965 (sic, it was 1865), the Fabra News Agency[10] had been an instrument of spiritual colonization of Spain by foreign interests in that it existed as no more than a "branch of the French Havas." Spain's voice was "of necessity adulterated" and diffused by foreign news agencies, "subservient to utilitarianism and imperialism, even in our brother nations like Portugal, the [Hispanic] Americas,[11] the Philippines and non-Spanish Morocco." The 2 great international expositions of Barcelona and Sevilla of 1929 found a hostile environment, which "condemned the first to calamity." The second fair in Sevilla had to be "saved" by the U.S. news agencies, which were pressured by the demands of their clients into installing their own services, "at incalculable sums —in an event no one in Spain was preoccupied with even though it was in the interest of Spain more than anyone else."

"Even in our Spanish South America, the [Nationalist] Spain has lost the war of propaganda." *La Vanguardia de Barcelona*, the leading Spanish daily, reported on 28 September 1938 on a Buenos Aires-based news service that supplied information favorable to the Spanish Republican cause to some 500 papers in South America, and some in Central and North America, including a few in San Francisco. The Republican news agency served 14 or more principal Argentine newspapers.[12] Even when some great South American papers assigned Spaniards as correspondents "in our own Fatherland," appointments invariably went to an enemy of the genuine Spain like in the case of Alvarez del Vayo, representative in Spain during many years of *La Nación* of Buenos Aires.

The document gushed angry words at "the leftist international propaganda network" that "alienated us from assistance and sympathy in such a way as to counteract the effect of the military victory." The *Catholic News* of New York published accounts on 18 October 1937 that 37 U.S. and Canadian professors, several politicians, and a number of religious figures sent letters to Generalísimo Franco and the military governor of Santander requesting that the lives of the 2,000 prisoners in Santander be spared, who they claimed were to be executed for remaining loyal to the government of Madrid. The document continued:

> After having assassinated 18,000 priests and laymen and destroyed more than 22,000 temples, and after trampling on all the norms of the human rights, the Bolshevik Committee of Barcelona has erected itself, without the least protest from the world press, as champion of the religious tolerance and civility. In spite of the so-called "Non-Intervention Principle," the International Brigades invaded our Fatherland. Day after day, the world press has applied to us the stigma of the bombing of the peaceful civilian populations.

The document then cited the case of "our most sincere friends who have indicated to us, in all languages, our inferiority in the subject of propaganda and the remedy, which is, above all, what is proposed in the 'present writing.'" The sympathetic British paper, the *Catholic Herald,* "surprised that some Catholics were not with Franco," had an explanation for the anti-Franco Catholic attitude: the intensity of propaganda against Franco, which was conducted by the newspapers 6 of the 7 days of the week —England has no Catholic dailies, only weeklies— and only the seventh day was not sufficient to counteract actions of the other 6 days. The organ of the Dutch fascism, the *Frente Negro (Black Front),* stated that Franco's foreign propaganda was not organized, for Franco underestimated its interest which made him suffer the subsequent damage.

The Swiss paper, *Action National,* said that, from the very beginning of the Spanish civil war, a certain part of the press systematically deformed the facts, or presented in a tendentious form, favorable to the Red government of Madrid and detrimental to Nationalist Spain. The Swiss Telegrafic Agency (Schweizerische Depeschenagentur) docilely took the same tone as the Havas agency. The Swiss agency never related the atrocities committed by the Republicans —church burnings, sackings of private buildings, and assassinations of hostages or noncombatant civilians. To the contrary, if Franco's air force executed bombing, the same Swiss agency gave each time the number of deaths— and never forgot to indicate that among the victims, there were noncombatants.

The document summed up the argument by emphasizing:

> While we have not created our own Agency, thus renounced our right to spread *our truth,* the Red Government has adopted a different

attitude and has kept the contracts with the Fabra Agency. Such an advantageous situation has not satisfied the Marxist Government, and it has created the propaganda network already mentioned above. That is why the Spain of Franco is presented as a territory invaded by the internal rivalry and struggle, where the sham Power is sustained only by terror, where the Italians and the Germans rob, kill and rape and in which the indigenous population gives the daily sign of its displeasure and of its rebellion (emphasis added).

GOVERNMENT–AGENCY RELATIONS

Getting down to the thorny problems of agency-state relationships, the EFE founding document envisaged an "independent and mercantile" agency, yet supported by the government. The EFE founders wanted to have it both ways. These EFE journalists aspired for the best of both worlds. They said the national agency was a "powerful instrument of external diffusion and influence, an authentic mouthpiece of the national feeling." For that reason, the national news agency should be "fundamentally at the service of the State and the Government." Yet, it must be organized as "a mercantile enterprise of private character" that would "function with a full autonomy." A news agency is "always a business in red." Its only revenue derives from the services given to papers or official, business, and private entities. The efficiency of those services requires the assembly of costly and complex news and technical organization. To minimize the loss, the news agency must adopt the structure of mercantile enterprises that extend the business to other commercial activities related to journalism.

Needless to say, government-press relationships were a troublesome to the EFE founders. To argue for governmental backing for their enterprise, they felt obligated to cite the legal bases of the French Havas and the British Reuters agencies and also to refer to the historical cases of national protection of the German Wolff and the British Reuters agencies. Yet, they wanted "freedom" from the Francoist government, then being consolidated, as far as their journalistic activities were concerned.

An "Officious" News Agency

The EFE founders came up with a uniquely Spanish solution to the apparent contradiction. They found a semantic solution to their problem. They characterized theirs as an "officious" news agency, as opposed to an "official" agency. The word *oficioso*, the Spanish equivalent to English *officious*, was a very convenient term for EFE's setup. The primary definition of the Spanish and English words is "zealous" or "meddlesome."

Also in diplomatic and human relations, English and Spanish have a similar usage. English *good offices* means a "friendly third-party mediation." Likewise in the Spanish usage, an *intervención oficiosa* (officious intervention) of a nation is employed to help solve a problem among other nations. But the Spanish *oficioso* has a third and strange meaning without an English equivalent usage. It refers to "unofficial things which someone with an official position does or says without formal exercise of that authority."[13] In the Spanish perception, the EFE news agency could be the "unofficial" acts that the Spanish government performs "without formal exercise of" but with informal recourse to its authority. It is in this sense, for example,that the Spanish journalists claim that they got some information from *fuentes oficiosas* (officious —not official— sources).

The EFE founders preferred to call their agency an "officious" agency. EFE should never be an "official" or even a "semiofficial" news agency. None of the great news agencies had official character, and the government and news agency "took great pains even to hide and cover up any kind of direct relations" —political, administrative, and economic— that could exist. The Nazi Germany's DNB (Deutsche Nachrichten-Buro) was a private business (limited stock company), even though its private stockholders were "in sympathy with" the government. Italy's Stefani agency declared in its statute: "STEFANI does not enjoy subsidy of the State nor of any other official or semi-official entities." It means that in Italy, as in Germany, "care is taken to bring to relief the private character" of the news agencies.

The EFE founders found it more difficult to explain away the "officious" nature of the agencies of so-called democratic nations, such as England, France, and the United States. These countries "naturally tend to accent still more expressively the private character of their agencies and the absence of all tie of dependence with the State." They, however, "do not conceal the relationships of 'officious type,' because, otherwise the news agency would cease to fulfill its fundamental objective, 'which is that of being an instrument of expansion to the service of the national interests.'"

Arguments bordered on the ludicrous, when the founders of EFE attempted to argue that even in the United States, "with its orthodox democratic Constitution," the "political relationships" between the government and news agencies are "officious" type. But the EFE document resorted to 2 authorities, who said the U.S agencies are also "officious." German journalism scholar Emil Dovifat had concluded that North American news agencies were also "de facto officious institutions." Princeton University's French professor Gilbert Chinard was also quoted as having said that the U.S. press serves in the end the policies of the federal government.

It is not clear whether the EFE founders convinced themselves that the news organizations in the United States were of an "officious" nature also, because of the White House press conferences and their use by the president. This argument, however, serves to demonstrate what a difficult time the EFE founders had in defining the nature of the relationship between the news agency they were creating and the Spanish Nationalist government. The difficulty emanated from an irreconcilable contradiction between the 2 things that they were seeking at once. On the one hand, they wanted EFE to have a "complete economic independence" from all, including the state entities, so that "its journalistic function be neutral and objective." But, on the other hand, they wanted the government to give EFE a news monopoly and necessary financial subsidy, because EFE should be "a truly authentic mouthpiece of the national sentiment at the service of the State and Government."

The "discovery" of the convenient Spanish term, *oficioso*, muddled the issue more than it solved the problem. It made the EFE news agency an easy prey of the 40-year Franco dictatorship, which used it as a simple instrument of political propaganda and press control. And the problem has persisted even in the post-Franco epoch. Even now it plagues the government and the EFE agency alike with the difficulty of defining the legal and financial status of the EFE.

SPY VERSUS REPORTERS

The founders of the EFE agency persistently advocated "the national interests of the 'New Spain' under the Caudillo Franco" but their "interests" may not have been purely patriotic. Their urgency and vehemence at least partially originated from a turf fight in the very field of journalism. The EFE group, including the powerful interior minister Serrano Súñer, was faced with a formidable rival in political jockeying for influence from none other than Franco's press office. Luis Bolin was the press office director, charged with accreditation of the foreign correspondents covering the Nationalist side of the civil war. Another of Bolin's duties was naturally that of Franco spokesman before the international press.

Bolin, however, was no mere press officer. He had fulfilled missions —complete with spy-thrillerlike plots— for the Franco forces in July 1936 which "were crucial to the successful launching of the Franco uprising."[14] Bolin made the arrangements for an airplane which took Franco —then military governor of the Canary Islands— from Las Palmas to Spanish Morocco on 18 July 1936. The next day, Bolin traveled to Rome with a commission from Franco to persuade "Il Duce," Mussolini, to provide the

Nationalists with the bombers and fighters that greatly helped the assault on the Spanish mainland by Franco's African forces on 5 August 1936.

Raised bilingually by his Spanish father and British-born mother (nee Bidwell), Luis Bolin Bidwell began work in 1920 as the press attaché at the Spanish embassy in London. Earlier, Bolin had served as a war correspondent with the British forces in the final years of World War I. With these extraordinary press-related credentials, Bolin returned to Spain to work as a regional delegate of the Spanish Tourist Board. Removed from this post by the socialist Second Republic, he returned to London. There he watched the events leading up to the Spanish civil war as correspondent for the right-wing Madrid daily *ABC*.

Two Blondes Go to Casablanca

ABC's publisher, Marques Juan Ignacio de Luca de Tena, and Juan March, a Majorcan businessman, masterminded and financed Bolin's mission to enlist Franco's leadership for the 18 July 1936 military uprising. On 5 July 1936, Marquess Luca de Tena called Bolin from the French border town of Biarritz (to avoid detection by the Madrid Republican government) with plans to transport Franco to the Spanish mainland. The *ABC* publisher instructed Bolin to hurry to Casablanca by 11 July with a plane capable of flying from the Canary Islands to the Spanish Moroccan town of Ceuta. In Casablanca, Bolin was to receive further instructions from an unidentified agent.

Bolin drew the funds needed for the clandestine mission from a Spaniard who worked at the London bank of Kleinwort. Now with sufficient money (2,000 pounds), Bolin could make further arrangements in London with the help of another Spaniard, Juan de la Cierva, the inventor of the autogiro,[15] a precursor to the modern helicopters then being manufactured by British and U.S. factories. De la Cierva and Bolin rented a 7-seater, twin-engine De Havilland plane.

To avoid arousing suspicions about the intent of their flight, they decided to have 2 blondes and another man accompany Bolin and the flight crew to give the appearance of 2 couples on a vacation trip. From an English publisher and writer, Douglas Jerrold, Bolin next received help in recruiting such passengers. Jerrold found an adventuresome, retired British army major, Hugh Pollard, to take on the offer. Moreover, Pollard persuaded his daughter Diana and her friend, Dorothy Watson, to go along. For the young women, free air travels to Casablanca and points beyond was an exciting adventure. "I did not know what was happening when we started out," the young daughter said later.

The small group left London on 11 July and, after unexpected delays in Lisbon, arrived in Casablanca on 12 July. The next day, newspapers reported the murder in Madrid of Calvo Sotelo, a leading fascist deputy in the Cortes (Spanish parliament). Fearing that tighter security measures would be taken by the Republic after the assassination of Calvo Sotelo, Bolin sent Pollard and the pilot alone to the Canaries to make contact with an intermediary. The plane, named *Dragon Rapide* and marked G-ACYR on its fuselage, reached Grand Canary on 15 July. The next day Franco placed the Canary Islands under martial law, which provoked some fighting among the military and the civil guards, delaying Franco's departure until 18 July.

The pilot drove to Las Palmas air strip in a rented car in which General Franco was riding, dressed in his funeral suit and wearing spectacles to confuse the casual observer. He was carrying in a valise his uniform, into which he changed aboard the *Dragon Rapide* upon takeoff. A day later Bolin received Franco and his party on the chartered British plane in Casablanca. The group proceeded to Tetuan, where Franco was joined by his Moorish and the Spanish foreign legion troops. Now the African military rebellion under Franco was fully on.

Franco next had to reach the Spanish mainland to join forces with the rest of the military insurgents. The crossing of the Gibraltar Straits was a dangerous operation, for which Franco needed air cover. On 19 July Franco dispatched Bolin to Rome to convince Mussolini to provide the Nationalists with an Italian air squadron. Bolin's Rome negotiations for the purchase of aircraft and supplies proved much more difficult than had been expected. Finally, on 30 July Bolin set out for Spanish Morocco with 12 Savoia-81 bombers. The bombers were heavily loaded with military supplies. Strong head winds caused 3 airplanes to run short of fuel and crash. The remaining 9 bombers and their Italian pilots enrolled in the Spanish foreign legion, thus creating an instant air force, which went into service in crossing the Straits of Gibraltar on 5 August.

Bolin served as the liaison officer between the Italian squadron and the Spanish military, and set up a press office in Sevilla to regulate and accredit foreign correspondents. In late September 1936, Bolin entered Toledo with the victorious armies of Africa and southern Spain commanded by Franco. In Toledo, Bolin recovered numerous art treasures, which had been hidden or were being crated for evacuation by the local Republican officials. Among the pieces recovered by Bolin was El Greco's *Burial of Count Orgaz*. For the 3 successful missions from the beginning of the Nationalist insurgency, Franco "owed an unending debt" to Luis Bolin, "who had made it all possible."

PRESS-POWER RIVALRY

From October 1936 at the Franco headquarters in Salamanca and later in Burgos, Bolin continued his old press-related services as press director with the tasks of organizing foreign correspondents for tours of battle areas. In this capacity, Bolin also functioned as the official spokesman for Franco on military and political matters. These duties placed Bolin in the center of newsmaking, always closely at the side of the Caudillo.

In this "glamorous" work, Bolin was helped by a diligent collaborator, Vicente Gay. A writer and university professor, Gay published articles on the Nationalist cause before and during the civil war. He eventually became chief of the press and propaganda department in Serrano Súñer's interior ministry, where he developed a massive propaganda effort directed at Spaniards within the Iberian peninsula and other countries.[16] But before Gay's cooptation by the EFE group, the Bolin–Gay duo occupied a perfect position to preempt the news agency scheme then being engendered by the Casino de Burgos *tertulia* group.

The hard-worked EFE journalists were jealous or even scared of Bolin, who was in the limelight of attention of the world press. The mutual contempt and hostility between Luis Bolin and Serrano Súñer —both indispensable, die-hard cronies of Franco's— are evidenced by their major memoirs of later years, in which each avoided conspicuously mentioning the other's name.[17] Both men played pivotal roles in the successful Franco insurrection, Nationalist victory in the civil war, and the subsequent Franco dictatorship. Yet they despised each other. Luis Bolin was by birth an Anglophile. Serrano Súñer openly advocated alliance with the Axis in World War II after Spain's civil war. These 2 men were allied under Franco only by their common enemies: socialists, anarchists, and communists, all of whom the Franco Nationalists lumped together under the sweeping rubric of "the Bolshevik Reds."

In the fight against the Reds during the civil war, Bolin was always closer physically and spiritually to the Franco power center than the EFE clique led by Serrano Súñer. Bolin served Franco from the very beginning of his military rebellion. Serrano Súñer, an "accidental" Franco brother-in-law, did not join Franco until February 1937 in Salamanca.

From this handicapped position, the EFE journalist group had to shout —always with shrill voices— the cause of the Nationalist Spain and glorify Franco's victories just to show that its work was more important and significant than the services of the Bolin–Gay duo. The fact that the EFE journalists had to wave incessantly the banner of "national interests of the New Spain" to advocate the creation of EFE doomed their agency from its very beginning to the role of government mouthpiece, the role its founders expressly disclaimed.

Chapter 2

Managing Three Wars
(1939-1945)

In the 15-year period between 1936 and 1951, Spain weathered 3 wars: the civil war, World War II, and the cold war. Franco emerged victorious from all 3 interconnected wars. The development of Spain's news agency EFE during its initial years closely paralleled the political vicissitudes of the Franco regime.

The Falange regime, led by Franco, won the cruel internecine war of 1936–1939. It was aided by direct intervention of fascist Italy and Nazi Germany. World War II came only 5 months later. At first, taken aback by the German-Soviet nonaggression pact of 23 August 1939, and a week later, shocked by Hitler's assault on Catholic Poland, Franco practiced cold realism, carefully avoiding direct diplomatic and military commitment in the Second World War.

Although the Franco regime remained definitely sympathetic to Germany and Italy, Spain did adroitly manage to balance herself between the Allies and the Axis, pirouetting from neutrality to nonbelligerence. For these maneuvers, Franco was labeled by the Western press as a fascist and a military dictator of the same stripe as Hitler and Mussolini, who wooed him, in personal interviews, for Spanish commitment in World War II.

That successful management out of World War II brought, in its aftermath, an international ostracism of Francoist Spain by the newly formed United Nations. The label of "the last surviving fascist" stuck with him and for a time Franco appeared to be the most hated Western head of state. In December 1946, the United Nations General Assembly condemned the Franco regime as "undemocratic" and recommended that member nations sever relations with Spain. Most countries withdrew their envoys from Madrid. But the period of international isolation was short-lived. Franco skillfully turned the UN's ostracism of Spain into a means of rallying domestic support in the name of national unity "faced with the international communist conspiracy."

Franco's self-confidence originated from an intuition that the Western powers could not long sustain their hostility to Spain, Europe's third largest country (194,885 square miles) located strategically between the Atlantic and the Mediterranean and a bridgehead to the African continent. The Franco regime survived the most difficult period of world boycott. The tide started turning in Spain's favor with the advent of the worsening relations between the Soviet camp and the West, which culminated in the cold war. Franco was once again ranked among the world's leading anticommunist statesmen. Relations with Western countries began the course of normalization in 1948. The Western powers reestablished diplomatic relations with Spain, led by the return to Madrid in 1951 of U.S. ambassador Stanton Griffis. It was only 2 short years away from the 1953 signing of a 10-year military assistance pact with the United States by which the Franco regime allowed 4 U.S. military bases in Spain.

Through these tumultuous years, the EFE news agency served the needs of the Franco regime, its creator, in surviving the crises. In the 1936–1939 civil war and its aftermath, EFE exalted the Franco Nationalist cause in domestic and international war propaganda. In the World War II years, EFE defended Franco's "skillful prudence" (*hábil prudencia*) of international neutrality and helped the Franco regime in consolidating its domestic control. The 1945–1951 international ostracism of Spain coincided with the EFE group's isolation among the rival factions in the Franco regime. EFE managed to survive the crisis in the same way Franco succeeded in vindicating himself by using the cold war.

WAR PROPAGANDA

The civil war began with the military uprising on 17 July 1936 and ended in the defeat of the Republic on 29 March 1939. The rebel military were supported by conservative groups such as the Falangists, traditionalists, monarchists, landowners, the Roman Catholic Church, and businessmen. When an initial garrison coup on 17 July 1936 failed to win swift control over all Spain, a bloody civil war ensued.

The rebelling Nationalists attacked on 3 fronts: the northern, southern, and central. In the north, General Emilio Mola took Burgos and pushed southward to Madrid. From the south, General Franco, leading the Army of Africa and other groups, including General Gonzalo Queipo de Llano, advanced north. By 15 August the rebels had linked their northern and southern zones. On 21 September these 3 generals —Franco, Mola, and Queipo de Llano— established the new triumvirate Technical Junta (*Junta*

Técnica). It declared Franco the "Generalissimo" and bestowed upon him the title of *El Caudillo* (the Chief) from 1 October 1936.

On the central front, the rebel forces advanced to the outskirts of Madrid by November 1936, but they could not get through the Republican defense lines at the University City area. The Madrid front then remained stable throughout the war. The Madrid defenders were supported by contingents of the International Brigades from 53 foreign countries. The Republicans were also assisted by the Soviet Union, which sent weapons and advisors. The Nationalists received aid from Italy and Nazi Germany. During its first months, the Spanish civil war acquired international political and ideological significance, representing, in microcosm, the polarization of the Western world into extreme left and radical right camps.

On 26 April 1937 German bombers of the notorious Condor Legion destroyed the Basque capital-village of Guernica, killing several hundred noncombatant civilians. The Nationalist army captured the Basque northern provinces in the summer of 1937 and by October 1937 it held the whole northern coast. A war of attrition began. In April 1938 the Nationalists drove eastward, reaching the Mediterranean and thus splitting the Republic into 2 zones, Madrid and Catalonia. At Christmas 1938, they moved upon Catalonia, capturing its capital, Barcelona, on 27 January 1939. The Republican government flew to exile in France on 28 March. The Nationalist forces entered Madrid that day. Franco declared the civil war officially over at 2:20 P.M., 29 March 1939.

Nationalist war propaganda during the 3-year civil war and its aftermath was staged in 3 distinct manners as the war went through 3 different phases. The first, a heterogeneous phase, started with the military uprisings on 3 fronts in July 1936. The second, a unified phase, started with formation of the first unified Nationalist government in January 1938. And the third, the war aftermath, came with the Day of Nationalist Victory (1 April 1939) and ended with the outbreak of World War II on 1 September 1939.

Radio War

During the first phase, each of the 3 rebellious fronts mounted its own war propaganda, until the EFE agency came into being and took control of the Nationalist press and propaganda in early 1938. On the southern front, the rebels led by General Queipo de Llano staged a daring strike in Sevilla on 18 July 1936. Through bluff and bravado, they had taken the small military post there and occupied the local radio station, from which Qeipo de Llano himself broadcast the rebel message to all of Spain —causing mass confusion among the ranks of the Popular Front. Queipo de Llano was among the most colorful of the Spanish military. He was inclined to talkative excesses and blustering propaganda.

He was not above repeating with relish rumors of the extramarital affairs of the opposition leadership. His accounts of Nationalist victory were often exaggerated. But his friends liked to be reassured and his enemies were thrown into terrified skepticism. Those bombastic, witty, and caustic broadcasts gave Queipo de Llano the nickname of "the Radio General." His use of radio was not limited to general propaganda, but was used in the frontline trenches as well. For this pioneer endeavor, the official civil war history credited Queipo de Llano with having introduced the radio as a new tactical instrument in modern warfare.[1]

The first Compañía de Radiodifusión y Propaganda was formed in the Madrid front and 8 units of radio announcers were stationed at the very first combat line in all sectors of the rebel forces surrounding the capital city. At first, army commanders took a jaundiced view of the radio unit, but the efficiency and enthusiasm demonstrated by the new units finally convinced them of the value of radio war. The Nationalist official war history even made the claim that the German technicians working with the Nationalists "imitated the Spanish mobile units, inspired by the plans by the Nationalist Command."

DUX News Agency

In the northern region the old-guard Falange carried out their own political propaganda war, even creating a news agency, *La Agencia Dux* (Dux News Agency). It was an official agency founded and run by the Delegacion Nacionál de Prensa y Propaganda of the Falange movement. DUX was established in October 1937 in Irún, a town on the northwest French-Spanish border, to which many Falangist leaders had fled from Republican persecution at the start of the civil war.[2]

For a year DUX functioned as the official organ of the Falange movement and an "officious" (*oficiosa*) news agency of the Nationalist government. DUX acted as the organ of political intervention over the foreign news supplied to the Spanish press in the Nationalist-held zones, a function later assumed by EFE. DUX was preoccupied with the war reporting and especially with the news destined for abroad and the Red Zone, which it infiltrated from its news bureaus spread around the Nationalist areas. News was transmitted by telephone, for DUX could not set up a radio service. The Dux News Agency was an important propaganda instrument for the initial periods of the National movement. When the Nationalist army expanded territory under its control, DUX proved insufficient to attend to

propaganda. Only 10 days after the military uprising, the Junta de
Nacional isssued an edict (*bando*) on 28 July 1936 which ordered
sorship on all printed materials under the "state of war" and gave
ribunals total jurisdiction over all crimes committed by publicity.[3]
May 1937, an order was issued to create —"to centralize the
p"— the Delegación del Estado para Prensa y Propaganda (State
on for Press and Propaganda), which was attached to the Secretaría
del Jefe del Estado (General Secretariat of the Chief of State).[4]
gation issued an 18 November 1937 order, upgrading itself to the
perior de Censura (Supreme Junta of Censorship).[5]

ne Press Law

ly April 1938, the Nationalist forces had cut the Republic into 2
zones. Sensing the looming victory in the civil war, the
Serrano Súñer regime delivered the coup de grace to the
an ideology, and decreed the Press Law (Ley de Prensa) of 22
38. The preamble of this fascist press law attacked the concept of
rth estate" as a decadent idea, declaring that "the existence of a
tate cannot be tolerated. It is inadmissible that the press can exist
he State. The press must always serve the national interests. It
e a national institution, a public enterprise in the service of the

press law of 23 articles, with its high-sounding preamble and
y disposition, was to "restore to the journalist, dignified worker at
ice of Spain, a sense of being apostle of thought and faith of the
' It delegated to the ministry of interior "the organization,
ion, and control of the national institution of the periodic press."
August 1938 order from the interior ministry created the Servicio
l de la Prensa (SNP). The SNP head, director-general de prensa
and his delegates across Spain could intervene in all printed
s in the Nationalist zones and later in all of Spain.[7] Serrano Súñer
l up "young persons in abundant supply then"[8] and organized an
e press-control apparatus. The "young persons in abundant supply,"
ed and persecuted by the leftist Second Republic, diligently went
heir way to reward the confidence deposited in them by the Franco
They approved and supported the voluntary services of the right-
rnalists who supplied war news accounts and photographs under the
title of EFE. They encouraged the incipient idea of news agency
d by the EFE journalists. They rounded up the financial backing for
s agency in the making from old bankers.

the necessary services. Its extreme northweste
fit to serve the press and radio in the northerı
Vascongadas, and the Old Castile. The DUX
the recently formed EFE group in October 1'

POLO – SISTERs' SPAIN

While Franco was engaged in military operat
politico-legal base was in the hands of Ramoı
in-law, and a Falangist lawyer. The captaincy
gradually assumed by Francisco Franco, who '
the head of state and of the military governme
Técnica del Estado" (Technical Junta of the S
of divergent Nationalist groups did not come
Franco in Salamanca on 20 February 1937. (F
married the Polo sisters, Carmen and Zita, re

When the 17 July revolt came, Serrano Súñe
After escaping from Madrid with assistaı
roundabout travels through France, he joined
in the same palace with Franco's family. In m
in March 1937, he discussed politics and prop
busy with military affairs. Serrano Súñer had
decree, which named Franco as *El Caudil*
totalitarian party. It forced the unification
Falange in to the FET y de las JONS —La Fala
y de las Juntas de Ofensiva Nacional-Sindicali

Politico – Legal Base

From April 1937, the war front expanded,
Nationalist forces remained in the hands of the
During August – October 1937 Franco mov
Salamanca to Burgos. Serrano Súñer gradual
control and on 30 January 1938 set up an
abolished and replaced the old triumvirate Jun
pre-Serrano days. This government served throu
Súñer assumed the powerful post of minis
propaganda, and public health.

Before this Franco – Serrano Súñer governr
band had spontaneously decreed various legal

press an
Defensa
prior ce
military

On 2'
censors
Delegat
General
This de
Junta S

Warti

By ea
isolated
Franco
Republi
April 1'
the "fo
fourth
outside
should
State."

This
transito
the ser
Nation.
supervi

A 10
Nacion
(DGP)
materi;
gathere
elabor;
mistrea
out of
regime
wing jc
service
presen
the ne

With elaborate legal provisions and intricate press-control bureaucracy —all a creation of Serrano Súñer— firmly in place, the ragtag group of right-wing journalists got a financial go-ahead on 1 October 1938 at an interiror ministry meeting to found La Agencia EFE, S.A. Two months later, on 3 December, EFE absorbed the old Fabra News Agency. The founding statute of "La Agencia EFE, S.A.," was notarized on 3 January 1939, at Burgos. Vicente Gállego Castro, director of the Catholic daily *Ya,* was named director of the new agency. War correspondent Pedro Gómez Aparicio was transferred from the position of chief of the SNP (National Press Service) and named EFE's subdirector. The "young Turk" from the Casino de Burgos group, José Luis García Gallego, was among the initial team of EFE reporters.

The first decision of the new EFE command was to continue the division of labor into 3 operational branches: (1) Foreign news, incoming as well as outgoing, was to be handled by the EFE proper. (2) The domestic operation would be entitled CIFRA (acronym for Crónicas, Informaciones, Fotografías y Reportajes de Actualidad, or Chronicles, News, Photographs and Reportage of the Present [News]).[9] (3) In spite of its inclusion in the long title CIFRA, the photography service of the EFE news agency was differentiated by its own logo, la CIFRA Gráfica (CIFRA Photo). After the civil war when sports became possible in Spain, a sports section was added with the logo ALFIL, meaning "bishop" in chess.

EFE GOES TO WAR

The newly born tripartite —EFE, CIFRA, and CIFRA Gráfica— news agency EFE went to war at Christmas 1938, in the Operation Catalonia of the Nationalist forces. Two days before Christmas, Franco ordered 6 army corps to converge on Barcelona to mop up feeble, disorganized resistance in the Catalonia region. Franco entered Barcelona on 26 January 1939 with a column of 50,000 soldiers.

To EFE, not formally constituted until 3 January 1939, the Operation Catalonia and the fall of Barcelona were the first official combat, although some of the confused, murky versions on the origin of EFE had it that "the name EFE appears already in the newspapers of the Franco zone in first months of 1938."[10] EFE director Gállego Castro declared, in a 1940 interview with a Spanish journalist, that EFE "magnificently gave the lie to" the news accounts overseas that the Catalonia offensive was directed by foreign generals. He said EFE had established photo services for foreign publications since 3 January 1939. Gállego Castro said the "copious photographic news" supplied to a "great English magazine" could demonstrate "the fabulous tales" on the fall of Barcelona in the foreign press.[11]

AP Man Visits EFE

In this 1940 interview Gállego Castro reminisced over the very first days of the EFE operation. EFE had to work out of a back room of a Burgos shop before moving into an office at the Palacio de Diputación building on Espolón Street. A North American AP man visited the EFE locale and proposed a news exchange, or a "reciprocity of services." Gállego Castro replied that he would "think about it." The EFE director was sure that the answer must have been a "great surprise to that AP man" who did not know that the dilapidated EFE setup was only "transitory" and it was not to be the "definitive" condition. He must not have been able to explain that "the EFE news agency, so obviously poor, would permit itself the luxury of 'considering' the proposal from a great American news agency." Surely, the man must have left with a quick remark about the "pride of the Spaniards."

But it was neither the poor physical condition of EFE nor the Spanish pride that prevented Gállego Castro from accepting the AP man's service exchange offer. The political decision had to come from a higher authority, interior minister Serrano Súñer, who was under the influence of the German propaganda office, already in operation since the early days of the civil war. Ramón Garriga, chief of news of the National Press Service (SNP) at the interior ministry, affirmed in his 1976 book that this Nazi office which was dependent on the German embassy, took care of the translation and editing of books and the distribution among the Spanish dailies of "all kinds of propaganda."[12] There had also been operating a branch of the German news agency, DNB (Deutsches Nachrichten-Buro), which supplied telegraphic news to the Spanish press through the EFE news agency.

German *Cross* Wins

The German propaganda office of Salamanca had employed several Spaniards. The "masterpiece of that office was a periodical publication called *ASPA* (*Cross*), which presented the latest German propaganda. The German press office, in addition to its own materials and the dispatches of DNB, supplied the fledgling EFE agency with news from the German Trans-Ocean, a wireless agency established in 1919. The Third Reich had acquired Trans-Ocean principally to serve overseas newspapers and foreign news agencies.[13] The Trans-Ocean News Agency made its appearance in Franco

Spain in the person of Hans Lazar. In September 1938 the Berlin government sent Lazar to Burgos as representative of Trans-Ocean. Goebbels had sent Lazar to Spain with the mission to "mount a great news service in the [Iberian] Peninsula with a fat salary as the representative of Trans-Ocean."

Retired EFE reporter García Gallego agreed with Garriga in the assessment of Hans Lazar's mission in Spain as the Trans-Ocean representative. García Gallego said[14] that there was pressure on EFE to contract the Trans-Ocean Agency, "dedicated generally to overseas and concretely to the Iberoamerican area." Although EFE resisted, not contracting its service, it was "obligated" to become the distributor of the Trans-Ocean service to the Spanish newspapers. García Gallego made the point that in the distribution of Trans-Ocean news, the EFE name was never attached; "we separated and delimited in a clear manner, so that it would not be mixed with the EFE news." Garriga said Hans Lazar did not spend too much time as the Trans-Ocean man. On termination of the civil war, Lazar was appointed press attaché of the German embassy, where he became the "most powerful agent of all those Germans, who toiled there to the service of the Hitlerian cause."

Meanwhile on the international political front, the fall on 27 January 1939 of Barcelona —the first military operation fully covered by the newly organized EFE agency— accorded legitimacy to the rebel Nationalists. A month later, on 27 February, the United Kingdom and France recognized the Franco government. Two days later, on 1 March, Marshal Philippe Petain arrived in Burgos as the French ambassador. On 17 March Spain signed a nonaggression treaty with Portugal, which had recognized the Franco regime in May 1938. The victorious Franco regime demonstrated to the world its pro-Axis stance by joining the Anti-Comintern pact on 27 March 1939, the day before its troops marched into Madrid.

WAR AFTERMATH

Little by little, event after event, the groping EFE journalists were proving the worth of the new officious agency. By the time Franco formed a new post-civil war government on 10 August 1939, EFE had been solidly established as the conduit of official bulletins. All Spanish newspapers of 11 August carried on the front pages a "boxed" bulletin bearing the logo or signature CIFRA, the domestic part of EFE.[15]

Except for the absolute authority in the hands of Generalissimo Franco, there was no other equal to the power wielded by Serrano Súñer, *cuñadísimo* (the superlative for *cuñado* or brother-in-law). *Cuñadísimo*'s fame was riding high. On his recommendation the Franco regime announced its withdrawal from the League of Nations on 8 May 1939, another step to accommodate the wishes of Berlin and Rome. Serrano Súñer had travled to Mussolini's capital, accompanying the Italian troops who were returning home from the Spanish expedition.

Serrano Súñer's Rome visit was quickly reciprocated with a return call to Spain by the notorious Italian foreign minister, Count Galeazzo Ciano, in mid-July 1939. The climax of that visit was the 13 July Ciano–Franco meeting at San Sebastián where cheering crowds greeted it with the loud cries of "Franco–Ciano" and *"Viva El Duce"* (Hail Il Duce).[16] The event was reported by all Spanish newspapers, served by EFE. Serrano Súñer could do no less than to mobilize Spain's whole press under his firm control to honor the visitor from Italy, which along with Germany, had made the Francoist victory possible.

Serrano Súñer's attention to the Axis capitals was not limited to "full liberty" allowed the Spanish press "to praise Germany and Italy."[17] He sent his top 2 press functionaries to Berlin and Rome as EFE correspondents in August 1939. José Antonio Giménez-Arnau, director-general of press (DGP) at the National Press Service (SNP) and the "creator" in 1938 of EFE, was sent to the Italian capital, and Ramón Garriga, SNP's news chief, was dispatched to Berlin. Both EFE correspondents also worked as press attachés at the Spanish embassies in these cities, emphasizing EFE as an official organ of the Spanish government. These 2 SNP officials were the first foreign correspondents of EFE.

Then came what Garriga called "a true bombshell"[18] in the form of the Hitler–Stalin nonaggression treaty signed on 24 August 1939, which caused Spain "complete consternation."

The event was the first test of EFE as the international agency it pretended to be. EFE, however, had claimed that its "sovereign information" mission was to promote anticommunist Falangism against the "encroaching leftist propaganda" directed at Franco's cause. The Soviet-German friendship entente was a troublesome story to report; "Nazi Germany making friends with communist Russia!" EFE found an easy way out of the dilemma. It distributed to the Spanish papers the diverse news analyses on the event coming out of the world news centers: Brussels, London, Berlin, Moscow, Warsaw, Oslo, Paris, Bucharest, Rome, Tokyo, Basel, Salzburg, and others.

EFE's Rome correspondent Giménez-Arnau sent in his own analysis of the Hitler–Stalin treaty, saying: "The nonaggression treaty signifies a new stumbling block that makes the [world power] equilibrium difficult to recover," according to a Spanish journalism scholar, Felipe Maraña Marcos.[19]

HITLER's FOUR TEETH

During the 6 years of World War II, Spain pursued the policy of "*hábil prudencia*" (skillful prudence) that Franco had announced to the National Falange Council on June 1939, as "the chief feature of our foreign policy."[20] By this policy, Franco kept Spain out of the world conflagration, practicing proclaimed "neutrality" with varying degrees of pro-Axis tilt, according to the tide of the war. Franco's noncommittal attitude infuriated Hitler so much that he is supposed to have uttered remarks that he "would rather have 4 teeth pulled than bargain with such a man again" after the Hitler–Franco meeting in October 1940.

In implementing this neutralist policy of "skillful prudence," Generalissimo Franco and *cuñadísimo* Serrano Súñer, (who had been appointed foreign minister the week before the Hitler–Franco meeting), fully utilized the services of the now firmly established EFE news agency. On the day of Anglo-French declaration of war on Germany, Franco broadcast from Radio Burgos an urgent appeal for peace, begging the belligerents to "localize the conflict." Franco spoke as a man of experience, pretending to be the "conscience of Europe."

On 5 September Franco dispatched through the EFE-CIFRA service to all Spanish newspapers a decree in which he imposed "the strictest neutrality on all Spanish subjects considering the state of war that unfortunately exists."[21]

Serrano Súñer took trips to Berlin and Rome in September and November 1940, respectively. On their heels followed the 23 October 1940 Franco–Hitler interview at the French town of Hendaye near the Spanish border, and the 12 February 1941 Franco–Mussolini meetings at the Italian city of Bordighera near the French border.

On 12 June 1940 —only 2 days after the Italian entrance into the war— Spain declared its nonbelligerency that, under international law, gave Spain much leeway to maneuver in favor of the Axis side. Soon after the Nazi attack on the Soviet Union in June 1941, Spain dispatched 47,000 Falangist "volunteers" put together as the "Blue Division" (División Azul) under General Agustín Muñoz Grandes to the Russian front to fight along with the German troops. Then, on 1 September 1942, the fascist *cuñadísimo* Serrano Súñer was dismissed as foreign minister. Closely watching the war trends now turning in the Allies' favor in 1943, Franco Spain jumped back on the tight rope of neutrality, acceding to a demand by British ambassador Sir Samuel Hoare that "Spain must assume an actual rather than a nominal neutrality."[22]

Spain desperately grasped at opportunities to get back on normal terms with the Allies. Presumably aroused by Japanese atrocity in the Philippines, Spain severed diplomatic relations with Japan. Cynically only a day before the German surrender, Spain severed relations with Germany on 7 May. (Spain had dissociated itself from Italy in September of 1943, only 2 months after the fall of Mussolini.) These quick-fix friendly overtures by Spain toward the Allies were vitiated by the Spanish attitude toward the Soviet Union, exemplified by Franco's statement that "we cannot believe in the good faith of communist Russia." At the July–August 1945 Potsdam Conference, the Allied powers declared that they "would not favor any application for membership" in the United Nations "put forward by the present Spanish government." Thus began the period of Spanish ostracism from the post-World War II UN community.

Soviet News Scoop

On 18 October 1939 —5 months after the 19 May victory celebration in Madrid— Franco left his wartime headquarters at Burgos for the capital city, where he settled at the Palace of El Pardo some 16 miles from the bustling downtown. The EFE agency followed the *Caudillo* into Madrid in December, and took up residence at 8 Espalter Street, the building belonging to the old Fabra agency. At this "small chalet"[23] at Espalter 8, EFE staged an international news scoop.

On 30 November 1939 the Soviet Union invaded Finland. After a 3-month stand, the Finns capitulated, and the Soviet-Finnish peace treaty was signed in Moscow during the night of 2–3 March. The text of the treaty in Russian was announced at 3 A.M. "Only 50 minutes later the EFE agency facilitated to the Spanish papers the news and the text translated into our language," bragged Gállego Castro, EFE founding director, in an interview on 10 September 1940. He proudly pointed out that, thanks to EFE's news scoop, "the Spanish dailies could give in their morning editions what the newspapers of all the rest of the world could not insert until the afternoon editions of the following day.[24]

Children of War. How was this unusual scoop possible for EFE yet unequipped with international news network except for its one-man bureaus attached to the embassies in Berlin and Rome? It was an unexpected benefit from a tragic civil war event. Faced with the oncoming Nationalist assault on Barcelona, the members of the defeated Republican government fled abroad, a majority of them to France. The Soviet Union welcomed about

2,000 Spanish communists along with some 5,000 Spanish children over the course of the war.[25] They were called the "children of war" (*niños de la guerra*). Some Spanish communist refugees in Moscow had learned Russian and also obtained high-ranking contacts in the Soviet party. They obtained the Soviet-Finnish treaty, translated it into Spanish, and cabled it to their families in Spain. The Spanish government intercepted it and gave it to EFE, which distributed it to Spain's newspapers. (Some 40 years later, at least 2 former "children of war," now Soviet citizens, worked at the Moscow bureau of EFE in December 1985.)

37 Years at Ayala

After this Russian news scoop, the EFE administrative council felt that the 5-story chalet at Espalter 8 did not have the capacity for developing a news agency of "national and international diffusion." EFE officials found a house at 5 Ayala Street. The building had 4 stories; EFE initially occupied only the ground floor, basement, and the first floor. The rest of the building was rented to other enterprises "to obtain economic resources." Several years passed and the agency needed the upper floors. The tenants were asked to leave and the EFE agency then occupied the whole building and stayed there until April 1977. This means that EFE spent some 37 years of its 50-year legal existence (1939–1989) at Ayala 5.

During the years 1940–1943 EFE expanded its operations and acquired material means. In 1940 the EFE office in Barcelona (Spain's second city and the leading industrial center) was elevated to the category of "delegación" (delegation, an equivalent of bureau). Besides its bureaus in Berlin and Rome in the hands of the press attachés at the Spanish embassies, EFE also dispatched a stringer each to New York City and the pro-German French Vichy.[26] In 1940 and 1941, EFE installed a radio broadcast station on Abedul Street in the north Madrid suburb of Chamartín de la Rosa, near the capital's north railway station. This radio station and its grounds were acquired to commence radio-telegraph communication with the Canary and Balearic Islands and the Americas at the cost of P700,000 (some US$77,000 then).

In 1943, EFE replaced the telephone with its first teletype machines.[27] EFE had used age-old telephones in all facets of its news-gathering and -dissemination activities. EFE's central newsroom had phone booths, where journalist-stenographers would receive and dispatch news —shouting at the top of their lungs— across the country. The CIFRA correspondents would be paid for their services at a certain rate for every 3 minutes of their telephone conference.[28] The stenographers were not clerical shorthand-takers but were an important component of Spanish the press. José Luis García Gallego, of the Casino de Burgos founders of EFE, for example, had begun his 60-year journalism career as a reporter-stenographer for the Catholic daily, *El Debate.*[29]

During the first year of its residence in Madrid, EFE added a branch to its operations. In May 1940, EFE director Gállego Castro started a weekly news magazine, *Mundo (World)*, himself becoming the magazine's director, and naming the EFE subdirector, Pedro Gómez Aparicio, to the position of *redactor-jefe* (chief writer) of the new magazine. Pedro Gómez Aparicio, the founding subdirector since 1938, took over the EFE directorship on 13 July 1944, to remain in that position until 1958. Another top EFE command change occurred in December 1940. The nominal presidency of the EFE agency had been held by the old Fabra owner, Celedonio de Noriega Ruiz, the Marquis of Torre Hoyos. The EFE presidency was unceremoniously transferred to Jesús Pabón y Suárez de Urbina, until then the foreign propaganda chief at the National Press Service (SNP) of the interior ministry. With these 2 changes, the government control of EFE was firmly established and the Pabón–Gómez duo would carry the agency through the next 15 years of consolidation. But the story of EFE during the years of World War II is not complete without looking at other facets of its activities.

Nazi Propaganda Organ

On 2 August 1940, German foreign minister Joachim von Ribbentrop informed his ambassador in Spain, Baron Eberhard von Stohrer, that "Spain's early entry into the war was desirable."[30] Ribbentrop extended a personal invitation to visit Berlin to Serrano Súñer who was allowed by Franco to accept the invitation ("Serrano had sought the invitation since early July"). In September 1940 Serrano Súñer visited Germany and Italy, laying groundwork for Franco's later meetings with Hitler and Mussolini.

EFE director Gállego Castro accompanied the Spanish mission to Berlin. EFE's correspondent in Berlin, Ramón Garriga, said, "Paul Schmidt, Ribbentrop's press minister," offered to the EFE director "all kinds of assistance, collaboration to prepare the things with the objective to carry out a great journalistic work [in the Americas], if one day, our Trans-Ocean Agency has to leave the positions that it has gained in the past years."[31] Schmidt told EFE director Gállego Castro that he only had to make "propositions with a guarantee that we will accept your offers, because we are determined to help you Spaniards in the conquest of extensive journalistic market in the Americas." Gállego did not want to understand the "sibylline language" of Schmidt and "played the fool," leaving the things "for study to discuss again later." When Gállego Castro and Garriga left Schmidt's office on Wilhelmstrasse, the indignant EFE director repeated to Garriga: "Franco and Serrano can do anything they want; but I will not sell the EFE Agency to Nazi gold."

Soon "several Berlin elements in the agencies DNB and Trans-Ocean and of the Ministries of Propaganda and the Foreign Affairs" started complaining about "the very little facilities that Gállego would give." These Germans would "put their hands on the heads [in incredulity]," for Gállego Castro would not accept "their generous offers to give the EFE news agency the very technical means that it needed to transmit by radio extensive news services to all the corners of the American continents." Garriga was fearful that Gállego would not keep the EFE directorship for long, for he was the target of "a terrible campaign" by the Falangists, sold to the side of the Third Reich.

Hitler Meets Franco

Gállego Castro would meet Schmidt 2 more times. During his September 1940 visit to Berlin, Serrano Súñer met Hitler, who expressed to Franco's brother-in-law his desire to meet Franco in German-occupied France. Franco and Hitler were to meet on 23 October 1940, at the railroad station Hendaye, the French town on the Spanish border. With this "accomplishment," Serrano Súñer was "promoted" to foreign minister on 18 October just before the planned Franco–Hitler meeting. The EFE director, Gállego Castro, accompanied the Franco trip along with the new foreign minister Serrano Súñer. EFE broke the news of the historic meeting to the Spanish press with a bulletin that was carried on the frontpage of all Spanish newspapers with huge headlines, large pictures of Franco and Hitler, and accompanying articles.

> IN FRANCE, 23—The Fuhrer has had today with the chief of the Spanish State, Generalissimo Franco, an interview on the Spanish-French frontier. The interview has taken place in the atmosphere of camaraderie and cordiality existing between both nations. The minister of Foreign Relations of the Reich, von Ribbentrop, and the minister of External Affairs of Spain, Sr. Serrano Súñer, took part in the conversation. —(EFE)[32]

A day later, on 25 October, the Spanish and German papers carried front-page photographs showing Franco with an exuberant smile on his face, as

Hitler met him at Hendaye station on 23 October, when the *Caudillo* —with his right arm stretched in Nazi-Falange salute— and the Fuhrer, strutting side by side, inspected the S.S. honor guard. People expected the next act would be Spanish entry into the war on the side of the Axis. However, in spite of smiles, the Hendaye meeting did not produce any clear-cut results. Many said Hitler and Franco did not take to each other.[33] Franco's train arrived an hour late. Franco had played a psychological trick on Hitler. One account has it that the Fuhrer was exasperated by portly little dark-eyed Franco, who, in his calm, monotonous sing-song voice, pleaded for economic aid and avoided committing Spain.

After 9 hours of hard bargaining, Hitler was supposed to have made the remark about his preference for 4-teeth extraction to another meeting with a man like Franco. Serrano Súñer disputed all these foreign accounts and claimed that Franco's train arrived only 8 or 9 minutes late and that Hitler had gotten there only 10 minutes earlier at 3:30 P.M."[34] Upon return from Hendaye, Serrano Súñer made another visit to Rome in November 1940. Within 3 months from the Hitler–Franco meeting, Franco traveled to Bordighera, in the Italian Riviera, to meet with Mussolini on 12 February 1941.

The Hitler–Franco meeting was not wholly negative from the German viewpoint. Paul Schmidt, Ribbentrop's foreign-press minister, again approached Serrano Súñer with the proposal to assist in the Spanish information operation in the Americas. Gállego Castro again balked at the idea. Then, Schmidt decided to attack the EFE director from the rear. Schmidt ordered Hans Lazar, the "agile" press attache in Madrid, to act quickly. Lazar was to stage "the battle of EFE" with Serrano Súñer and Antonio Tovar, his subsecretary of press and propaganda, instead of trying to convince Gállego Castro to cooperate. In a short time Lazar achieved this aim. Agreements were worked out and Schmidt flew to Madrid to sign the Schmidt–Tovar Agreement in early March 1941.

The agreement stipulated that the Spanish government would order the EFE news agency to establish branches in the Americas with a double mission: (1) to transmit to Madrid all kinds of journalistic information on events in the Americas; and (2) to receive and distribute among all kinds of people a news service that would be sent by radio from Madrid. The Germans would contribute the needed currency for the expenses of mounting and operating this great news service. Garriga could presently observe in Berlin the complaints of the Germans on "the parsimony of EFE's Gállego in carrying out the Schmidt–Tovar Agreement."

Now impatient, Hans Lazar took actions without EFE's cooperation. He drew up a list of about 30 Spaniards who would travel to the Americas as correpondents; made special studies about technical services EFE needed;

and prepared a roster of materiel that Germany could furnish. The Germans were "in a hurry" and Gállego Castro would only present "difficulties." Finally, Gállego Castro had to do something. Four Spanish journalists left for the Americas to act as correspondents in the United States, Chile, Argentina, and Guatemala. But EFE did not accept the generous technical and financial assistance offered by Berlin. Gállego Castro supported his 4 journalists with EFE's own money, and the radio transmission never materialized. The EFE director "won the title of saboteur of the Schmidt–Tovar Agreement," Garriga said. This and other things would lead to the dismissal of Gállego Castro as the EFE director later.

About the time that the Schmidt–Tovar Agreement was being implemented, EFE news personnel demonstrated resistance to German encroachment by small but significant acts of courage and sound judgment. In April 1941, the German Afrika Corps under the brilliant command of Marshal Erwin Rommel conquered the entire Cyrenaica province of Libya, except for the Tubruq (or Tobruk) garrison. It held out against months of Rommel's siege. On 11 April, the Nazi Trans-Ocean news agency reported that Tobruk had been taken. The Madrid daily, *Informaciones* (*News*) carried the Trans-Ocean news. EFE, which had been forced to distribute the Trans-Ocean news service to Spanish newspapers, did not give that false "German propaganda" in its own service. This small act of resistance was proudly pointed out by José Luis García Gallego.[35]

THE *CONSIGNAS*

On 8 November 1939, an assassination attempt was made on Adolf Hitler's life. A German carpenter named Georg Elser had planted a bomb at the hall of the Burgerbraukeller in Munich, where Hitler delivered an anti-British speech. (The bomb blast missed Hitler by about 12 minutes.) The news literally was a bombshell to the Spanish government, which abhorred the possibility of a similar attempt on Franco. Early the next day, the National Press Service (SNP) of the interior ministry issued an order to all Spanish newspapers through the dispatches of EFE. This order, denominated *consigna*, read: "All commentary about the violence of Munich against Chancellor Hitler is absolutely prohibited. In this respect, only the communications of the EFE Agency will be published, without giving them excessive importance." The terse order was followed up by a reminder: "We utilize this circumstance to recall the prohibition on publication of all news supplied by the listening of foreign [radio] stations."

Such *consigna* orders were enforced with the stringency of orders in the military from which the term had originated. The military term *consigna* was "incorporated into the totalitarian concept of the press, and performs specific functions," says Manuel Prados y López, Spanish scholar of journalism ethics. He describes the functions this way: "The *CONSIGNA* —distributed simultaneously to newspapers— unifies them, dignifies them, and orients them toward only one vigorous love. . . . The *CONSIGNA* is for the newspapers light on the horizon, sign of security, timely guide."[36]

The *consigna*s worked this way, says another Spanish press law scholar, Gonzalo Dueñas: "The newspaper would receive a ministerial communication accompanied with a series of directives. The document carried letterhead of the Ministry, signature of the Minister, and the date. Also received was a separate, unmarked and unsigned sheet that gave the *CONSIGNA*s —instructions— to follow."[37] The *consigna* was, without a doubt, the principal instrument of "the Spanish formula of the Oriented Press (Prensa Orientada)," a phrase coined by Arias-Salgado, when he later became the minister of information and tourism. He claimed: "Between uncontrolled and 'theoretically free' Press and 'statutorized and prefabricated Press,' subservient to an iron-clad directivism, the Spanish formula is the Oriented Press."[38]

Article 19 of the 1938 Press Law said the state would penalize "any and all deviation from the NORM dictated by the competent services in the subject of Press." The *consigna*s were among the norms, says Manuel Fernández Areal, vehement opponent and critic of the Francoist press regime. He was the dierctor of the *Diario Regional* (*Regional Daily*) of Valladolid province, and even as late as November 1964, he was jailed for 19 days for an editorial "insulting the Army."[39] He described what an iron rule without any escape the entire 1938 Press Law was. It was codified on the general principles that "the Press ought to serve the State, the Press is not a group of private or private and public enterprises, each of which has its rights and obligations, but a 'national institution' and 'service,' something which —not paid by the State— depends on it. The State orders it, employs it for high purpose, controls it, determines how many and what newspapers should exist, who will be directors of the different newspapers —diverse in number and unified in the political orientation— and when they should cease to exist." Fernández Areal pointed out the same general principles of the 1938 press law dictated:

> The state will supply the news through only one channel, the EFE Agency (that will adopt the names of CIFRA for the national news and ALFIL for the sports news), directly tied to the governmental Press services.[40]

There was nothing secretive about the use of EFE for distribution of the government *consigna*s. Though occasionally critical of heavy-handed and clumsy measures adopted by government censors, many "independent" journalists of EFE openly admitted to the use of the agency by the government. In a 1945 document, which asked for more governmental supports, EFE administrators even went so far as to enumerate the distribution of *consigna*s conspicuously among the services they claimed that EFE rendered to the government.

These government orders to the press varied in physical form and content. They would be variously denominated: "orders, circulars, *consigna*s, orientations, requests, suggestions," and so forth. No matter what the titles, when they were not followed 100%, they would promptly trigger such actions as "threats, warnings, and sanctions" which would be issued in another official communication. The sanctions would be "economic" (fines), "coercion by restriction on newsprint supply," or "blustering dismissals."[41]

Hollywood Banned

The most interesting *consigna*s to the Anglo-American observer was a "circular" issued on 2 April 1940 against the 29 Hollywood-related "professionals who publicly supported the Second Republic." This circular-*consigna* prohibited "the enumeration of their names in publicity, in articles and in film distribution." These celebrities made the blacklist: (1) actors-actresses: Bing Crosby, Joan Crawford, James Cagney, Bette Davis, John Garfield, Constance Cummings, Edward Arnold, Eddie Cantor, Florence Eldridge, Frances Farmer, Douglas Fairbanks, Jr., Frederic March, Ann Miller, Paul Muni, Burgess Meredith, Franchot Tone, Louise Rainer, Silvia Sidney, Paul Robeson, and Rudy Valle; (2) directors-producers: Charlie Chaplin, Lewis Milestone, and Frank Tutle; and (3) script-writers: Upton Sinclair, Kenneth McGowan, Humphrey Cobb, Clifford Odets, Dudley Nichols, and Liam O'Flatherty.[42]

The Francoist regime had reason to resent these show-business personalities, for most of Hollywood supported the Republican cause in many ways: "Some 80 actors, writers, and directors had signed an open letter to President Roosevelt in February 1937 protesting the Nationalist bombing of Barcelona; a big rally in the summer of 1937 raised $1.5 million for the Republic; and three full-length feature films were made in defense of the Republic —*Last Train from Madrid* (1937), *Love under Fire* (1937), and *Blockade* (1938). In *Blockade*, produced by Walter Wagner, Henry Fonda played the role of a member of the International Brigades who, at the end of the film, delivered an impassioned soliloquy —praising the Republic and denouncing the [unevenly enforced] Non-Intervention Agreement."[43]

A military decree issued early in the civil war (23 December 1936) had sweepingly declared illicit "productions of pornographic, socialist, communist, libertarian, and 'generally dissolvent' literature."[44] This "degenerative" literature included the books authored by such foreign writers as Ernest Hemingway, Arthur Koestler, Thomas Mann, Andre Gide, George Orwell, Andre Malraux, Romain Rolland, Aldous Huxley, Louis Aragon, Alexis Tolstoy, Octavio Paz, Pablo Neruda, Malcolm Cowley, and John Dos Passos. They had either attended or supported the Congress of the International Association of Antifascist Writers, celebrated in the Republican-occupied zone in July 1937.[45]

It boggles one's mind to imagine how many *consigna*s were issued during the more than 40 years of their existence. They were, however, all distributed by the national agency EFE. The other Valladolid editor, once-jailed Fernández Areal, observed that "literally millions, and millions, of *consigna*s were transmitted to the Spanish newspapers through the teletypes, that were necessarily and obligatorily connected with the only agency supplying national and international news, EFE —directed first by Vicente Gállego and later, 'with more fidelity,' by Pedro Gámez Aparicio, who deserved the National Journalism Prize and still later, was appointed 'journalist of honor' by the Ministry or by EFE's provincial bureaus."[46]

It is impossible —or ludicrously futile— to attempt to trace the millions of *consigna*s dispatched by the censors during the 40-year existence of this institution. However, it is useful to review a sampling of them to present a profile of this uniquely Spanish phenomenon during the second half of the 1940s.

"Masterpiece" Censors

Several *consigna*s dealt with national and international politics. One of these was a lengthy *consigna* received at *El Norte de Castilla* of Valladolid in late 1943. The editor could not place the precise date, for, as stated earlier, all *consigna*s were issued on undated, unsigned plain sheets of paper. The long and tedious text of this *consigna* is presented in its entirety so that the reader will taste the flavor of these "masterpieces" of bureaucratic literature. It read:

> That newspaper shall publish in next 15 days 9 articles by your better collaborators, on the first page, commenting [on] the speech

pronounced by His Excellency, the Chief of state, on the day 1 of October before the National Council. It shall be divided for these objectives in various sections that are detailed below, each writer fitting the corresponding theme, subjected to the fundamental orientation given by the Generalissimo. The sense of the speech should be commented upon with reference and illustrations fit to the theme, selecting fundamental phrases, but without loading the article with numerous and lengthy transcriptions of the speech itself. Commentaries should have original tune and should not limit to emphasizing phrases with tone of journalistic compromise.

Then the *consigna* determined the titles and the content of those 9 articles as well as the fragments of the speech by Franco on which the articles should be based:

Theme 1:   The world and the Spanish momentum. Vigilant neutrality and national reality. From "Councilmen and comrades" to "of our regime."

Theme 2: The enemies overseas. Hispanoamerica and our policy. Internal policy and the Spaniards. From "That is fruit in great part" to "why disfigure them."

Theme 3: Principles of our Movement: unity, authority and liberty. The Movement is not a program. From "Our regime has not hidden" to "Will not be sterile. . . ."

Theme 4: The communist menace. From "As the war progresses" to "of communist chaos."

Theme 5: Liberalism, communism and Marxism. Catholic truth and economic realism. From "A Catholic sentiment of the life" to "commercials of our Fatherland."

Theme 6: The wealth, the Christian moral and the service to the interest of the society and of the fatherland. Limits of the property, concern for social redemption of the Falange. From "The wealths of a nation" to "social betterment of the humans."

Theme 7: Laws and social works. From "This is the example" to "tyranny of our regime."

Theme 8: The problems of the Spanish agriculture and their solution. From "Two are the big problems" to "redemption of our field."

Theme 9: Unity, youth and relief. From "In this way" to "the end."[47]

This *consigna* came from the Dirección General de Prensa (DGP) and was transmitted through the EFE teletypes. That editor —jailed in 1964— of the other Valladolid daily, *Diario Regional*, described a *consigna* which originated from and was distributed directly by the EFE agency on 21 February 1950. That month in Rome the Third International Congress of the Catholic Press was celebrated. In his usual message to the congress the Pope Pius XII alluded to the "unjust situation in nations" where the Catholic press was gagged for the lack of freedom of expression. A few U.S. journalists inferred that the pope's words could be in reference to the situation in Spain, where the 1938 Press Law was still imposing vigilance and control. The EFE news agency quickly stepped in and diffused to the Spanish press a Rome dispatch, which read:

ROME, 20. — Several North American journalists have approached a distinguished personality in the Vatican circles, asking if certain concepts of the message of the Holy Father, addressed to the International Congress of Catholic Journalists, should be understood to make reference to several Latin countries, like Argentina, Portugal and Spain, in which the governments maintain certain censorship. The personality consulted replied negatively, manifesting that in the cited countries the censorship was limited only to the political order, maintaining an ample respect for the Catholic Press of the respective countries. — EFE.[48]

Not all the *consigna*s dealt with such momentous themes as these 2 examples. Some dug into technical details showing that some censors had journalistic expertise equal, or even better, than that of professional news editors on the copydesk. A *consigna* sent to *El Norte de Castilla* in December 1941 not only ordered obligatory insertion of a speech by the subsecretary of popular education, but it gave these technical details:

It should be published in bold or italic types and with different subheads in the text copy. The speech can start on the front page, in four columns at least, then to jump the news to any other pages of the paper. The photograph should also be published. The headlines should pick out the phrases of the essential paragraphs of the speech.

At times, these meticulous instructions would backfire and become the cause for consternation among all concerned. Some editors —frightened because they did not know how to read the censors' minds— thought that the initial letters *DGP* (for Dirección General de Prensa), indicating obligatory insertion, should be included as the logo EFE or CIFRA were. This erroneous conclusion triggered the following advice:

> In some Spanish newspapers, there appear, from time to time, at the end of some news or information, the initials D.G.P., which, without doubt, signify 'Dirección General de Prensa,' perhaps for the same reason that some texts appear signed by the EFE agency that transmits the news. In any case and however it may be, NO news should ever appear signed with the initials D.G.P. from whatever news source it may have proceeded.[49]

The reasoning of this advice was that the newspapers should not let the reading public have an inkling that those items were "inserted" by the order of the DGP; the newspapers should give an appearance that they themselves wrote those articles. The censors might have thought that either the Spanish public was so innocent, or the newspaper editors were putting up some passive resistance, or both.

HELL—REUTERS—U.P.

As far as Spain was concerned, 2 German agencies —DNB and Trans-Ocean— were the primary sources of international news. Before it installed its first teletypes in 1943, EFE-CIFRA news used the German radiotelegraph system known as "Hell." Alberto Poveda —with EFE since 1944 and secretary of the administrative council since 1977— explained that Hell (short for *Hellschreiber*, or Hell-writer) was "a kind of radio-teletype, not exactly teletype as we conceive of now, with typing keys but with a ribbon, a drum filled with ink and a blade."[50] The blade marked letters, which were sometimes "difficult to read, but after all they were letters, not Morse signals, and could be read."

These Hell machines were used by the EFE offices installed in Madrid in 1940 to communicate with many provincial newspapers, especially with the ones in the distant Balearic and Canary Ialands through the radio station at the Chamartín de la Rosa outskirts of Madrid. The radio station was also

utilized to broadcast Spanish news to the European news agencies. Poveda
said he knows that the Italian agency Stefani received the broadcasts by a
Hell radioteletype.

Change was slow not only because of economic and material shortages.
The slow innovation process was well described by Francisco del Valle
Arroyo, who worked for EFE from 1939 to 1982.[51] The directors of "our
papers were accustomed to receiving the news delivered by cyclists," Del
Valle said, and they had to be "almost forced to accept an innovation, the
teletypes," as they obviously cost them a small investment, too. Poveda
remembered that when EFE connected the whole Spanish territory with
teletypes, the Hell system was sold to the *Guardia Civil* (the Civil Guard),
the notorious paramilitary police force established in 1844 to patrol the
rural communities of Spain.

When the tide of World War II changed in favor of the Allies, EFE took
measures to move away from the German news services and to introduce
Anglo-American agencies. The British Reuters was the first to come.
Gállego Castro, the first EFE director —"who was a great journalist, great
professional but not a political man"— thought that EFE hardly had any
international coverage; it had 4 correspondents —2 in the Americas, one in
Rome, and one in Lisbon. Gállego Castro made this [exchange] operation
with Reuters because it was "the most indicated: First, it was a European
agency. The French HAVAS Agency was in the Nazi-occupied territory,
therefore all its news was controlled. The only agency in 'independent
Europe' in that sense was Reuters." The point was that EFE —even in the
early days of World War II— attempted to achieve a balance in its news.

AP – UP Rivalry

In 1945, the Spanish government (and EFE itself) made an important
decision to contract the North American news service, the United Press
(UP). There are again contradictory versions about why UP, instead of the
Associated Press (AP), was chosen. First, the Poveda version: Within EFE's
news policy to have "an amplest possible service overseas, it was thought
that a North American agency was needed." An agreement with UP was
reached in January 1945, after long negotiations because it was very
expensive and the economic resources of EFE were then constrained. UP
service cost some P800,000 a year or some $88,000, a hefty sum. Poveda
emphasized that the EFE-UP contract was considered important, because
"we would have more complete news." All this, however, does not quite
explain why UP was preferred over AP.

Henry F. Schulte, journalism scholar and former (1956–1962) manager of the Madrid bureau of UP (UPI since 1958), presented a second version in his 1968 book.[52] With an imminent Allied victory on the horizon, Franco "incorporated the press into a campaign to gain 'free world' favor." EFE was "encouraged, if not ordered, to create ties with major Western wire services." After the British agency Reuters, it was decided in 1945 "to add an American agency, and detailed study was undertaken over the relative merits" of both AP and UP. Schulte could "only conjecture that the Spanish government was hopeful that UP would be more malleable, less likely to be anti-Franco" than AP. UP was a private news agency "obligated only by business ties to its clients" while AP was an "organization constituted by member U.S. newspapers," which "might be inclined to reflect the anti-Francoism believed rampant" in that country then. Schulte observed the "feeling that the purchase of the UP service entitled Spain to favorable treatment certainly permeated some areas of government."

Schulte, however, did not think that the EFE-UP contract "ever influenced UP news reports on Spanish subjects." UP news was provided to EFE by radioteletype broadcasts, some directly from London and others from New York relayed by a Mackay station in Tangier.

Ramón Garriga, an EFE Berlin correspondent during World War II, gave yet a third "insider" version of the EFE-UP pact.[53] The period between the EFE-Reuters agreement in 1940 or 1944 and the EFE-UP contract coincided with the transition. On 13 July 1944, EFE changed command from Vicente Gállego Castro to Pedro Gómez Aparicio, then EFE subdirector. Garriga considered Gómez Aparicio "a journalist of second rank." Gómez Aparicio reached the top by "demonstrating a great agility in knowing how to follow the current." His pen was "far from being in consonance with his vanity." Each week Gómez Aparicio would write an extensive article signed with his name on national and foreign subjects in the *Hoja Oficial del Lunes* (*Official Monday Sheet*) of Madrid.[54] Gómez Aparicio was the person with whom AP and UP had to deal in their competing bids for the succulent EFE contract.

UP Fawns over EFE

UP's Madrid bureau director at the time was Ralph E. Forte —Garriga called him "a dynamic man"— who knew all the "ins and outs" of the power system of the Franco regime. Forte was helped by A. L. Bradford, UP's director of foreign service, who made a special trip to Madrid in late November 1944. Having been informed by Forte of "the psychology of Gómez Aparicio," UP's Bradford knew how to deal with the EFE director. Bradford started his first interview with Gómez Aparicio with these words:

"I have the satisfaction of saluting the first journalist of Spain. In Washington, we await every Monday to know the text of your weekly article to find out what Spain thinks." "After these words were pronounced," Garriga claimed, there did not arise any stumbling block to the signing of the contract, which incidentally was regarded "the very best deal signed by UP since the entry of the United states into World War II."

Two years after signing the service contract with UP, EFE entered into an agreement to exchange news photographs of its CIFRA-Gráfica with the photo agencies of France, England, Italy, Holland, Switzerland, Sweden, the United States, and Argentina.[55] It cannot be ascertained whether those agreements with the European agencies already were part of the European Pressphoto Union being organized. These 1946 press photo exchange agreements put some limitation on the later expansion of the EFE-UP contract. In July 1950 EFE was given exclusive rights to the use of UP's ACME News Pictures and Planet News. EFE could not give to UP exclusive right to the CIFRA-Gráfica photographs, because of the 1946 agreements among the European agencies.[56]

The 1945 EFE-UP contract represented a 180-degree turn from EFE's news sources of the recent past, those of the Nazi German agencies. To observers with 1980s hindsight, the 1945 EFE-UP agreement also marked an epoch because EFE would not enter into exchange agreements with any other foreign agencies for more than 13 years. Only in 1958 did EFE sign another exchange pact with the West German Deutsche Presse-Agentur (dpa).[57] This EFE-dpa agreement was followed by another signed in 1962 with Agence France-Presse (AFP).

The Associated Press (AP) trailed its 1945 competitor by about 20 years, only to obtain an EFE contract in 1964, although the EFE executives attempted in November 1946 to persuade the Spanish government to "placate the Associated Press now resenting and troubled for not having being the one selected" in 1944.[58] It was a political consideration, of course. As of this writing (April 1989), EFE has more than 35 exchange agreements with agencies of all political tendencies, that will be enumerated as the history of EFE unfolds. (That number, 35 —of EFE's news exchange agreements— compares with 41 for AP, 55 for dpa, 65 for the Italian ANSA, and 77 for the Soviet Union's TASS.[59]

Chapter 3

EFE's Cold War
(1945-1950)

ISOLATION

Spain's ostracism from the international community started with the defeat in 1945 of the Axis powers by the Allies. Though the Franco regime had claimed to maintain neutrality, it was more of a case of nonbelligerence with a definite tilt toward the Axis. This stance resulted in an international ostracism of Franco as the last surviving fascist. In December 1946 the United Nations condemned the Franco regime as "undemocratic" and recommended that members break off relations with Spain. Most withdrew their envoys from Spain. But the isolation was short-lived. Spain survived the boycott. The tide turned with the advent in 1948 of the cold war. Spain was now needed.

Relations with the Western nations began to normalize, led by the U.S.-Spanish agreement on 27 December 1950 to exchange envoys. The rapprochement was not a one-way deal. Spain also loosened up on its stiff fascist stance. Sensing the Allied victory, Franco began relaxing his tight press control in 1944. He ordered exemption of censorship on scientific and technical materials, and more significantly for this book, on overseas press dispatches. He engendered a climate favorable for EFE to contract the Reuters and UP services.

Spanish "Bill of Rights"

In a master stroke to fence off world criticism of his dictatorship, Franco decreed on 17 July 1945 "Fuero de los Españoles" (Right of the Spaniards)[1] —"Spanish Bill of Rights," as some would call it. Article 12 declared, "All Spaniards shall be able to express freely their ideas while they do not assault the fundamental principles of the State." In addition to the built-in counter proviso in the same article, the "Fuero" —promulgated on the ninth anniversary of the military uprising which had initiated the civil war— was strewn with enough riders to arrest excessive liberalization. Article 33 stipulated: "The exercise of the rights that are recognized in this 'Fuero' shall not assault the spiritual, national and social unity of Spain."

The Ministry of National Education issued an order on 23 March 1946 to implement the "Fuero" provisions on press matters. The order softened and attenuated the prior censorship somewhat. But Article 161 clarified that "the liberty conceded to the press could not attempt against the unity of the Fatherland and its external and internal security, the fundamental institutions of the State and the persons who incarnate it, . . . the principles of the Dogma and Catholic moral and the ecclesiastic persons and institutions."[2] Franco would not give in totally.

When the General Assembly of the United Nations barred Spain from membership on 23 December 1946, Franco responded with a mass demonstration. He told Falange-mobilized throngs from the balcony of the royal palace in Madrid: "We, the Spanish, must never be surprised at what took place in the United Nations, for a wave of Communist terror is devastating Europe." The crowd of 300,000 Spanish, their ego bruised by the UN decision, applauded Franco, chanting, "Franco, sí! Comunismo, no!"[3] The Spanish press carried intensive anti-UN propaganda items distributed by the EFE agency.

World ostracism did not last long. It was cracked first by friendly gestures from Argentina of Juan Domingo Perón in 1947. Switzerland, Portugal, and the Vatican never had withdrawn their ambassadors and nuncio from Madrid. International events occurred in a quick succession. Political crises in Greece and Turkey were followed by the Berlin blockade in July 1948. The German Democratic Republic was established and China was taken over by Mao Tse-Tung in 1949. The Korean War broke out in June 1950. The Western nations needed Franco more than he needed them by then. Spain's isolation hardly lasted 2 full years, as the May 1949 UN vote motioned to restore diplomatic relations with Franco's Spain. The U.S. Senate approved a $100-million loan by the Export-Import Bank in 1950. The U.S. ambassador Stanton Griffis returned to Madrid in February 1951. Spain sent ambassador José Felix de Lequerica to Washington in April. Franco had weathered the international boycott.

EFE Without "Godfather"

Covering these events, in faithful defense of the Franco line against world opinion, EFE went through its own 5-year post-World War II isolation among the domestic groups jockeying for power. The remote origin of its crises went back to 18 October 1940, when Serrano Súñer was moved from the interior ministry to the foreign ministry. At his new post Serrano Súñer tried to temper those Falange's anti-Allies press actions too crude and heavy-handed even to his own pro-Nazi taste. He retained control over international news at his new foreign ministry, to keep it out of the hands of rabidly fascist Arias-Salgado, vice minister of popular education. By then, press control had been passed over to the vice ministry of popular education. Two years later, in September 1942, Serrano Súñer was fired by Franco as foreign minister and left the government for good.

The EFE news agency was now without its "godfather." The EFE journalists found themselves hemmed between the foreign ministry's "lefts" —were such a term possible in the Franco Spain— and the "rights" at the Vicesecretaría de Educación Popular. On the one hand, the foreign ministry circle, led by the "moderate" ministers José Félix de Lequerica and Alberto Martín-Artajo y Alvarea, despised the Falangist past of EFE and openly challenged the "de facto monopoly EFE might have come enjoying" over foreign news.[4] On the other hand, Arias-Salgado initiated a campaign to assume complete control of EFE and make a total official mouthpiece out of it.

"Press Czar" DGP

Arias-Salgado, in fact, succeeded Serrano Súñner as the Spanish "press czar" in 1941 to continue in that position for 21 years. Serrano Súñer had founded the Falange press system for the civil war Spain. Arias-Salgado consolidated the legacy of his predecessor and controlled it with an iron fist. The position of "press czar" had had various names and belonged to different ministries since the beginning of the civil war. In the military "Junta Técnica" of 3 October 1936, General Millan-Astray with Juan Pujol as aide briefly operated "La Oficina de Prensa y Propaganda." The military order of 14 January 1937 set up "La Secretaría General del Jefe del Estado," which, in turn, created "La Delegación del Estado para Prensa y Propaganda" on 29 May. In the civilian government of 30 January 1938, interior minister Serrano Súñer created the "Subsecretaría de Prensa y Propaganda," in which "El Servicio Nacional de Prensa" (SNP) operated. Serrano Súñer had several "young people who were in abundant supply" work for him at the different SNP sections as noted in chapter 2.

In the reorganized government of 10 August 1939, Serrano Súñer gave himself the title of minister of the government (*gobernación* —practically the same as the interior). He renamed the press office "Dirección General de Prensa" (DGP). When Serrano Súñer moved to the foreign ministry in

October 1940, Generalissimo Franco himself assumed the affairs of "the government." As the foreign minister, Serrano Súñer retained control over international news. Remaining press matters were moved to a new ministry, "Secretaría General del Movimiento," which took over and upgraded the DGP to the "Vice Secretaría de Educación Popular" under the law decreed on 20 May 1941.

Gabriel Arias-Salgado de Cubas, former civil governor of Salamanca province and 37 years old, was named vice secretary of popular education, assisted by "Director General de Prensa" (DGP) Juan Aparicio. A decree law of 27 July 1945 changed the title of the office held by Arias-Salgado to "Subsecretaría de Educación Popular" (SEP) and placed it under "Ministerio de Educación Nacional." (It is symptomatic that Arias-Salgado's press-control functions be conceptualized as those of "popular education." In the authoritarian precept, the press was an instrument to educate the popular mass.) When the "Ministerio de Información y Turismo" (MIT) was created on 19 July 1951, Arias-Salgado was promoted to and stayed as MIT "boss" until succeeded by Manuel Fraga Iribarne on 10 July 1962. Arias-Salgado died a short 2 weeks later.

Control of the press in Franco's Spain (1936–1975) was in the hands of 3 men: Serrano Súñer, Arias-Salgado, and Fraga Iribarne. All the censors were regularly called by the Spaniards DGP, because that title —whether "el Director General" or "la Dirección General"— persisted throughout the many protean shifts in the bureaucracy of press control.

(This history of the Spanish "press czardom" is no doubt tortuous and confusing to most non-Spanish and even to many Spanish readers. But the real "torture" was suffered by the Spanish journalists, who had, in despair, to exclaim frequently: "These [expletive deleted] DGP censors are all the same, no matter what their names and titles." The confusion of the reader will be alleviated by references to Figure 2 provided below.)

Two Enemies of EFE

To get back to the precarious position EFE was in under Arias-Salgado, the self-claimed "independent" EFE journalists now found themselves really "independent" —probably not in ideology— but of any champion supporting their cause. Politically hamstrung and financially strapped, the EFE group had to fight for survival through its isolation which coincided with Spain's international ostracism. The problem facing the EFE executives was not merely the fact that Arias-Salgado would not countenance their pretense of professional independence. Detecting their weakened political position, attempts were made to take over the role of the EFE news agency by rival

PRESS CZARS

SHIFTING BUREAUCRACY OF PRESS CONTROL (1936–1989)

TITLE	SUB-UNIT	UNIT	MINISTRY	LAW	Press CZAR
AUTOCRACY (1936–1975)					
Jefe		Oficina de Prensa y Propaganda	Junta Técnica del Estado	Orden 1936/10/01	Millán-Astray
Delegado		Delegación del Estado de Prensa-Propaganda	Secretaría General del Jefe del Estado	Orden 1937/01/14	Millán-Astray
Jefe	Servicio Nacional de Prensa **SNP**	Subsecretaría de Prensa y Propaganda	Ministerio del Interior	Orden 1938/01/29	Serrano Súñer
Director General de Prensa **DGP**	Dirección General de Prensa **DGP**		Ministerio de Gobernación	Decreto 1939/08/10	Serrano Súñer
Director	Oficina Diplomática	Ministerio de Asuntos	Exteriores	Decreto 1940/10/18	Serrano Súñer -sharing powers with Arias-Salgado
Vice Secretario de Educación Popular		Vice Secretaría de Educación Popular	Secretaría General del Movimiento	Decreto 1941/05/20	
Delegado Nacional de Prensa-periódica **DGP**	Delegación Nacional de Prensa-periódica **DGP**				
		Vice Secretaría de Educación Popular	Secretaría General del Jefe del Estado	Decreto 1941/10/10	Arias-Salgado + Aparicio
Delegado Nacional de Prensa-no periódica	Delegación Nacional de Prensa-no periódica				
Director General de Prensa **DGP**	Dirección General de Prensa **DGP**	Sub-Secretaría de Educación Popular **SEP**	Ministerio de Educación Nacional	Decreto 1945/07/27	Arias-Salgado + Aparicio & Cerro
Director General de Prensa-periódica **DGP**	Dirección General de Prensa-periódica **DGP**				Arias-Salgado + Aparicio
			Ministerio de Información y Turismo **MIT**	Decreto 1951/07/19	—1961/07/10
Director General de Información	Dirección General de Información				Fraga + Beneyto & Jiménez
			MIT		Sánchez Bella + Cerro
DEMOCRACY (1976–1989)					
Dirección General de Información	Dirección General de Información	**MCSE**		Constitución 1978/12/06	

FIGURE 2: Franco's **Press Czars** exercised legal control over EFE and press with the title: **SNP** (National Press Service), **DGP** (Director General of the Press), **SEP** (Secretary of Popular Education) and **MIT** (Minister of Information and Tourism). **MCSE** (Social Communication Media of the State) is the post-Franco Constitutional apparatus of the press, which has operated since 1976 to the present, 1989.

groups which were more in line with the press philosophy of Arias-Salgado. The "Prensa del Movimiento" of the Falange and an obscure entity called the "Instituto de Cultura Hispánica" (ICH) were 2 such groups.

The Falange movement press, officially inaugurated on 13 June 1940,[5] had grown by 1946 to own 38 dailies, 5 Monday press-association papers (*Hojas del Lunes*), 8 weekly magazines, and 7 monthlies, all of which were controlled by the "Delegación Nacional de Prensa y Propaganda." This "Movimiento" press group was served by an agency called PYRESA,[6] which attempted to compete against and even to take over the position of EFE. At the same time, the "Instituto de Cultura Hispánica" (ICH) also loomed as a potential rival to EFE. The ICH was a 1941 product of "El Consejo de Hispanidad" (Council of Hispanism), born of attempts to link Hispanic America to Spain under the local units of the Falange. The Hispanism was strongly promoted by the Franco regime as a counterbalance to the Pan-Americanism under the U.S. aegis, perceived to be hostile to Spain.

ICH campaigns received a nationalistic stimulus in 1947, the 400th anniversary of the birth of Miguel de Cervantes Saávedra (of *Don Quixote*). During the year there were celebrations and commemorations in all of Spain and a worldwide Cervantine Congress ("Asamblea Cervantina de la Lengua") was attended by many Hispanic delegates. Elements in PYRESA and ICH appeared to team up together to pose a threat to the EFE agency. EFE had to fight for its life.

EFE WHITE PAPERS

The EFE executives were justifiably alarmed. Raising shrill voices, they presented to government authorities at least 7 formal documents of proposals —which sounded more like a protest— between 1944 and 1949. These 7 EFE "White Papers" alleged the following points.

1. EFE's Complaints. EFE protested "irresponsible acts" by the government in political, economic, materiels, and information "spheres."

Political misconducts were many. Arias Salgado's "Subsecretaría de Educación Popular (SEP)" planted, with false EFE signature, stories in Spanish newspapers denigrating the book by former U.S. ambassador Carlton Hayes to Spain,[7] and distorting the statement made by U.S. ambassador Norman Armour on his arrival in New York when he was recalled from Spain under the UN resolution. The EFE executives protested that the SEP "has done everything possible" to damage EFE's "prestige" which was indispensable to a news agency. A proof of this was that EFE

New York correspondent Francisco Cifuentes "has not been recognized as such by the United States authorities but only as an agent of the Spanish government."

Economic breaches were as numerous. The Falange and the government owed EFE millions of pesetas in unpaid bills. Worst of all, the SEP firmly denied EFE's several requests for permission to raise its service quotas, despite the 60% price increase which the SEP authorized for the Spanish newspapers and 2 labor pay hikes the government imposed in 1941 and 1944. The EFE quotas "have been the same as established in 1939!"

Materiels area was just as bleak. The EFE news agency had to build its own power supply because the National Electric Company would not exempt EFE from the "restrictions on power supply." The foreign ministry requested installation of a teletype receiver. EFE was told by the National Telephone Company it could not spare circuits even for the foreign ministry. For "radiographic transmission," EFE obtained from the United States a set of "radio tubes." The national customs service "has taken 3 months in clearance, without dispatching any to date." The EFE agency "does not ask for a favorable treatment" by the government, "but it should be given minimum considerations." One of those "minimum facilities" would be allowing EFE easy access to foreign currency for its materiels importation, and payments of its correspondents abroad. There was no sign of that yet.

In the information area, the EFE executives claimed that EFE was discriminated against worse than foreign news people: Since 1944, censorship on press materials destined overseas had been relaxed considerably. The EFE executives felt that since it did not apply to EFE, the relaxation placed their news-gathering activities at a distinct disadvantage in the competition with the foreign press. They complained that EFE was subjected to "the same censorship shackle as any Spanish newspaper." That was a "grave obstacle" to EFE, since it needed to compete against the foreign agencies and correspondents enjoyed "absolute freedom" in their news transmission.

2. EFE's Successes. As the "news centralizer," EFE provided all Spanish as well as foreign news to the state as the "very first beneficiary" of its information services. This did not happen in any of the Hispano-American countries.

EFE was the official "message distributor" in service to the state, whose documents, information, *consignas*, and other communications were sent through the most rapid means of transmission to all the Spanish press in the peninsular mainland as well as the outlying islands. This was especially valuable in the distribution by EFE of the foreign news obtained through the Reuters and United Press agencies. EFE subjected the foreign news from Reuters and UP to "a process of selection and revision, with arrangement in accord with the instructions received from the Superior Authority." It could not occur if the newspapers could directly contract these services of "the foreign agencies referred to." In this regard, the EFE executives were openly extolling the news censors' role as one of their State-assigned functions: the transmission of *consigna* and "gatekeeping" process on UP and Reuters wires.

In these White Papers the EFE executives valued very highly their role as Spain's "external relationers" or public relations men for the government in promotion of Spain's image in the foreign press. The EFE executives were positive that UP-EFE service contract "noticeably influenced" Spain's image abroad, especially in the United States.

EFE's role as the "political propagandizer" was also important. EFE's papers underlined the propaganda value that EFE attached to all the trips taken by "el Caudillo" and "quite a few of them" by the ministers, by always sending reporters and photographers to these trips "without being invited and without being refunded for the expenses."

3. EFE's Service Offers. The EFE White Papers also made different contract offers for EFE services, so that EFE would be financially viable yet would not have to depend on government subsidy. This, of course, was the premise of EFE when it was founded during the early civil war days. But during the war, rules were bent and EFE did not really have to earn its keep. Now, it was peacetime. EFE had to prove its worth to the government by services rendered. This had become all the more important if EFE was to survive the political infighting among the several power blocks that made up the Franco regime.

4. EFE's Expansion Plans. The EFE White Papers went back to the genesis of the EFE news agency, and harped on the founding goal of "information sovereignty." EFE could add to present services some 5,200 words daily of news from 12 cities in Hispanic America, Manila, and Cairo with which "we are joined by religious, racial, and cultural ties." EFE could assign its own full-time correspondents to 13 cities in Europe and the Americas; build an 8-point distribution network, from which to branch out to the rest of the Americas; and begin a radio-photographic service between Spain and Hispanic America by strengthening the existing broadcasting capacity to a 20-kilowatt station.

5. EFE Rejects Reproaches. The EFE executives were not sanguine about hoped-for success of their White Papers with the government authorities, nor could they be indifferent to the rumored creation of a second national news agency. They affirmed that "on occasion, the EFE agency is reproached for exercising news monopoly in Spain" by the authorities and the press. They rejected those reproaches, because, they claimed, there existed "at least 2 other well known" agencies and "a few not so well recognized" agencies. They also resisted criticism that EFE "has not achieved all it set out to do" in 10 years, for "EFE has been denied the means needed to fulfill" the original goals. They emphasized that EFE not only did not receive any state subsidies, but did not even receive adequate compensation for the services it rendered.

The EFE executives roundly condemned rumored plans to "set up other similar news agencies that would put up internal competition" and cause "dispersion of efforts, instead of revitalizing" the EFE agency, so that it could better accomplish its objectives. The "two well known agencies" they referred to were the PYRESA of the Falange press and "El Instituto de Cultura Hispánica" (ICH).

EFE "Jilted" by DGP

In their survival efforts, the EFE executives did not limit approaches to the government to the White Papers. Whenever occasions arose, they attempted to make the most of those events, in the style of modern publicity and public relations promoters. For example, when a group of obscure Cuban journalists visited Madrid in late November 1946, EFE did not miss the chance. EFE director Gómez Aparicio offered a big reception for the Cubans at the Ayala 5 headquarters of EFE, making sure to invite the Madrid journalism circles, including the SEP officials.[8]

On another occasion, the EFE executives went out of their way to make noise about what EFE was engaged in. In August 1947, EFE's New York correspondent, Francisco Lucientes, who EFE had said was treated as a government agent by U.S. authorities through SEP's fault, returned to Madrid on a business leave. The EFE agency honored "the illustrious journalist of great international prestige" by mounting a gigantic party, to which no fewer than 200 persons were invited.

On both occasions, however, the vice minister of SEP, Arias-Salgado, ominously made known his displeasure with EFE by his conspicuous absence. He was the person that EFE had to win over, yet he adamantly refused to be ingratiated by official and unofficial gestures coming from EFE.

ENTER US's INS

Then came the last straw. The International News Service (INS) of New York made its appearance on the Spanish press scene. INS, the smallest and latest-comer, and for that reason, the most active among the 3 U.S. press associations, was engaged in an aggressive market expansion plan. INS had won prominence for its competitive spirit,[9] true to the tradition of its precursor and founder, the Hearst newspaper chain. INS had already gained a foothold in Spain by supplying to the Falange Movimiento press literary and feature-filler services, which had expired for little use. It now wanted to make a formal full-time entry into the Spanish market through the Falange press. INS initiated its move in May 1950, bringing to a climax the crisis EFE was going through. There was no room for INS in EFE which had the Reuters and UP services already and considered adding AP, as had been suggested in one of the White Papers.

INS put H. E. Knoblaugh in charge of its campaign in the Spanish market. Knoblaugh was an old "Spain hand" who had covered the Spanish civil war for AP from the Republican side.[10] INS had hired Knoblaugh from AP in New York and dispatched him on a Madrid mission. Intimately knowledgeable about the inner workings of the Spanish bureaucracy, Knoblaugh first conferred with the Spanish ambassador in Washington, José Félix de Lequerica. The envoy gave him the guarantee that Spanish newspapers had "the liberty to contract the services of any agency other than the EFE." Lequerica, who had previously been the foreign minister, promised INS's Knoblaugh his support, so that INS would "enjoy the same treatment as the United Press" and so informed his successor.

Armed with this blessing, Knoblaugh went to Madrid, where he first interviewed the foreign minister, Alberto Martín Artajo, and information chief Luis María de Lojendio. The minister told Knoblaugh that "all foreign agencies were fully authorized to contract their services to any newspaper of Spain under the same conditions as EFE, which did not have right to any monopoly, although it had come enjoying it de facto." It was a bombshell to the EFE agency. That is, it would have been one to the EFE executives, had they gotten wind of the INS contract offer to the "Movimiento" newspapers. Bartolomé Mostaza, chief of the "Collaborations" of the Falange press, made a detailed report[11] on the conversation he had with INS's Knoblaugh on 3 May 1950, to Lucio del Alamo, chief Delegado Nacional de Prensa y Propaganda of the Falange FET-JONS.

As noted earlier, the Falange press had grown to become a giant chain —"the largest of periodical publishers of the country"— with a total circulation of some 1.1 million copies in 1946 of its 38 daily newspapers. It continued to grow, and its aggregate "publishing potential" came to 41 million a year.[12]

Knoblaugh made an attractive offer to the Falange press. For US$3,000 a month, INS would give an exclusive service on political, economic, cultural, literary, and stock market news. For $4,000 it would install, as Falange property, a system of radioteletype necessary to receive all the news at 60 words per minute. While these arrangements were completed, INS would revive its expired feature-filler service for monthly fees of only $1,000.

Mostaza, the Falange negotiator, compared the INS offer with the EFE contract, pointing out in his report that the INS services would cost only $36,000 a year. He recalled that EFE cost the Falange press P2.25 million or $162,000 annually. EFE cost the Falange press 4.5 times as much as INS would! Mostaza said that the INS offer also included economic news that the EFE service did not. More importantly, Mostaza emphasized that the INS deal "would free us of the obstacles [*trabas*] we now have with the EFE agency and we could make news according to our standard."

He added that in case the INS offer would be accepted, the Falange press "would have to organize PYRESA as an agency" to receive INS news, on which "we would impose a kind of censorship or control to give it Spanish form." It would be an easy task "with 2, 3 or more elements added to the writing staff that we now have." Mostaza cautioned that the FET-JONS delegate should "assure the precise legality of the statements that Mr. Knoblaugh alleged to have got from the foreign minister and he says Sr. Lojendio could credit also." Behind the backs of the EFE officials, the biggest press chain in the country was scheming to subvert EFE. What emerges from these INS–Falange plots is that the embattled EFE was not or could not be an "exclusive official" State news agency at all.

Despite these many tribulations the EFE agency survived the onslaught of its enemies, not because the Falange press in the end did not subvert EFE with the help from INS. A strange, unexpected turn of events saved EFE.

MINISTRY OF INFORMATION

EFE survived the crises of the 5-year period of 1945–1950 because its "enemies" needed it, just as Franco's Spain was needed by the Western powers in their cold war strategy. In the year 1950, normalization of diplomatic relations with UN member nations was in the air. Spain was admitted to the UN Food and Agriculture Organization (FAO). A U.S.-Spanish pact was reached on 27 December 1950 to exchange ambassadors.

The U.S. Congress approved a $100-million loan to Spain. In order to better chart Spain in all these international dealings, Franco was contemplating a government shakeup of major proportions, the first since 1942, when Serrano Súñer was ousted from power. In the cards was the formation of brand new ministries, that of the presidency (designed to relieve Franco of routine business), of commerce, and the Falange party.

When the government reconstitution was finally announced on 19 July 1951, Franco had created the ministry of information and tourism (MIT), with Gabriel Arias-Salgado as the new minister. When he contemplated the coming cabinet shakeup during the months of 1950, Franco naturally consulted Arias-Salgado as the "subsecretario" of popular education in charge of press control. Sensing an almost sure promotion into a ministerial suzerainty, Arias-Salgado was not about to reduce the size and reach of his domain. EFE was one of the biggest branches —if, in fact, not the only one— in his new fief, MIT. Besides, with the new ministry of the Falange party in operation, the press chain of the Falange was most definitely not to belong under his direct control. Arias- Salgado needed EFE. The life of an institution takes curious turns. Arias-Salgado had to save the EFE agency to save his own continued press czardom.

Life, of course, went on at the embattled EFE during these isolation years. In one aspect, the life at EFE was more than just continuing. In 1946, while the EFE executives were in the frenzy of writing up all those service offers in the White Papers to the government, EFE broke new ground in its services. After long negotiations and consultations with Spanish business circles, EFE founded a commercial news service, the COMTELSA ("Comercial Telegráfica, S.A.") with a 50-50 capital coinvestment with the British Reuters. It came from the learning experience the EFE executives had gained during the years of news service dealings with Reuters.

EFE's 1950 Finances

By 1950 EFE's finances had grown "astronomically" from the ragtag days of the civil war years of 1938 and 1939. EFE's gross revenues had reached the millions, at least in "pesetas." In 1949 and 1950, respectively, EFE grossed P4.03 million and P4.84 million (or about US$368,100 and $431,400 at the 10.95 and 11.22 exchange rates). That was an impressive 20% growth in a year. (As the DGP authorized a 100% tariff increase on 1 October 1950 by a 26 September order, EFE's revenues in the coming decade would rise by leaps and bounds.) But the outlays of EFE jumped a bit faster than the incomes. Payrolls, which took up more than 75% of all expenses, increased by 21.5%, given the 1949 and 1950 payroll expenditures of P3.06 million and

P3.71 million ($279,140 and $330,520). These 1949 and 1950 payroll figures compare with that of 1940, for example, which amounted to only P969,000 (or $106,100 at a 9.13 exchange rate).

In 10 years' time, EFE's payroll alone had almost quadrupled —383%— from below P1 million to a whopping P3.71 million. The 1941 EFE annual memorial was a scanty 3.3-page statement, and the only substantive matter in it was an P81,000 ($7,400) pay hike caused by the minimum salary decreed by DGP in 1938. In the 1941 financial statement, the EFE management whined about the "tremendous economic burden of P81,000." In 1950, EFE was handling a payroll increase 10 times as big. The EFE agency had some 200 national correspondents who supplied 15,000 words of national news daily to Spanish and foreign media and its contracts with both Reuters and UP were providing 35,000 to 40,000 words of foreign news daily to all Spanish news organizations. In 1936, the Fabra news agency had distributed only 2,500 to 3,000 words a day received from the French Havas.[13]

La Agencia EFE, S.A. had come a long way.

Chapter 4

Fifteen Years of Peace (1951–1965)

On 1 April 1964, the ministry of information and tourism launched a gigantic propaganda campaign, marking the 25th anniversary of the Franco victory. The day had been celebrated as "El Día de la Victoria" (Victory Day) every year since the end of the civil war. But the one for 1964 was special. It had now been a quarter century. The slogan, "25 Years of Peace," was commemorating the "peace" Spaniards had "enjoyed" since that victory march in Madrid in 1939. Though the slogan was catchy, the first 10 of those 25 years were anything but "peaceful" for Spain. The civil war was followed by World War II in 5 short months. During the 6 years of World War II (1939–1945), Spain nervously oscillated from "neutrality" to "non-belligerence" and pranced back to "neutrality" between the Allies and the Axis powers.

An international isolation marked the lustrum of 1945–1950, in which Spain suffered both spiritually and materially. To an objective observer, it would be obvious that Spain had been under peace for only about 15 years since 1950. A more truthful slogan might have read "15 Years of Peace."

To La Agencia EFE, S.A., a creature of the Franco regime, the year 1964 marked the 25-year anniversary of its existence too. But EFE's first 10 years were anything but "peaceful." It had passed most years of its infancy, 1939–1945, as a Nazi propaganda organ. In its adolescent years of 1946–1950 EFE had to fight for its survival, subjected to internal isolation in Spain's power politics. Now the 15 years of EFE's life from 1951 through 1965 can fittingly be characterized as the "15 Years of Peace." EFE did not achieve any extraordinary feat; it just lived, and in the process, grew into adulthood.

COMMAND CHANGES

During the 15-year peace period, EFE gradually consolidated its foundations by twists and turns. Jesús Pabón (y Suárez de Urbina), civil war foreign press chief under *cuñadísimo* Serrano Súñer, held the ceremonial EFE presidency throughout this 15-year period; indeed Pabón had held that position since 1940. The founding director of EFE, Vicente Gállego, resigned in 1944 under combined pressure from the Nazi German propaganda apparatus and the press czar Gabriel Arias-Salgado. Pedro Gómez Aparicio, the EFE founding subdirector, took over and carried out the agency's fight for survival, when the EFE executives flooded the government with the White Papers discussed in the preceding chapter. The hostility of both the government and the Falange could not be placated by any of the "good" arguments the White Papers might have presented. Arias-Salgado of the newly created ministry of information and tourism (MIT) protected EFE against the Institute of Hispanic Culture (ICH) and the Falange news agency PYRESA. They had put up a very real joint competition to EFE with possible help from the third-ranked U.S. International News Service (INS). MIT Arias-Salgado thus demanded total obedience from EFE, not the "professional independence" that the EFE journalists sought. His encroachment of EFE was such that even Pedro Gómez Aparicio, much more docile than his predecessor Gállego Castro could not take the pressure.[1] So, Gómez Aparicio repeatedly and reasonably requested that the EFE director, "who must assume the direction of the most complicated professional and technical tasks," be free of "the preoccupations and chores of management."

On 25 April 1950 the EFE administrative council finally resolved that the EFE president assume the functions of management. It was actually a "cop out" on the part of Gómez Aparicio. He let Jesús Pabón, EFE president, take over the relations with Arias-Salgado. But thorny problems did not subside. For the MIT required that news written and distributed by the EFE agency be totally in line with his "oriented press" precepts. Pedro Gómez Aparicio gave up the EFE directorship on 5 February 1958. But his days had already been numbered long before that, as the MIT was recruiting its own man for the directorship of EFE.

EFE Direction Limps

In late 1956, the director general of press (DGP) of the MIT, Juan Aparicio, contacted Waldo de Mier García-Maza, director of the Palma de Mallorca daily *Baleares*, and offered him the job as subdirector of EFE. De Mier had fought first in the Spanish Legion, and later as an officer on the Nationalist side in the civil war, where he was wounded in the left leg. (He is proud of his limping gait.) An ultraright Franco follower, De Mier accepted the job offer and began working as subdirector of EFE in January

1957. Only a year later, Gómez Aparicio quit. But MIT Arias-Salgado could not promote De Mier to the EFE directorship for 2 reasons. One was that the EFE director needed a little more stature than that of De Mier.

The second reason was more complex. The years 1956–1957 saw much unrest among Spanish students, intellectuals, and workers who demanded more political liberalization. Another cabinet change was rumored. The major cabinet shakeup came on 25 February 1957, instituting big changes in the economic and financial spheres to end the stagnant autarchic economy of Spain. MIT Arias-Salgado stayed on, surviving yet another cabinet change. But the new cabinet imposed on Arias-Salgado the dismissal of his loyal aide, Juan Aparicio, replacing him as the director general of press (DGP) with university professor Juan Beneyto. Beneyto had been "a top student of the Spanish press,"[2] and the Spanish pioneer in the novel social science of mass communications.[3] His appointment as the new DGP meant a certain liberal tilt in the new cabinet. In his short tenure —only 9 months until January 1958— Beneyto "attempted to give the EFE agency autonomy."[4] He did not succeed because Arias-Salgado in no time regained control of the MIT and appointed Adolfo Muñoz Alonso as the DGP in January 1958. The following month Arias-Salgado named Manuel Aznar as EFE director.

The 7 years from 1958 to 1965 saw a see-saw battle between the moderates and the ultraright in the MIT and at EFE. Redoubtable Arias-Salgado at last gave out and was replaced as MIT on 10 July 1962 by Manuel Fraga Iribarne. The changes at MIT also put the EFE directorship through a rocky period.

MIT–EFE Whizzes

Manuel Fraga Iribarne was a young (not yet 40) technocrat. A former law professor at Madrid University, Fraga tackled his double charge (information and tourism) "with breathtaking energy and an undue optimism for the speed of the change in the Franco regime of 1962."[5] Within a few days of assuming the MIT post, Fraga declared that "a new information [i.e., press] law will be presented to the Cortes in December."[6] Though that did not occur until 3 years later in 1965, he produced a new press law eventually in 1966. It would later be dubbed the "Fraga Press Law," versus "the Serrano Súñer Press Law" of 1938. In addition to enacting the new press law, New MIT Fraga demonstrated his quality of a quick study and immediately plunged into the modernization of the Spanish press. His actions had a profound effect on the Spanish mass media industry during his MIT tenure until 1969.

When his architecture of a new press law was practically finished, Fraga made one of the most important appointments in the entire history of the EFE agency. He sought an ideal man to carry out the task of modernization of EFE. And he found a young Spanish just fit for the task in Carlos Mendo Baos, as prodigiously talented as he himself. Fraga named Mendo as EFE director on 10 June 1965. Mendo, not quite 32 yet, was then the Madrid bureau chief of the United Press International (UPI), "the only Spanish man who ever 'boasted' (ostentated) such a position."[7] Starting in December 1965, Mendo, "with a total political backing and financial support from Fraga," launched historical foreign expansion programs for EFE.

EFE OPERATIONS

In these 15 years EFE grew slowly but steadily. This section will describe EFE growth in physical plants, news and exchange agreements, economic scale, technical fields, and other sundry aspects. (Table 8.4 gives a comparative overview of these aspects throughout EFE's 50-year existence.)

Construction Works

Two construction projects were undertaken. Of the 6 stories of the Ayala 5 building, EFE had occupied only half. New arrangements on the ground floor gave a better grouping of transmission and news services of EFE-foreign, CIFRA-national, and Special Services (features). A new nave was built to accommodate teletypes and the Hell radio-writers adjacent to the control room. Along with the building work, EFE installed new teletypes, tape perforators, Hell radios, and other equipment. Since the mid-1940s EFE had operated a makeshift radio station at the Chamartín suburbs of Madrid, both for news transmission to the Balearic and Canary islands, and also for radio broadcast overseas. With the steady growth of its operations, EFE had to convert this broadcasting station into a permanent facility.

News Services

By 1962 EFE-International was distributing annually some 9.7 million words mainly from Reuters and UPI. The United Press (UP) and the International News Service (INS) merged in May 1958 to become UPI. CIFRA-National transmitted some 1.8 million words to the newspapers (plus a few non-news clients like the foreign ministry) in Madrid and about 4.4

million words to the provincial newspapers, giving the CIFRA total of 6.2 million words. The ALFIL-Sports section transmitted some 5 million words. Special Features distributed almost a half-million words, especially for such big international events as the 1961 Bay of Pigs (Cuba) invasion and the Soviet Sputnik satellite and 1962 Cuban missile crisis. Comtelsa, the economic news service, with the British Reuters financial news supplied almost 205,000 words in 1962. EFE Radio retransmitted some 380,000 words of the Radio Vatican broadcasts. Adding all these together, the EFE news services in 1962 totaled some 21.5 million words. That 1962 wordage was not much of an increase over the 1950 figures of 18 million to 20 million words. The CIFRA-Gráfica section supplied some 25,000 photographs to the Spanish papers and 10,000 to foreign agencies.[8]

EFE News Personnel

These verbal news services were rendered by some 400 correspondents in Spain and some 10 part-timers in the north African Spanish colonial outposts and one in Andorra, an autonomous principality in the French-Spanish Pyrenees. Correspondents in the provinces included government bureaucrats, teachers, and court clerks. At the Madrid headquarters and the Barcelona bureau, about 200 journalists received, edited, and wrote the news stories. CIFRA-Gráfica had its own team of some 300 full- and part-time photographers in Madrid and in the provinces. About 70 of the 300 photographers nationwide worked out of the Bilbao and Barcelona bureaus.[9]

The MIT helped EFE keep employee morale high by ordering a substantial salary increase for all employees in the press industry, including the news agencies. The new regulations of 1 November 1962 gave EFE employees a 20% pay hike. The EFE payroll of 1961 was P12,198,794 ($203,313) and it went up to P14,678,249 ($244,637) in 1962, which amounted to 44% of total outlays —the largest category of all expenditures as seen below.

EFE's Finances

EFE's news operations experienced amazing quantum jumps in the decade of 1950s. EFE's finances grew by almost 550% during the 12-year period from 1950. In 1962, EFE showed a negative balance of 1,890,952 ($31,516). This resulted from the revenues of P31,327,813 ($522,131) and the outlays of P33,218,765 ($533,645). In 1950 EFE had perceived gross revenues of P4.84 million.

Technical Aspects

The Madrid transmission room received about 65,000 words daily to send out to EFE clients. The subscribers were 87 newspapers, 36 *Hojas del Lunes* (*Monday Sheets*), 5 foreign news agencies, and 5 non-press clients like the foreign ministry. The Barcelona bureau would retransmit what it received from Madrid to the newspapers in Catalonia. The 65,000 words sent daily to transmission amounted to some 24 million words (65,000 x 365 = 23,725,000) a year. As EFE clients were given differentiated news services, the Madrid technical section (transmission room) dispatched actually 100,000 words a day, 36.5 million annual wordage.

News Exchanges

During the 1940s, EFE had signed exchange agreements with the British Reuters and and U.S. United Press (UP), which had become United Press International (UPI) in 1958. By the time Carlos Mendo took over the EFE directorship in mid-1965, EFE had acquired agreement with the Deutsche Presse-Agentur (dpa) in 1958. Four years later in 1962, EFE signed exchange agreements with the Agence France-Presse (AFP), the successor to the pre-World War II international news giant, the Havas.

On 11 March 1964 EFE acquired the services of the last and the largest of the Western agencies, the Associated Press (AP). Signing the exchange contract were EFE director Carlos Sentís and AP's Madrid bureau chief, Harold Milks. The same year EFE signed an exchange agreement with the Italian Agenzia Nazionale Stampa Associata (ANSA) and others. Meanwhile, the old United Press (Intenational) was not dormantly observing events. UP improved its 1945 contract with a new agreement on 8 June 1956. It extended its teletype circuit to Paris and Lisbon and also updated its telephoto service, UNIFAX, several times.

"BUFFALO KILLED McKINLEY"

Early in 1955, EFE director Pedro Gómez Aparicio gave a talk at the Press Club "Jaime Balmes" in Madrid,[10] in which the speaker emphasized that the news agency was a Spanish "national mania." He meant to say that there were many news agencies in Spain because of the "particular Spanish inclination." As if to prove these interpretations by the EFE director of the national traits, Spain indeed had had its share of news agencies since the mid-19th century, long before EFE was formed in 1938 during the civil war.

News-Agency Mania

A Spanish journalism historian gives the following accounts of the 19th-century growth of news agencies in Spain.[11]

One-Man Telegraph Agencies. Most of these news agencies mushroomed as ephemeral ventures of enterprising spirits who set out to make a fast peseta from provincial newspapers without doing much work. They were really single-correspondent agencies. Busy with the daily chore of a Madrid daily or sometimes engaged in something completely unrelated to journalism, the "correspondent" would have friends "telegraph in his name" news to client newspapers or write daily political letters, for which he paid a little money. The correspondent-agent would thus make a goodly amount doing nothing. He did not have an office, staff, or any other necessary facilities. Or, if he himself did the work, all he did was to go to the telegraph offices and send the newspapers along with some advertising inserts he obtained, skeletal messages of "news" items cut short to save on telegraph fees. Receiving editors had to "translate or bloat" the scarce message. An example of the "translated news": "Buffalo, McKinley assassinated" was "expanded" to, "According to information from Washington, a buffalo has killed the president of the United States!"

Singing Telephone Conferences. Beginning in 1913, telephones gradually replaced telegraphed "news" transmissions. The news correspondent-agencies would now use telephone conferences of 3 to 15 minutes. This created in Madrid the "singer" (*cantador*) or "conference singers" (*canta-conferencias*), who "read" news to the provincial newspapers from Madrid's "Press Studio of Telephones" (Gabinete de Prensa de Teléfonos). These "readers" would pass hours on end, shouting into telephones —"thus subjecting their throats and the lungs to a trial of resistance"— the clips from the Madrid newspapers, given to them by the "correspondent-agents." They had to read fast, eliminating prepositions and articles to shorten the sentences. These "readers" were poorly paid, and poorly read, and often did not comprehend what they were reading. One read: "His Majesty received in audience Argentine ambassador and minister

... minister from, here it says, Czechoslovakia here, must be an error of the [printing] machine" (he obviously did not know the word *Czechoslovakia*).

Solid News Agencies

Out of these innumerable and unrecorded one-man agencies, there emerged a few formally organized news agencies that left a definite mark on Spanish journalism. A few such agencies are still operating today. These certainly did not belong to the group of news agencies that Pedro Gómez Aparicio saw as products of a Spanish news-agency mania "inclination." Before the EFE agency was formed as the Franco organ in 1938, Spain had produced a half-dozen solid news agencies: Fabra, Mencheta, Agencia Prensa Asociada (Associated Press Agency, APA), Febus, Logos, and DUX.[12] The first Spanish news service, Fabra, founded in 1865, was absorbed by the EFE agency in 1938. The DUX agency was formed by Falange partisans in the northern Franco-occupied zone in the early days of the civil war and it too disappeared in 1938.

Agencia Mencheta. The second important news agency after Fabra was founded by Francisco Peris Mencheta about 1876. The Mencheta[13] agency contributed to Spanish journalism by its adoption of the newspaper consortium system —like the cooperative system used by AP of the United States. The original consortium of his 3 newspapers grew to include some 30 newspapers by 1900, and 50 dailies by 1936. This cooperative consortium operation was followed later by most other Spanish agencies (except for EFE, which could not adopt it, for its clients preferred the cheap state-subsidized price, as will be discussed in the next chapter.)[14] Operated by enterprising Peris Mencheta brothers and their children, who enlisted help from luminaries of Spanish journalism, Mencheta was famous for its speed, dedication, and resourcefulness.

At a Christmas lottery-drawing ceremony —an important annual Spanish slam-bang event— Mencheta reporters were nowhere around. The competition and the public wondered why. Mencheta had placed a telephone at the feet of the children who sang out the winning lottery numbers, thus beating all others in speed of transmission.

When French President Sadi Carnot was assassinated in Lyon in 1894, the Mencheta agency had one correspondent in Lyon and Paris. Despite the French government's closure of telecommunications out of Lyon, the Mencheta correspodent in Paris could report to Spanish client papers. Among them, *El Heraldo de Madrid* put out an extra, quoting Mencheta.

Director Peris Mencheta tried to confirm the news in Madrid with the Spanish government and the French embassy, neither of which was forthcoming. The director had to go home badly shaken —"with his teeth rattling"— and had to take to his bed with thermometer in mouth because of the fever he had for the enormity of the event. It was not until 4 in the afternoon that the Spanish minister of state called to tell him that "Carnot has been the victim of a crime." Mencheta let out, "Oh, am I glad!" And his fever was gone. "The life is hard! The journalism is cruel!"

Mencheta thus became known as a practical school of "hard, cruel journalism" among the many Spanish journalists it had produced.[15] Mencheta, still operating in 1989 as the dean of Spanish news agencies from its Madrid headquarters, has its bureau in Barcelona and correspondents in Spain, Hispanic America, and Europe. Mencheta's domestic coverage is good, and its foreign sports service is popular, as it receives news from the Agence France-Presse (AFP).

Agencia Prensa Asociada (Associated Press Agency, APA). The first Catholic church agency to appear in Spain originated from the "Mision de la Bonne Presse" (Mission of the Good Press), an international popular Catholic press movement, so denominated by the Augustine friars in 1873 in Paris, or the "Buena Prensa" in its Spanish version. Two "Good Press" national assemblies were held in 1904 in Sevilla and in 1908 in Zaragoza. The second one voted to create a Catholic press agency. The Spanish church started in May 1909 its "Good Press" agency, giving it the name "Agencia Prensa Asociada" (Associated Press Agency) or APA, with P1 million investment of its own capital. The church's goal for founding APA was to combat the "impious and irreligious" Spanish press, for the church leaders had perceived that the lay press

> on all levels and in all forms, increases its sly and brazen attacks on the Church of Jesus Christ, incessantly vomiting forth an infinitude of dailies and magazines, roadsides and pamphlets which reach even the most peaceful and remote homes, shooting down the old, redeeming beliefs, or, at best, leaving the poisonous dart of doubt or of immortality [sic, immorality] in their hearts. . . .[16]

By 1930, APA had some 70 subscribing church papers, among which *El Debate* was the leading paper with its 70,000 circulation. In mid-1935, APA belonged to the "Junta Nacional de Acción Católica" (National Council of Catholic Action), and was slowly absorbed almost totally by the Logos agency in 1936. In 1955, APA was rescucitated by priest Jesús Iribarren, editor-in-chief of *Ecclesia*, the official Catholic organ. At this writing, APA is functioning as a literary collaboration agency.

Agencia Febus. Nicolas María de Urgoiti founded in 1916[17] the morning daily of Madrid, *El Sol* (*The Sun*), regarded as "one of the best newspapers of Europe and the best ever in Spain" by press historian Antonio Espina.[18] This paper had among its editors and contributors such intellectual luminaries as José Ortega y Gasset, Miguel de Unamuno, and Salvador de Madariaga. The editors of *El Sol* founded the agency Febus in 1919, and they also launched an evening daily, *La Voz* (*The Voice*) in 1920. *La Voz* was intended as an evening paper for Madrid only but when the liberal *El Sol* was suspended by the government in August 1920, *La Voz* changed to a national-circulation paper to substitute for its silenced sister newspaper, and continued so even after *El Sol* reopened. The Febus agency serviced the 2 dailies of the same enterprise, plus 30 odd dailies in a consortium system started earlier by Mencheta.

The left-leaning Febus agency went through vicissitudes in the tumultuous years of transition between the left and right around the Second Republic. Just before the Second Republic was proclaimed in 1931, 2 monarchist noblemen purchased Febus and its 2 newspapers to use these news media for the monarchist cause. But it was too late. The Febus agency and the 2 papers changed their owners to the left and right. In October 1933, the second year of the Republic, the anarchist-syndicalist interior minister, Eloy Vaquero, nicknamed "Matacristo" (Jesus Killer), suspended Febus. But Febus ignored him and kept the operation.

When Franco and his cohorts rebelled in July 1936, Febus editor Fernando Sánchez Monreal, an "extreme leftist,"[19] left the capital to go to Tetouan, the Spanish Moroccan port, where the rebellion was being staged. Upon arrival in Córdoba, he found it under Nationalist military control. He suspended his planned reporting excursion and was captured on his way home in Valladolid by the Nationalists, who shot him for alleged espionage for the Republic. During the Second Republic and the civil war, Febus and its 2 sister papers supported the Republican cause, until they were confiscated by the Franco regime upon the March 1939 fall of Madrid. The properties of *El Sol, La Voz*, and Febus were taken over by the Falangist newspaper, *Arriba* (*Hurrah*), which had been founded in 1935, to be suspended by the Republican government in 1936. Such was the fate run by intellectual endeavors like Febus, *El Sol*, and *La Voz* in the Spain of the 1930s.

Agencia Logos. In the summer of 1929, the publishing house of the church, "La Editorial Católica," set up another Catholic news service, the Agencia Logos. The guiding genius behind Logos was the editor of the daily *El Debate*, Bishop Angel Herrera Oria, who was later promoted to cardinal. Logos was founded by the church to have its own information organ to serve its newspapers. The church was determined to shield its newspapers against the stories supplied by the various news agencies, "which some were doubtful and the rest frankly of the left."[20] The old "Prensa Asociada" was not performing its job adequately; the church needed new blood. Logos was the fourth agency —after Mencheta, APA, and Febus— in Spain to operate under the consortium among member newspapers.

The financial unison of the chain of "La Editorial Católica" dailies gave Logos the needed volume of capital to maintain itself. And the expenses divided by all members resulted in economy. Logos, however, grew so fast that it had to be separated from the other papers. In 1934 it became an autonomous entity in the "Editorial Catolica," which appointed, as first Logos director, the editorial writer of *El Debate*, Vicente Gállego Castro. He became the founding director of the EFE agency in 1938. This new independent life gave Logos an impulse for quick development, and by 1936 it had more than 50 newspapers subscribing to its news service, provided by 25 writers, 250 correspondents, and a radio telegraphic station by which Logos received the foreign news. At this writing in 1989, the Agencia Logos is still operating as a private agency of Spain.

Ibero-American News Agency

The "news-agency mania" may not be a particularly Spanish inclination as was claimed by EFE director Pedro Gómez Aparicio in 1955. If it were any national or cultural trait, it was certainly shared by Spain's Iberian neighbor, Portugal. The seafaring conquerors of the 4 seas in their glorious past, the Spaniards and Portuguese shared in a dream to build an information empire by means of the modern news agency. Such an "Iberian dream" was entertained formally by 2 powerful men. Ramón Serrano Súñer, the erstwhile *cuñadísimo* of Spain, and Antonio de Oliveira Salazar, the 36-year (1932–1968) dictator of Portugal, together put this Iberian dream into the scenario described below.

The geographic proximity of Spain and Portugal has naturally given the 2 countries all sorts of intimate ties through the eon. During the difficult days of World War II, the Franco regime signed a nonaggression pact with

Portugal to mitigate its international isolation. Portugal would always render full support to the perpetual Spanish claim on the British-occupied Rock of Gibraltar. EFE's first foreign contact was with the Portuguese press union in August 1945. EFE also had had contact with the Portuguese national news service, Agencia de Noticias e Informacoes (ANI).[21] The EFE agency was long an object of admiration by Portuguese journalists.

During his May 1963 visit to Spain, Portuguese Premier Salazar broached a grandiose scheme to none other than *cuñadísimo*, Ramón Serrano Súñer. Serrano Súñer recalled, in an interview,[22] that "Dr. Oliveira Salazar, with whom I always had very good relationship," had "great illusions to create an agency among Portugal, Spain, and some country in the Americas —related with us— Argentina then, in order to have in the world a 'presence' a little bigger than EFE." Serrano Súñer explained why that great Ibero-American news agency did not become a reality:[23]

> Look, it was not made principally for the fault of Spain. For there arose small groups of here [Spain] with the idea of nationalism, saying that it would be [a] loss for the agency EFE, that was to lose importance. Salazar saw all the importance of the matter, with all enthusiasm. . . . We, he and I, suffered the deception that little considerations here, small interests of the country, frustrated this idea.

Salazar and Serrano Súñer were empire builders, and they both dreamed a great dream of the Iberian conquistadores of past centuries, who pushed open the enormous expanses of the Americas. Some would call the idea a megalomania. It is interesting, however, that the same ideas were entertained by these experienced power-wielders of Iberia —not the poetic fiction writers— and in the middle of the 1960s. The Iberians would eternally entertain that Quixotesque impulse, which was to motivate Carlos Mendo and his successors of the EFE agency in their enterprising expansion in the decades to come.

SCHOOLS OF JOURNALISM

Among the top EFE executives who have taken part in EFE's 25-year history thus far, Carlos Mendo was the first full graduate of the Official School of Journalism. Mendo in that sense was of the new generation of EFE and Spanish journalists, a generation that received a formally structured journalism education. Since about the mid-1950s on down to the present, practically all of the journalistic workers of EFE have been graduates of the Official School of Journalism operated first by the director general of press (DGP) of the vice secretariat of popular education of Arias-

Salgado, and later by the ministry of information and tourism (MIT) established in 1951. The generation of the EFE journalists of the 1980s have all been graduates of the Colleges of Information Sciences (Facultades de Ciencias de la Información), which gradually took over from the old schools of journalism after Franco's death in 1975.

The older generation of the top EFE management had learned the journalism profession on the job, and they became teachers of the journalism school(s). The first director-manager, Gállego Castro, became a journalist while working for bishop-editor Angel Herrera Oria of the Catholic paper *El Debate*. Then, Gállego Castro himself taught at *El Debate* journalism school, "the first in Spain"[24] already functioning some years before the civil war. When he became the first EFE director in 1939 at age 43, subdirector Gómez Aparicio, who was 36, had been a student of Gállego Castro. Later both Gállego Castro and Gómez Aparicio taught, while working for the EFE agency, at the Official School of Journalism, established formally by the 17 November 1941 law of the vice secretariat of popular education of the interior ministry.

The first of the top EFE management who was on record to have studied at the Official School of Journalism ("Escuela Oficial de Periodismo" —EOP, henceforward) was Waldo de Mier, subdirector of EFE during 1957–1970. He took "brief courses in 1943–1944, offered for those of us who were already working at the newspapers."[25] De Mier was too old to have gone through the full EOP curriculum, which was still being organized when he studied. The EOP was founded, as indicated above, in November 1941, on "experiences of *El Debate*'s journalism school, which had had its influence on technical improvement of *El Debate* journalism school."

To control the Spanish press, the Franco regime decreed a series of dispositions, codifying the journalism profession from the early days of the civil war. The 1938 Press Law created the Official Registry of Journalists and regulated the curriculum of journalism education. After the journalists' registration was finished in October 1939, interior minister Serrano Súñer issued an order in August 1940 to begin "the celebration of courses" as "the only process which is recognized hereafter for entry into the Official Registry of Journalists." This 1940 order ruled that journalism courses would be "convened annually . . . , reserved to those who possess a university degree, the status of active Army officer or a title from the Higher School." This meant that the journalism courses, as well as the Journalist Registry, were more a means of control than for professional training.

The first journalism course of 1940–1941, which had begun at a Madrid academy, finished at the Ayala 5 location of the EFE agency. (The Hispanic "course" is an academic year rather than the subjects of study.) EFE's director Gállego Castro assumed the direction, and subdirector Gómez Aparicio the secretariat of the "course." They also taught "journalistic technique" and "reporterism" (reportage) respectively. EFE president Jesús Pabón also taught "contemporary history." The 1940–1941 cycle produced 20 graduates, who "later occupied outstanding positions in the journalistic profession and outside of it."[26] Based on this first-year experience, subsecretary of popular education Arias-Salgado definitely ordered the formation of the EOP on 17 November 1941. His loyal aide, DGP Juan Aparicio, became the first director and "its true craftsman." Enrollment was limited to 20 students, half of whom were given scholarships by journalistic "entities in order to give access to the persons of limited economic resources."

All applicants had to be graduates of high schools, normal schools, or equivalents.[27] For the 20 available seats in the first "course" starting on 2 January 1942 more than 230 applied. The curricular contents —which later were expanded to 3 years plus a thesis (*tesina* or little thesis) to graduate— included such dogmatic courses as "Life and Doctrine of National-Syndicalism," "National-Syndicalist Policy," and others taught by none other than DGP Juan Aparicio. General education courses included political science, philosophy, contemporary history, geopolitics, national economy, history of the universal literature, and religious culture. The EOP did naturally offer several journalistic courses: headlining and make-up, journalism history and press legislation, literary writing, news and reportage, typography, and others. During World War II, German was the required foreign language, which later became French and still later included English. Students had to acquire typing and stenography skills on their own.

Imposed on top of the very degree-conscious culture of Spain, EOP graduation became a prerequisite for employment as a journalist in any Spanish media, for only with an EOP degree could one be enrolled in the Official Registry of Journalists, which in turn was a requirement to work in the profession. The EOP was reformed and updated several times by laws decreed in 1951, 1952, 1953, 1957, 1958, and 1960. The 1958 reform authorized the founding of 2 Catholic church-operated schools of journalism in Madrid and Barcelona. In 1960, a third church-run journalism institute was accredited at the Navarra University in Pamplona. But the graduates of these unofficial schools had to pass an equivalency examination conducted by the EOP to be enrolled in the Official Registry of Journalists.

That provoked angry protests from the church hierarchy, which was becoming increasingly reform-minded. The church's protest was based on the 1953 concordat between Spain and the Vatican that granted special privileges to the church's literary and educational activities. The church and Arias-Salgado's MIT clashed directly. To dramatize their protest, the church representatives in February 1961 began a prolonged boycott of the meetings of a commission which had been charged with drawing up a new press law.

These open church – MIT quarrels of 1961 were the beginning of the end to the MIT tenure of Arias-Salgado. He was fired in July 1962 to be replaced by Fraga Iribarne

Agency-Journalism School

There was another wrinkle to the involvement of the EFE agency in journalism education. Toward the end of the Franco era, the old journalism schools were taken over by the new Faculties of Information Sciences with more generalized academic curricula that did not concentrate on the on-the-job performance of graduates. In January 1977, the EFE news agency formed its own journalism school to meet its needs. At the time, EFE was going through its second overseas expansion, reaching out to the non-Hispanic world. EFE gave the 2-year training program a long-winded title: "Escuela de Especialización de Periodismo de Agencia" (Specialized School of Agency Journalism).

Applicants now had to be graduates (*licenciados*) of the Faculties of Information Sciences of the Spanish universities or of the church. Teachers were selected from practicing EFE journalists and "professional specialization" placed emphasis on the practical aspects of news-agency activities. Works produced by students in the practice became the property of EFE and could be included in the news dispatches of the agency. EFE promised to compensate the students for any works used. Most of the graduates of the 2-year program were employed by EFE to replenish the supply of reporters and correspondents badly needed in the late 1970s and the early 1980s.

DEMANDS FOR CHANGE

The Catholic church's protest against the "discrimination" of graduates of its school of journalism during 1961 – 1962 was not an isolated event, and the discontent over the autocratic Franco regime was not limited to the religious hierarchy. Far from it. Indeed, the church belonged to the privileged class in Falange Spain. The facade of "25 Years of Peace" hid many a problem behind it. Promised improvements in the economic and social life did not materialize as quickly and widely as hoped for, despite the influx of U.S. economic "aids in exchange for the military bases surrendered to a foreign power alien to the Spanish interests."[28] Every year, starting in 1956, saw evidences of general unrest. University students, professors, and other intellectuals clamored for liberalization of the stifling control and press censorship.

Labor and farm troubles cropped up, culminating in miners' strikes in 1962 and 1963. In these conflicts, the church started to take the side of the repressed majority. The repression and punishments could not solve the underlying problems. Indeed, the major government shakeups —at least 6 during 1951–1965— were an indication of the regime's effort to come to grips with the turmoil through some measure of reform, along with reactionary crackdown on the protest. The Franco regime oscillated between the factions representing reform and reaction. The stronger the repression, the more outspoken the protest became. The Spaniards are famous for indomitable spirit of rebellion. The Franco regime itself was a rebel creature.

The Franco regime established such a stifling autocracy that Spanish intellectuals rebelled against it. Pablo Picasso produced the world-renowned *Guernica* in protest against the April 1937 German bombing of the Spanish town of the same name. He would not let the masterpiece return to Spain as long as Franco was alive. Miguel de Unamuno openly defied the Francoist military in 1938. He was put under house arrest and soon died. José Ortega y Gasset wrote *La Rebelión de Masas* (*The Rebellion of Masses*) against the Francoist oppression. On his death in 1955, MIT Arias-Salgado issued, through an EFE dispatch, a stern *consigna* that all Spanish papers include his many lifetime errors in his obituaries.[29] This *consigna* gave such macabre details as to permit the publication of pictures of the death mask or body of Ortega but not the ones made during his lifetime.

Intellectual protest against the regime was not limited to these well-known figures, students, and professors. Under the meticulous censorship, Spanish writers and journalists invented "a minor ingenious art of writing between the lines."[30] The newspaper *Juventud* (*Youth*) aired an angry protest against the censorship by using the camouflage of such worn slogans as the "information sovereignty" and "news colonialism" against the Western "liberal" news media, the epithet constantly waved by Falangists and EFE journalists alike. A long *Juventud* article on 11 December 1953, accompanied by a piquant cartoon, accused the North American news agencies of a conspiracy of silence against Spain and the Hispanic world. Hiding behind the Spanish nationalism and patriotic outcry against "information colonialism," the article denounced the EFE agency for "surrendering itself" to the United Press (UP). It asserted:

> We do not have our own news agencies, but when we begin to have them, we surrender them, shamefully, to those same agencies that have us submitted to a true information colonialism, as happens

specifically in Spain with the subordination of the EFE agency to the United Press, while [EFE] does not have a single correspondent of its own in any part of Hispano America or overseas.[31]

Even Salvador Dali ridiculed the EFE agency, using its London dispatch dealing with the Profumo Case on the cover of his book, *Diario de Un Genio* (*Diary of a Genius*), published in 1964 from his self-imposed exile in Paris. Dali, the surrealist painter, had earlier taken exception to the Spanish intelligentsia which was generally opposed to the Franco regime. But in 1964, the year of the "25 Years of Spanish Peace" campaign, Dali painted a news dispatch with the signature of "EFE, the first news agency of the world that was ever carried to a canvas" for the cover design of his book.[32] Dali picked, of all the EFE dispatches, one on the spy-sex scandal-laden Profumo Case, news that lacked in substance but was filled with sensationalism, because it was about a British caper safe from Spanish censors. It was Dali's indirect criticism of press control in his native Spain, which he believed had gone out of all the justifications of the wartime needs.

Press and Print Law (1966)

Demand for change was astir in Spain during the late 1950s, when EFE was growing into its adulthood. EFE director Carlos Mendo, who took the Spanish news agency to Europe and the Americas during his 1965–1969 tenure, believed that important changes originated toward the end of the 1950s, when "the economic autarchy ends."[33] It presupposed "evidently a total change in attitude of the Government and of the Spanish people." It presupposed, at the same time, "the beginning of the end of the dictatorship, because it is impossible, as has been amply demonstrated, to maintain a political dictatorship with an economic liberty, for they are 2 terms completely antithetic." That movement toward liberalization was advanced by a cabinet change in 1962, when "some reformers entered with an idea to reform the system from within." The "most important for his youth —age 39— was Manuel Fraga Iribarne" who entered the cabinet as minister of information and tourism. Mendo said Fraga confided to him —"for we made ourselves such good friends"— that General Franco asked Fraga to make a new press law.

Obviously, Franco would never think that Fraga would dare to make a press law very liberal, but thought that it would be limited to changing the obsolete Press Law of 1938. Fraga Iribarne presented a press law which was very liberal for the standards of the Franco regime, improving upon an Arias-Salgado project of 1959. Mendo said the Fraga project was

"tremendously liberal"; it was to end the prior censorship. It was to allow
the freedom to establish press enterprises; "in Spain then, it was impossible
to begin a new newspaper, unless there was the title [imprimatur]." That
triggered a battle within the government, which was so pitched that it took
Fraga 4 full years to obtain the new press law. There was official opposition
to the new law, and liberalization was countenanced only by a small segment
of the government. Fraga and his liberal partisans were caught in the middle.
They had to oscillate between the liberal reformers and hard-line
conservatives. Possibly to placate the reaction, Fraga himself took many a
contradictory action.

Zigzagging left and right with an often inexplicable ambivalence, Fraga
Iribarne still forged on with the press law reform. Late in the fall of 1965,
MIT Fraga celebrated meetings with the directors of newspapers and news
agencies on the progess of the press law reform. He also answered questions
from the press people, when Madrid and provincial journalists had a
reception at the EFE locale.[34] It took until the following year for the MIT
to get the new press law through the Spanish Cortes. MIT Fraga delivered
an eloquent historic speech on 15 March 1966 to the Plenary session of the
Cortes,[35] which gave its prearranged approval 3 days later to the "Law of
Press and Print" (La Ley de Prensa e Imprenta or LPI) of 18 March 1966.
It had been almost 30 years since the wartime Press Law of 1938 had been
instituted.

Not So "New" Press Law

The "new" press and print law of 1966 was hailed as something
revolutionary. Most U.S. trade journals, for example, cited the 1966
enactment of the law "as the end of long-time censorship in Spain and the
beginning of an era of a more independent press."[36] Such assessments
revealed ignorance on the part of outside observers. The law, among
hundreds of new "reformist" provisions, was supposed to have: (1)
eliminated the prior censorship; (2) returned to the journalistic businesses
the right to name their own directors and management personnel; and (3)
abrogated the requirements for an official permit to start a periodical. But
the practicing Spanish journalists and press managers could not see the law
with such optimistic eyes.

The prepublication censorship had already been replaced by "delegated
censorship" since 1957. A 14 June 1957 law created within the MIT the
"National Council of Press" (Consejo Nacional de Prensa) as the "supreme
organ of consultation." By that decree, the MIT "delegated to the directors
of publications the role of the DGP censor on the basis of consultation."[37]

The consultation was "much worse than the censorship" in practice. Waldo de Mier, the EFE subdirector, remembered that "with the censors, we could play fool and crazy —'jugar tontos o locos'— alleging that the *consigna* was not received in time or lost. If it was an urgent telephoned *consigna* we could even pretend that we could not hear, for telephone connections were often bad, fortunately." But with the "delegated censorship with the 'right' —actually 'duty'— to consult, we could not find any escape. We self-censored much more than DGP censors would have done."[38]

That consultation provision was kept intact in the 1966 Press Law in Article 4, entitled cynically "Voluntary Consultation." The new law retained the *consigna* rule in Article 6 that kept the provision to require "the periodic publications to insert and the news agencies to distribute" information deemed to be of general interest to the public by, of course, the government.

On the supposedly "autonomous appointment" of directors and other management personnel of the news organizations, Chapter V —entitled "Of the Journalistic Profession and of the Directors of Periodic Publications"— stipulated that the directors had to be enrolled in the Official Registry of Journalists, which could be and was subjected to MIT-DGP control. Article 36 (Prohibitions) of the same chapter listed so many qualifications for a newspaper or a news agency director that the MIT-DGP could at will boycott any person so appointed.

The new law's Chapter IV (Of the Registry of Journalistic Enterprises) had so many rules and steps on "inscription" that they could be manipulated by the government. Its Article 29 (Causes for Denial and for Cancellation of the Inscriptions) was so fraught with ambiguity that the MIT-DGP could block opening of any journalistic businesses, if it would so deem.

After all, it was not the written provisions of the law but how those provisions would be applied that might bring about a change. All was dependent on the politico-social climate, and the climate of the 1960s Spain which produced this new law, not the law itself, appeared to augur well for Spanish journalism in general. The climate certainly brought a windfall to the EFE news agency.

Exclusive Foreign-News Agency

Chapter VI of the new press law dealt with the subject "Of the Foreign News." It said: "The distribution of the news proceeding from foreign agencies, 'with exclusivity' and without any discrimination, 'can be conceded' to a national agency with representation of the public Entities and of the news media or in cooperative management of these last." To implement the provisions contained in Chapter VI, a decree was issued 2 weeks after the law on 31 March 196 on the "Inscription in the Registry of News Agencies."[39]

Two months later, a windfall order came down for the EFE news agency. The short order (with only 2 articles) of 1 September 1966 conceded to the EFE agency "the exclusive distribution in all the national territory, of the news proceeding from foreign agencies." Without any ambiguity, the EFE agency was given the exclusive right of distribution of all foreign news. This was a paramount victory for EFE. Up until then EFE had enjoyed only a de facto exclusivity on foreign news. No competition was possible now, for example, from PYRESA, with help from foreign news agencies like U.S.'s INS (International News Service), as had been attempted in 1950. MIT Fraga Iribarne saw to it that the EFE news agency would have free and exclusive control over foreign news in the country, under the direction of Carlos Mendo, who had become his friend and protégé.

The preamble to the 1 September 1966 order also referred to EFE's "current international expansion, which permits it to obtain its own and objective news, without any other orientation than that of satisfying faithfully the journalistic interests of Spain and of the Hispanoamerican world, thus complementing the services of the world agencies that it distributes at the present time." The world agencies whose "services it [EFE] distributes" were, of course, AP, UPI, Reuters, AFP, dpa, and ANSA. The EFE agency's "current international expansion" for "the journalistic interests of Spain and of the Hispanoamerican world" was a reference to an EFE expansion program to South America being carried out since December 1965 by the new EFE director, Carlos Mendo. MIT Fraga Iribarne, sure that his press law reform would soon come about, approached Carlos Mendo in mid-1965 with an idea of expanding EFE services to Hispanic America, asking:

> Why should we not achieve to exploit the community of millions of persons who speak the same Spanish, in Hispanic America as well as in Spain? Having a vehicle of a news agency, it looks like a lie that this EFE agency should be limited by the Pyrenees and the Strait of Gibraltar when Spain always has had a very ultra-marine vocation, very much toward the other parts of the seas. Do you think that it would be possible, that it is not an insanity, to try to sell the services of EFE to the Hispano American communication media?[40]

Mendo, then UPI Madrid bureau manager, told Fraga that he did not know, that he would have to study it, and that he did not like to improvise. Mendo studied the plan and later gave a positive reply to Fraga. But he also told Fraga that it would need money and authority. Fraga told Mendo: "Authority, I can give you very much, but money, very little." Mendo said:

"The truth is that they gave me very little money. And then, Fraga offered me the management of this house [of EFE]." Mendo took over the EFE directorship on 10 June 1965.

At the time, monetary provision for the EFE agency was not at all lacking; EFE, in reality, was well provided for. In the year 1963 —with Fraga already in the MIT post— the EFE administrative council was authorized to increase its capital by 100% to P20 million. This measure was to allow EFE to keep up with the devalued purchasing power of the Spanish peseta that went from P9.13 in 1939 to P60 to a U.S. dollar. Two years later, on 9 March 1965, Franco authorized the finance ministry to buy up 4,666 shares of the EFE agency, owned by private entities. This would carry the state share of EFE ownership to the legal maximum of one-third of the total capital, allowing more financial leeway to the EFE administrative council.[41]

Before the year 1965 was out, Mendo went to Argentina to open daily news service between Spain and Ibero America through EFE's Buenos Aires bureau, which was to serve in the months ahead as the general headquarters of the EFE news agency in the Americas. The Spain – Argentina connection was established on 20 December 1965. It brought to reality the dream much argued by the EFE executives even before EFE's foundation in January 1939. It had taken 26 years to realize that dream. It also needed a "revolutionary" reform in the Spanish press law, from the one decreed in the wartime Spain of 1938 to the Spain of 1966, which was largely at peace with itself and the world. La Agencia EFE, S.A. had again traveled a long way.

Chapter 5

Heart in the Americas
(1966–1969)

In the 40-year Franco rule, the second half of the 1960s was the most upbeat, yet the most frustrating period. In this lustrum the regime attempted several liberalizing reforms from within, which were countered quickly by the reactionary elements in the same system. Consequently, EFE zigzagged between prosperity and poverty.

In 1966 a new press law was passed, eliminating prior censorship. The laborer's right to strike was recognized by a 1965 law. The country was enjoying a spectacular expansion, which was classified as an economic miracle. In 1968 the second quadrennial development plan was launched after the first 4-year plan concluded, which had brought about the highest growth rate in all Europe.[1] Political liberalization was codified in the 1966 Organic Law of the State. The regime seemed to prepare for a peaceful transfer of power, when Juan Carlos was declared the Crown Prince in 1969.

But this was only one side of Spain. Vibrant hopes were fast dashed. The conservative wing of the regime would countenance only "cosmetic" changes. The penal code was tightened in 1967, on whose heel followed the 1968 "Law of Official Secrets." Labor and student strikes were as harshly repressed as ever, under the pretext that they were not legitimate "economic" strikes, but "purely political" ones. To arrest the unrest, a 3-month "state of exception" was declared in January 1969 throughout the country. Along with the economic boom came sharp increases in prices. The peseta was devalued 14.3% in 1967. A slow deceleration set in, and uncertainty became the economic keynote. Prince Juan Carlos was "obligated" to break with his father in a statement to EFE.[2] Yet his ultimate ascension —not restoration— to the throne was entirely subject to the Franco regime.

The EFE news agency was championed by the minister of information and tourism (MIT), Manuel Fraga Iribarne, who was no less obedient to *El Caudillo*; his servitude was, however, more sophisticated. For most of the 1960s, MIT Fraga rode the crest of the liberalizing trend. And EFE under the direction of his protégé, Carlos Mendo, could strike out to Latin America. EFE's "American" feat was possible because Fraga encouraged Franco to believe —and so declare, as will be seen shortly— that "Spain has its heart in the Americas." But when the reaction set in, beginning already in 1967, the Fraga–Mendo duo was swiftly removed from power in 1969. This chapter will deal with the accomplishments of the Fraga-Mendo MIT-EFE apparatus.

H-BOMB LOST

An incident of dramatic repercussions opened this 1966–1969 period and placed Spain again on the world news scene. On 17 January a giant B-52 jet bomber of the U.S. Strategic Air Command collided with a KC-135 jet tanker, which was refueling it, at an altitude of 30,000 feet (9,000 meters) over the Almeria region on the Mediterranean Sea. Three 20-megaton hydrogen bombs dropped inland near the fishing village of Palomares —meaning "dovecots" ironically— approximately 180 miles east of Gibraltar. The fourth bomb fell into the sea a few miles off the coast. One of 3 bombs was recovered intact. The other 2 bombs cracked open and spread their frightening contents on the dry earth, contaminating it with plutonium and uranium. About 1,500 tons of topsoil were shipped to an atomic power plant in South Carolina for disposal, and another 5,000 tons had to be buried in Spain itself.

It took an extensive 79-day search to discover and salvage the fourth bomb from the sea bottom with special equipment on 7 April. At Palomares, the working life had to languish while U.S. scientists and technicians set up detector equipment. The 1,200 inhabitants of the Palomares farm and fishing community were informed later that medical checks would have to continue indefinitely. No radiation on humans and animals was detected immediately, but tomato and many other crops had to be destroyed. In spite of total censorship, the news slowly filtered through, and indignation and anxiety went beyond the frontiers of Spain. Digging continued all around Palomares. Anti-U.S. leaflets were distributed in Madrid, Barcelona, and other cities and towns. A popular song, *La Bomba Perdida* (*The Lost Bomb*), was composed and sung around the country. The official censors could not suffocate the news of the tragedy.

The Spanish government had to cope with the panic, silence alarmist rumors, and forestall the anxiety of foreign tourists fast, tourism being one of the big sources of foreign exchange for Spain. Press and tourism campaign tasks fell on the shoulders of minister of information and tourism (MIT), Manuel Fraga Iribarne. MIT Fraga concocted a scheme. He invited the U.S.

ambassador Angier Biddle Duke and the family to join him and his children for a swimming trip near Palomares on a March Sunday. Newspapers all over the country carried EFE-supplied stories and CIFRA-Gráfica photos, and the official, and only, Television Española broadcast the pictures of the brave minister and obliging ambassador plunging into the icy March water of the Mediterranean. This tragicomic incident illustrated well the new methodology of MIT Fraga's information service, resolutely savvy and gleefully concealing, by way of a spectacular EFE news campaign, the real problem: the nuclear peril exposing Spain and the rest of Europe.

De Gaulle "Closes" *Madrid*

A short time after the Fraga – Duke Mediterranean "nuclear" dip, the new Press and Print Law (LPI), of 18 March 1966, laid down the rules governing the Spanish press in an apparently more liberal way, but they were more skillfully repressive. The regime shifted left and right in its policy toward the press. In spite of its many flaws, the 1966 LPI liberalized the press system to a considerable degree. But only a year later the 8 April 1967 reform of the penal code tightened the limits of freedom of expression. The regime followed it up only a year later with the 5 April 1968 Law of Official Secrets. It permitted the government to restrict many key areas to the press.

An extreme example of regression is the case of the daily *Madrid*. The afternoon paper was closed for months from May 1968 as a punishment for an editorial which called the French President Charles de Gaulle "an old man clinging obstinately to power." The editor was heavily fined, for the Franco regime could not stomach the obvious parallel that the Spaniards could draw between De Gaulle and the Spanish "old man" also clinging to dictatorial power for more than 30 years by then.

MENDO ERA

Director-manager Mendo worked in 2 stages to effect the transformation of EFE from a lethargic domestic organ into an active international news service. He knew that the area of strength of the agency lay in Latin America, her former colonies, with which she held intimate cultural affinities and close economic relations. He set out to "reconquer" it first. But Mendo realized that Spain by herself did not generate much news to offer the Latin American market. To supply Hispanic American clients with sufficient and meaningful information mix, EFE had to establish a European news-gathering network. Mendo accomplished both the American and European phases of his mission with dispatch.

Exploring the Americas

Franco declared to the Madrid correspondent of the French daily *Le Figaro* on 16 December 1963 that "Spain, that has her feet in Europe and her heart in [the] Americas, can constitute [itself as] a bridge between the 2 continents."[3] Mendo's heart was set on establishsing a direct news transmission link between Madrid and Buenos Aires. A week of difficult trial runs during the Argentine summer months enabled the young EFE director to "initiate the link in 'officious' (oficioso) mode."

The permanent services of 3 hours of daily transmission began on 2 January 1966. In a 20-month period, EFE set up its overseas network in 3 phases characterized as the "EFE miracle."[4] In the first phase, by June 1966, EFE-Madrid got to transmit news 20 hours per day to Buenos Aires, which, in turn, retransmitted it to EFE bureaus set up in Asuncion, Lima, Santiago, and Montevideo. Concurrently, the European service started 14 hours of daily transmission by telephone connections from the EFE bureaus in Paris, London, Brussels, Bonn, and Rome.

From the news supplied by these European points and the Spanish news provided by CIFRA (national), EFE (foreign) selected its European service to Buenos Aires. In May 1966 the New York bureau with its Washington branch commenced a 20-hour daily service through Transatlantic cables.

The second phase commenced in June 1966, when New York entered into direct radio contact with Mexico City, Caracas, and all other EFE bureaus in the Americas. Within a year —by July 1967— EFE's American network had 2 "currents" (*corrientes*). The Northern current ran: Madrid – New York – Mexico – Caracas – Guayaquil – Bogota – Quito. The Southern current connected Madrid – Buenos Aires – Santiago – Montevideo – Rio de Janeiro – Asuncion – La Paz – Lima.

In the third phase —starting in August 1967— EFE opened its Asian extension, centralizing at its Manila bureau, the Far Eastern news from Saigon, Hong Kong, and Tokyo. Manila radioed via San Francisco Asian news 12 hours a day to New York City which in turn sent it to the Iberoamerican capitals and to Madrid through the London – Paris channel. The Asia service was still the weakest of all EFE networks.

Astride Europe

EFE director Mendo, when he launched on the American expansion in 1966, quickly realized that EFE had to take European news to the Americas. As spiritual new consuistarores of Hispanic America, EFE had to transport European riches to the former Spanish colonies in a process "reverse" to that of the erstwhile conquistadores. Only 2 months after he returned from Argentina, Mendo set out to establish EFE bureaus in 5 principal cities in Western Europe.

Mendo started on an 18-day European tour on 12 March 1966 with 2 fellow travelers, both high EFE executives: EFE secretary-general Alberto Poveda Longo, 50, and administrator Jose Luis García Gallego, 53, who had been a young-Turk member of the 1938 Casino de Burgos group. The 3 top EFE manangers were equipped with authority and financial wherewithal bestowed by MIT Fraga Iribarne.

In Paris they rented "a very good office right behind the Elysee Palace on Rue Montalivert" to house an EFE correspondent. EFE's London office was already lodged in a building which also housed the United Press International. In Brussels, EFE set up an office in the building of the daily *La Lanterne* (*The Lantern*). In Bonn the EFE group found an office. In the last city on their itinerary, Rome, they installed the EFE bureau in "La Obra Pia" (Pious Work) in La Piazza Navonna.

During Mendo's 18-day absence from Spain, the new Press and Print Law had been promulgated (on 18 March) under MIT Fraga Iribarne. Before his European travel, Mendo had been amply apprised of the new press law by his mentor, MIT Fraga. Yet, Mendo still had to consider the full impact of the new law. On 31 March, Mendo's first day on the job back from the European swing, the government issued a decree to implement the provisions of Article 6 of the new press law. The article —and the implementing decree— stipulated that news media including news agencies, had the obligation to insert information supplied by the government. The decree gave detailed procedures on how to comply with the government order. Mendo had to comprehend them and study the effects they would have on his job as the director of the nation's premier news agency.

EFE 1969 Statistics

Director-manager Carlos Mendo, by his dynamism, drive, and expertise, effected a metamorphosis of EFE from a domestic agency to an international news organization during the 1965–1969 Mendo–Fraga era. Toward the end of his tenure, EFE had grown to show the following statistics in its organization, performance, and finance.[5] (To be meaningful, these figures should be looked at from hitorical perspectives against the comparable data from the different eras in EFE history, as presented in Table 8.4.

EFE news staff had increased to 500 persons —counting 200 men working abroad— including journalists, translators, and technical people. In addition, EFE hired more than 1,100 part-time national correspondents working in provinces across peninsular Spain and her island possessions. Of the 500 full-time employees, 250 worked out of the Madrid central offices, and 50 at the 4 domestic bureaus in Barcelona, Bilbao, Sevilla, and Santiago de Compostela. About 200 were engaged as individual foreign correspondents, or staff members, of 32 foreign bureaus located in Bonn, Brussels, Paris, Rome, London, Lisbon, The Hague, and Geneva in Europe; Tokyo, Manila, and Taipei in Asia, with news also fed from Hong Kong and Singapore; Rabat and Bata in North Africa; New York, Washington, Mexico, Cali, Quito, La Paz, Guayaquil, San Jose de Costa Rica, Santo Domingo, Panama, Santiago de Chile, Caracas, Bogota, Medellin, Montevideo, Lima, Rio de Janeiro, Asuncion, and the Buenos Aires hubpoint for the bureaus in the Americas.

These EFE news people, in Spain and abroad, provided verbal and photographic news. Total annual wordage was 135.1 million: 25.6 million going to foreign clients, and 109.5 million sent to domestic subscribers. The 109.5 million domestic wordage broke down to: 22.4 million in EFE-Basic (EFE's and UPI and Reuters news), 35.4 million in complementary EFE-AP and EFE-AFP services, 22.3 million in CIFRA (national) news, 12.2 million ALFIL sports (domestic and foreign) news, and 17.2 million economic-finance news. The CIFRA-Gráfica photo service supplied 109,500 photographs in original and 912,500 copies annually.

The verbal and photographic news items were distributed to 446 subscribers, 163 in Spain and 283 abroad. The 163 Spanish clients comprised 115 newspapers, 11 radio stations, one television channel, and 36 other clients such as magazines, and government offices. The 283 foreign clients were: 75 newspapers, 100 radios, 8 television channels, and 100 magazines and others.

These figures on the EFE bureaus (36), annual wordage (135.1 million), and subscribers (446) should be cast in relative terms compared to other international agencies that the EFE people looked up to as world giants. Miguel Higueras Cleries, who by 1986 had become the EFE executive editor, presented interesting figures on AP, UPI, TASS, Reuters, and AFP in his 1967 thesis:[6]

Table 5.1
EFE Compared to Other Agencies

Agency	EFE	AP	UPI	TASS	Reuters	AFP
Bureaus	36	169	237	184	108	115
Wordage (M)	135.1	1095	912.5	365	292	273.8
Clients	446	4250	7000	184	610	569

(M is annual wordage in millions.)

EFE 1969 Finances

These domestic and overseas apparatuses and their services incurred EFE the total expenditure of P175.4 million (some $2.5 million at $1=P70 rate) annually. On the other hand, the total gross revenues from subscribers totaled P168.8 million (some $2.41 million) a year for various EFE services. Higueras complained that the EFE news agency's annual news-related expenditures —P175.4 million ($2.5 million)— "scarcely reached 2% of the annual budget of the giant U.S. agency, AP."[7] All told, the EFE expenses outstripped the revenues, giving the Spanish agency a negative balance of P6.6 million ($94,286).

The loss of P6.6 million is only 3.91% of the gross revenues of EFE (P168.8 million). Less than 4% annual loss in a state enterprise may not appear to be a serious matter when the concern is supposed to serve national goals, such as the much-touted "information sovereignty" and Spain's influence in its erstwhile American colonies. But the 1968 figures flaunted by various documents and declarations by the EFE management glossed over the grave economic status of the EFE agency.

As shown in Table 5.2, the Spanish government paid EFE P31.3 million of the P86.3 million domestic revenues. Now add the P31.3 million to the P6.6 million "admitted" loss picked up by the government and EFE receipts from the government amounted to P37.9 million. The P37.9 million government receipts were almost 6 times as big as the "admitted" loss of P6.6 million.

Table 5.2
EFE's Finances, 1969

TOTAL EXPENDITURE:		P175.4 M	
REVENUES from:	Domestic News	P86.3 M = P55.0 M (MEDIA)
		+ P31.3 M (GOV'T)
	Foreign News	P71.4 M
	Other Revenues	P11.1 M
TOTAL REVENUES:		P168.8 M
BALANCE:		(-P6.6 M) (GOVT' SUBSIDY)
TOTAL GOVERNMENT PAYMENTS:		P6.6 M + P31.3 M = P37.9 M

Furthermore, there were many other "hidden" expenditures from the government treasury. The government paid EFE much more than P37.9 million. Of the 115 newspapers which contributed toward P55.0 million for the EFE services, 39 belonged to the Falange press. The Falange press was hardly a business enterprise; it was another government-subsidized organ just like the EFE news agency. There also were 11 radio stations and one television channel, both totally belongling to the government. Consequently, what the dailies of the Falange press and government-run radio/television paid for EFE's news and photo services had to be added to the P37.9 million. No one knows how much —or how "little"— of the P55.0 million media revenues originated from private clientele. In the purposely murky record keeping, these state-subsidized entities of Spain under Franco left no way to trace the financial transactions among one another.

As if to justify this obvious drain on the state treasury, EFE documents from these years always resort to enumerating in glowing terms what a wonderful system the EFE agency had become. In transmission system, EFE had grown through the modern wonders of satellites, microwave, transoceanic cables, telephotos, and mobile photo-lab units. EFE now (in 1969) had "Hispanitized" 60% of its foreign news supplied to its Spanish clients, because EFE's own correspondents gathered the news. This was "information independence, news sovereignty, spiritual decolonization" as compared to the olden days, when the news from abroad was merely translation of the Reuters and UPI services. Was that worth all those millions of pesetas of government expenditure?

Mendo's Commercial Dream

In the early stage EFE director Mendo was not yet very sure of the success of the EFE expansion programs to Hispanic America. He knew from his previous work experiences with UPI that that part of the world was an area of predominance of the U.S. agencies AP and UPI. He could not pretend to compete against these giants. Mendo declared that "the secret of EFE's success was to fill an important 'news hole' left by the large international agencies, against which we do not intend to compete." Competing against those giants with the same news they also gave would be "falling into the same error into which some European agencies have fallen, when they tried to enter the [Hispanic] American market," Mendo added.[8] EFE's mission was to supply a Hispanoamerican focus to the news for the Hispanoamerican media.

But, in mid-1967,[9] he assessed the position of EFE and determined that it was now in a "healthy competition and the Spanish press must be proud to have a news entity that has an international ranking among the news agencies." This manifest wish to share the credit for EFE's success with the Spanish press was neither casual nor simply ceremonial. He was already in a long-range campaign to transform EFE into a real commercial news agency, totally free of state ties. Mendo had already started on a hidden agenda for EFE. Frequent remarks Mendo made at press interviews during 1968–1969 reflected his ideas of starting a cooperative setup for the EFE news agency among client newspapers.[10]

Mendo always tried to bring to the fore the "business character" of the EFE news agency. Mendo emphasized EFE paid all taxes "just like any other 'incorporated business' (*sociedad anónima*)" without any kind of exemption. During 1968–1969, Mendo underlined time after time that the EFE administrative council was composed of majority (8 of 15) members, "including its president —representing practically the totality of the Spanish press." He avoided discussing EFE's capital composition even in the euphemistic way it was presented in the EFE documents in those days: two-thirds of EFE's P20 million capital belonged to "the media businesses and the telecommunication enterprises," only 2% was owned by a group of private persons, and the rest —a little less than one-third— fell to the state's share. Mendo knew as well as everyone else that "the telecommunication enterprises" were also of the Spanish state.

Mendo's Legal Maneuvers

In his pursuit of privatization or "commercialization" of the EFE news agency, Mendo did not limit himself to dreaming or to blowing EFE's own horn. He had enough business acumen to know that merely dreaming or talking about it would not bring about the result he sought. Throughout his EFE tenure, he took several legal measures toward the commercialization of EFE. The extraordinary EFE general assembly of 27 June 1966 approved fundamental reforms to the EFE statutes, ostensibly to comply with the provisions of the new Press and Print Law of March of that year. Three important reform measures were: (1) the number of EFE's administrative councilors would be between 6 and 15; (2) EFE stocks could be owned by any private Spanish nationals or legal persons (companies); and most importantly —although not written into the EFE statutes— (3) the junta accorded Mendo a totally free hand in his management of the news agency.[11]

The importance of these steps to transform the EFE news agency into a possible press cooperative was not that Mendo took these measures but the significance was the speed in which he went about implementing them.

Mendo was leading the government in these actions to make EFE a press cooperative.

Mendo's "Business" Ventures

Mendo also expanded and consolidated EFE's business scope. On 21 June 1968, Mendo's EFE bought up Fiel, a private agency specializing in feature, reportage, and photographic services. EFE bought 75% of the Fiel stocks and the Fiel employees were integrated into the special services of the EFE agency.

After Fiel, Mendo also attempted to buy up Europa Press, which had been founded in 1960 and was one of the only 2 remaining truly "private" news agencies, the other being the Mencheta agency. (Even Mendo could not dare touch the other 2 news agencies existing then. PYRESA was the Falange news agency and Logos belonged to the Catholic church.) The tiny Europa Press valiantly resisted the takeover attempt by the state giant EFE.[12]

Mendo took another "business" venture. The EFE extraordinary general assembly of 9 July 1969 increased by a whopping 150% the "social capital" of La Agencia EFE, S.A., to P50 million ($0.7 million) from the P20 million ($0.29 million). However, little did Mendo know that this move was his last hurrah. As will be discussed later in this chapter, his mentor, MIT Fraga Iribarne lost his job on 29 October 1969, and Mendo consequently lost his a month later.

Mendo's horn blowing, his dreams, and his legal maneuvers all failed. Mendo failed in his 1966–1969 attempts to gradually transform EFE into a cooperative system among the Spanish papers, like the AP system. But to his "consternation and despair"[13] the failure of his attempt to commercialize the EFE news agency was not due to the resistance of the autocratic Franco regime but to the reluctance of the Spanish press. Mendo did not find among Spanish newspaper people much interest to participate in cooperative ownership of EFE. The Spanish press had grown accustomed and comfortable with the extremely low political prices that they were paying for EFE services, thanks to government subsidies given to EFE. Some newspapers were paying the EFE agency as little as P4,000 ($57) per month or about a third of the state-mandated minimum wage for a reporter.

CONSIGNAS II

Mendo should have known better and recognized the limits to which he could go. Mendo should have known that the Franco regime would never have permitted the EFE news agency to become a liberal, commercialized, and uncontrolled news organization. The "liberalizing" Press and Print Law of March 1966 was quickly followed by 2 reactionary measures: the regressive reforms in April 1967 to the penal code, and the promulgation in April 1968 of the Law of Official Secrets. These repressive laws were enacted to negate the liberal gains obtained in the 1966 LPI. But even before that, the Spanish government saw fit to apply the restrictive provisions of the 1966 LPI with more vigor than its positive aspects.

As if to show that the MIT meant business, MIT agents carried out the seizure of an edition of Madrid's leading illustrated magazine, *Actualidad Española* (*Spanish Present*) at 5 A.M. on 11 January 1967. It was the first time since the new LPI went into effect that the MIT applied such drastic sanctionary measures authorized by its Articles 25 and 64. Throughout the years when Mendo was merrily engaged in EFE's expansion abroad, the regime's press policy enforced by his mentor, MIT Fraga, showed only a hardening tendency. In the third year of the new LPI, 1969 —the year in which the Fraga–Mendo duo fell from power— the MIT under Fraga Iribarne had proved to be as repressive as the the press regime before the 1966 law.

Mendo's *Consigna*

Under these circumstances, Mendo's efforts and dream to change the EFE agency into a business cooperative among the Spanish papers was doomed from the very beginning. Furthermore, Mendo not only was obligated to manage EFE as a transmitter of *consigna*s from the MIT, but he himself wrote at least one *consigna* of his own. The following is an account of the most outstanding cases of press control occurring during Mendo's 1965–1969 tenure as EFE director.

The 1966 EFE annual memorial showed as a major accomplishment the distribution of 380 news items, totaling some 85,000 words, in 19 hours on 14 December 1966. The occasion was the national referendum conducted that day to approve the "Organic Law of the State" that Franco had presented to the Cortes on 22 November. (The law, among other provisions, contemplated a division of the executive powers between the *Caudillo* and his appointed premier still to be named, and the direct "family" election of 100 of the 600 deputies of the Cortes.) The government staged intensive 3-week campaigns with these MIT slogans: "Vote Yes for Spain's Progress \\ To Vote Yes Means to Vote for Our Caudillo \\ To Vote No Signifies to Follow Orders of Moscow or Prague \\ To Vote Yes Means to Vote for 18 July 1936."

The 14 December referendum was a staged election in which, for instance, the civil guards told rural voters which ballots to use, and traveling people (*transuentes*) could vote wherever they were. Even in Madrid, a French *Le Monde* reporter[14] succeeded in voting 5 times in 5 polling stations. The resulting "victory" was a foregone conclusion. It turned out to be even beyond the MIT's expectations. The MIT won the propaganda war of the referendum: 89% of the population voted and 95.6% cast YES![15] In such a sham election, the 380 EFE "news" items in 19 hours —20 news an hour!— could only have been meaningless reports of the polling reresults, that were, in turn, printed dutifully by the Spanish newspapers, which no one read.[16] Those 380 and hundreds of other "news" items during the "election" campaigns were in reality *consignas* for Spanish newspapers to follow, official directives issued by the EFE news agency that Mendo wanted to "commercialize."

Not only was Mendo obligated to supervise the *consigna*-issuing functions of the EFE agency, but he also wrote "news commentaries" that his agency distributed, which, consequently newspapers had to treat just like any other *consignas*. Mendo wrote a "commentary" on 15 June 1967, in which he scathingly attacked the announced British plebiscite among the populace of Gibraltar. At issue here is not whether the 10-inch Mendo column presented an equitable view on the British–Spanish controversy.[17] The point is that the EFE director wrote an extremely xenophobic article and distributed that propaganda to the Spanish newspapers, which had no other choice but to print it. Of course, a man of Mendo's position and stature would not write out a simple bureaucratic *consigna*, like many simple MIT censors, but presented the "Spanish position" on an international issue.

Mendo must have lived in agony because of the obvious conflict between his "liberal" press view and his daily management of government-organ news agency. Mendo's anguish was reflected in an EFE wire datelined Mexico City, which he transmitted on 21 August 1967 through the CIFRA circuit to Spanish papers and EFE's Latin American network to its overseas subscribers. UNESCO had held its biennial conference in Mexico, and published a study on the press. The UNESCO study concluded that:

> The profession of journalist is the most dangerous, after that of test pilot. The journalist lives in the uncertainty and the unexpected, which causes that he die relatively soon, the principal causes being: excessive nervous tension, bad nourishment and, above all, the permanent anguish, as a result of the many problems which he has to confront.[18]

EFE's 30th Birthday

On the evening of Saturday, 11 January 1969, a dinner was given at the plush downtown Madrid Hotel Meliá for about 300 persons who made up the personnel roster of EFE. It was to celebrate the 30th anniversary of EFE's 1939 founding in Burgos. It was not so much to remember its beginning in the wartime Spain of 30 years before. EFE had had it good over the past few years. It had firmly established itself in Hispanic America and Europe. It was now looking ahead to more adventures. It was a buoyant 30th birthday. It was a Happy 30th Birthday. Confucius once said: "At 15 I set my heart on learning; at 30 I was firmly established." The 30-year-old EFE was now a "firmly established" adult.

FRAGA–MENDO FALL

MIT Fraga's progressive bent to liberalize the Spanish press never sat well with the right wing of the Franco regime. Mendo's efforts to commercialize the EFE agency into a newspaper cooperative also were anathema to the regime. And EFE's fortunes always ran in parallel with those of the MIT. This is a fact that does not require much explanation. The "joint" fall in late 1969 of the Fraga–Mendo team at MIT–EFE will speak volumes. Given the system, the EFE management could not operate on long-range plans, but tried to achieve what it could. Under the circumstances, Mendo and his EFE people did manage to accomplish "surprising feats" to expand and modernize the state "news" agency.

The MIT tenure of the versatile, energetic Fraga Iribarne came to an end on 29 October 1969 amid the most serious scandal among the ruling elites of Spain thus far recorded in its history. The "Maquinaria Textil del Norte de España, S.A. (MATESA)" (Textile Machinery of the Northern Spain, Ltd.) was Spain's biggest textile-machine manufacturer. MATESA had been so successful in the export field that the government had granted the company credits and tax refunds amounting to P10 billion ($143 million), fabulous figures beyond the comprehension of the average Spaniard.[19] Textile machinery, however, was exported not to foreign buyers, but to the company's own subsidiaries abroad where most of the "exported" machinery was stocked, while MATESA used the funds to purchase shares in foreign businesses. While EFE downplayed the story, Spain's newspapers showed an extraordinary vigor in disclosing the scandal.

The press would not accept that the fraud of such a huge scale was perpetrated without arousing suspicions of official credit institutions. Six MATESA executives were jailed and a senior official resigned. The press took the unprecedented step of demanding that cabinet heads roll, for —the papers insisted— the economics ministers, or the whole cabinet, had to be involved. Fraga resigned.

Within a month, Mendo "resigned" as EFE director. Fraga had wielded power as the MIT for 7 years, 2 months, and 20 days. Mendo, in turn, had managed EFE for 4 years, 5 months, and 20 days. Druing their MIT–EFE tenure, the Fraga–Mendo duo had briefly inspired a "liberalizing" breath into the Spanish press.

Revolving EFE Presidents

In the Fraga–Mendo era, the ceremonial EFE presidency started on a stop-and-go trail, not coming to settle down to a semblance of permanence until 1968. Upon Mendo's assumption of the EFE directorship, his predecessor Carlos Sentís was kicked upstairs to the EFE presidency. Sentís served 16 months until 3 October 1966, when he resigned to become the director of the large daily *Tele-Express*. A journalist of Sentís's professional background could not coexist with another of similar caliber formally under him but not at his bidding.

The EFE council named its eldest member, Romualdo de Toledo y Robles, as the interim president, who functioned for 2 months until the end of 1966. The EFE presidency remained vacant until 23 February 1967, when Miguel Mateu Plá was appointed to the post. Mateu Plá, an industrial entrepreneur, had been mayor of Barcelona and ambassador to France. Mateú owned the Castle of Perelada in Gerona province, to which he liked to invite EFE councilors for management conferences. Mateu Plá had also to resign some 19 months later on 23 September 1968, because a new law decreed that his membership in other incorporated companies (or *sociedades anónimas* = S.A.) was incompatible with his position as president of la Agencia EFE, S.A.

The EFE news agency then brought in as its president former (1958–1960) EFE director Manuel Aznar. This former journalist and diplomat was an ideal person for the figurehead presidency of EFE. He served for 7.5 years until 12 February 1976, about 3 months beyond the demise of the Franco regime. Aznar was respected by EFE director Mendo. He believed that the EFE president must be a "very respectable figure from the Spanish press or the diplomacy" and Aznar "combined wonderfully the 2 capacities, journalism and diplomacy and, therefore, Aznar was a great and exceptional president."[20]

Aznar was also liked by Waldo de Mier, who had himself provided the
EFE news agency with a semblance of continuity by serving as subdirector
and/or acting director since January 1957. In an interview, De Mier called
Aznar "a teacher of journalists, a man of a 'most brilliant [*brillantísima*]
pen,' and ambassador of special missions like that to the United Nations."[21]
During Aznar's absentee EFE directorship because of his UN mission, and
3 years beyond, De Mier functioned as the acting director. With Mendo
gone, president Aznar and acting director De Mier carried EFE into the
next Armesto era.

Chapter 6

Isthmian Little Giant (1970–1975)

Francisco Franco died on 20 November 1975 at age 83.[1] The old dictator, in his doggedly slow journey to demise, effected many a political change in the 1970–1975 lustrum. Spain was being prepared for the period after his departure. The country continued to enjoy the economic expansion begun in the preceding decade. The 15-year period (1960–1975) saw a tripling of the real per capita income for Spaniards.[2] But prosperity brought with it rising prices and a revival of labor trouble. Students and intellectuals joined ranks with laborers. The intractable Basque nationalists developed a terrorist wing. The young elements of the Catholic clergy sympathized with the labor, student, and Basque movements.

Popular unrest persisted throughout 1970. So, on 14 December 1970, the regime suspended for 6 months —compared to 3-month suspension in 1969— Article 18 of the Spanish "Bill of Rights" (*Fuero de los Españoles*), allowing the police to arrest suspects without warrants. The EFE news agency did not give these events conspicuous coverage. EFE itself was muzzled by censorship, which it facilitated by faithful distribution of the MIT's *consignas* on the 1969 and 1970 occasions of imposition of a state of emergency. (In the 1970 months of non-news, EFE and the general Spanish press welcomed the August renewal of the U.S.–Spain military pact, and the October visit of U.S. President Nixon.)

The Spanish government's anti-press measures continued through the state of emergency. The magazine *Sábado Gráfico* (*Graphic Saturday*) was subjected to repeated suspensions, 4 months in all. The magazine finally had to come out with a new version. The government allowed the state of emergency to expire on its 6-month deadline, 14 June 1971.

Franco reached his 80th birthday during 1972, the year which marked the start of slow transition to the post-*Caudillo* era. A July decree named Admiral Luis Carrero Blanco as vice premier to succeed Premier Franco on his death or departure from politics. A year later, on 9 June 1973, Carrero Blanco was appointed premier, or *presidente del gobierno* (president of government), the post held by Franco since the civil war. Franco retained his position as chief of state. But, before 1973 was out, Carrero Blanco was killed by a bomb planted under his car on 20 December. Franco stuck doggedly to his carefully laid plan of steady move into the period after his death. On 29 December, he named Carlos Arias Navarro, civilian interior minister, as new premier. Each of these events was accompanied by the appointment of new cabinet.

On 12 February 1974, the new premier delivered a speech to the Cortes, widely interpreted as heralding the opening of a new era. A phrase —"the Spirit of 12 February"— was coined. But the iron grip of autocracy was always felt amid the changes. On 29 October 1974, Franco angrily fired new MIT Pío Cabanillas Gallas for having allowed the press "excessive freedom." Cabanillas, however, had suspended the Málaga daily, *El Sol de España* (*The Sun of Spain*).[3] And, until Franco died on 20 November 1975, press censorship continued. The regime confiscated the 3 January 1975 issue of the Madrid magazine, *Nuevos Fotogramas* (*New Photograms*), for revealing the names of the MIT film censors.[4]

COMMAND CHANGES II

Each political change during 1970–1975 at the top was accompanied naturally by appointment of a new minister of information and tourism (MIT). Toward the end of the Franco era, the position of the MIT was the most unstable. The lustrum of 1970–1975 saw 6 MITs come and go. After the MATESA scandal, Alfredo Sánchez Bella took over the MIT on 30 October 1969. The Spanish mass communications media had progressed, as the Spaniards were informed of cabinet changes, including that of the MIT, over the Televisión Española on the eve of the changeover.

New MIT Sánchez Bella spoke of "the continuity" in the MIT and promised to follow up on the work accomplished by his predecessor. The 2 MITs had many coincidental points in their careers that seemed to guarantee formal continuity. But their philosophies were at complete odds. Whereas Fraga Iribarne was a "liberal-minded reformer," Sánchez Bella was an avid Francoist partisan. The only demonstrable continuity between the 2 succeeding MITs was their administration —by the EFE conduit— of the *consignas* for press control.

CONSIGNAs III

The practice of using the EFE agency as the conduit for MIT's *consignas* continued after the Fraga – Mendo duo fell from power at the end of 1969, as it had continued after the "new" Press Law of 1966, which was supposed to have done away with censorship. In early 1970 the EFE agency published a book summarizing the major news events of the previous year, a common practice among the world news media. The book, *1969: Un Año de Desarrollo Constitucional (1969: One Year of Constitutional Development)*[5] smacked of official propaganda. By emphasizing "constitutional" development, it avoided discussing the 1969 MATESA scandal, which had been Spain's biggest political-financial fraud ever recorded until then.

The EFE book skirted the press censorship and a 3-month state of exception declared in January 1969 throughout the country. Confronted with the adverse impact the measure had on foreign tourism and investment, the state of exception was lifted a month early on 25 March. This point was emphasized by the EFE book. Despite the state of exception, college students, professors, and mine workers erupted in repeated dissent, with clear support from the young sector of the Catholic Church. The Franco regime responded with repression. On New Year's Day 1970 the new MIT, Alfredo Sánchez Bella, confiscated the first and the only issue of the daily *Nivel (Level)*, thus killing the new paper.

Fateful Rome Connection

In these measures against the press, new MIT Sánchez Bella was more ferocious and less apologetic than his predecessor. His career had prepared him for that. With a degree in law, philosophy, and letters, he had been president of "La Juventud de Acción Católica" (Catholic Action Youth), vice president of "La Federación de Estudiantes Católicos," and secretary general of the "Pax Romana." He was then a member of the Asociación Católica Nacional de Propagandistas. But the new MIT —unlike his predecessor— had also been a professional journalist. He practiced a militant and combative journalism for the insurgent Francoist cause in the civil war. Sánchez Bella had been educated and lived in Valencia, the Mediterranean city to which the Republican government had fled from Madrid in November 1936 and remained until the war's end.

Days before the entrance of Franco troops into Valencia on 30 March 1939 —the day after the "official end" of the civil war— Sánchez Bella had taken over a local daily paper and begun to edit it as *Avance (Advance)*

—"advance" of the Franco army. He also seized 2 local stations, Radio Valencia and Radio Mediterráneo; of both he named himself the director.
 In 1956 Sánchez Bella's diplomatic career commenced, first as ambassador to the Dominican Republic, next to Colombia, and then to the Vatican City and Italy in 1962. His 7 years in Rome —while Fraga reigned over the Spanish press— had given "Sánchez Bella a vision on the problems of information 'from outside Spain' which was without doubt useful for his new job" as the MIT.[6]

For the EFE news agency, Sánchez Bella's sojourn in Rome served as a "fateful connection." When Ambassador Sánchez Bella got to the Eternal City in early 1962, Carlos Mendo, the future EFE director, had been there since 1958 as UPI's correspondent. As a Spanish national, Mendo was under the Spanish ambassador's jurisdiction. But he was also an employee of the powerful U.S. company, not at easy beck and call of the ambassador of his own country. Though Mendo left Rome in late 1962 to assume the UPI Madrid bureau, Mendo "had had two or three incidents" with Sánchez Bella.[7] In January 1963, then MIT Fraga Iribarne made a proposal to the foreign ministry that a journalist be assigned to the Rome embassy as the counsellor of information, and recommended the director of a sports daily from his home province of Galicia. The man's name was Alejandro Armesto, who would replace Fraga's protégé Mendo. The "connection" among the 4 men was one of those rare human ironies.

During the next 6 years Armesto faithfully served the ambassador, who was 10 years his senior. The 2 men developed a mutual trust and there was born a formidable duo in a mentor-protégé relationship, which Fraga helped forge, and would eventually replace the Fraga–Mendo pair. On 30 October 1969, Sánchez Bella took over the MIT. Only a month later, he fired Mendo and named Armesto as the new EFE director. The Sánchez–Armesto era began on 1 December 1969. In early January 1970, Waldo de Mier was removed from the EFE subdirectorship, the position he had held for 13 years since 1957. Armesto was now firmly in command of EFE as the new director-manager.

As the situation developed over the next 6 years, Armesto turned out to be less perishable even than his mentor, MIT Sánchez Bella. Armesto enjoyed remarkable political longevity during the shaky terminal period of the rule of the aging *Caudillo*. Frequent cabinet shakeups brought in new MITs, 5 of them, —counting one acting MIT— during Armesto's tenure at EFE from 1969 through 1975. These ephemeral MITs never did get a chance to meddle in EFE affairs, leaving it to Armesto.

Franco's death on 20 Novmeber 1975 opened up a new era. And former MIT Fraga Iribarne made a dramatic —although short-lived— political comeback, being appointed interior minister and vice premier for domestic affairs on 10 December 1975. Adolfo Martín-Gamero González-Posada was appointed as the MIT. On 12 February 1976, the new powerful interior minister Fraga had his old protégé Mendo reappointed as EFE director. The second Fraga – Mendo duo, however, did not thrive long, being swept up in the post-Franco political swirl.

THE ARMESTO ERA

Alejandro Armesto Buz, named by MIT Sánchez Bella to the EFE directorship on 1 December 1969, had not had a career as brilliant as that of his predecessor Mendo. Armesto had been graduated from Madrid's Official School of Journalism. He was the president of Galicia's Provincial Syndicate of Paper, Press, and Graphic Arts, and a provincial councilor of the Falange movement of Lugo, the capital of Lugo province in the northwestern Galician region. He was chief writer of the Lugo newspaper *El Progreso* (*The Progess*) in 1956. In April 1961, Armesto became the subdirector of *El Faro de Vigo* (*The Lighthouse of Vigo*) and later became the director of its sister paper, *El Faro Deportivo* (*The Sports Lighthouse*). He was sent to the Rome embassy in 1964, to team up with the ambassador and future MIT Sánchez Bella.

The 2 succeeding MIT – EFE duos during 1966 – 1975 (the Fraga – Mendo and Sánchez – Armesto teams) represented sharp contrasts. The second duo was not as flashy as the first. The first MIT – EFE team has been credited with probably a bigger-than-life image for what was accomplished for the Spanish press in general and the EFE news agency in particular. MIT Fraga had the 1966 Press and Print Law to show off as his achievement. It was even dubbed the "Fraga Law." EFE director Mendo had the Latin American network to display as his conquest. The Sánchez – Armesto pair was a more down-to-earth team. Though the couple accomplished quite a deal, it has been accorded smaller-than-reality publicity. This second MIT – EFE duo, and later Armesto by himself, took care of numerous technical details for the EFE agency, but they did it quietly and without fanfare.

Technical Modernization

The EFE agency was keeping up with progress in telecommunications technology. In May 1971 EFE started using space satellites for trans-Atlantic communication. EFE was connected to the INTELSAT relay station at Buitrago with a backup antenna on Gran Canary Islands. INTELSAT connected EFE-Madrid by 8 direct and permanent hookups with Buenos

Aires, Lima, Santiago de Chile, Caracas, Rio de Janeiro, Panama, Mexico, and Washington. Microwave relays were set up between Buenos Aires and Montevideo, and from Caracas to Bogotá and Quito. But Caracas still had to use submarine cable to Santo Domingo. EFE used the Central America microwave systems from Panama City to San José de Costa Rica, Managua, San Salvador, and Guatemala. Only Paraguay, Bolivia, and Honduras continued on radioteletype system.

In January 1972, CIFRA (EFE-National) established a permanent bureau in Valencia to serve the southeastern region of Spain. This brought to 5 the number of domestic EFE bureaus at Barcelona, Bilbao, Sevilla, Santiago de Compostela, and Valencia.

In mid-1973 EFE started using computers for news transmission. On 22 June 1973, Fernando de Linán y Zofio, the new MIT only since 6 June, visited EFE headquarters at Ayala 5 and flipped on the new ADX computer to inaugurate a computerized transmission system. The system connected all points in the Americas with 3 dozen 2-way lines. Twelve of these 36 lines operated at 75 bauds and the remainder at 50 bauds, sending 100 and 60 words a minute each. The ADX mainframe had a 20,000-word memory capacity.

The Comtelsa (Comercial Telegráfica, S.A.) was the economy- finance news service of EFE begun in 1946 as a 50-50 joint venture with the British Reuters. The Comtelsa began on 1 February 1974 the SEFICOM (Servicio Económico Financiero, SEF), a 5-day weekly service covering international stock markets, economic and financial items appearing in the state official bulletin and autonomous communities' official bulletins; monetary quotations on the Spanish *peseta*, U.S. dollar, major European currencies, and ECU (or European currency unit); national and international news, and news on other business activities.

NEWS EXCHANGES II

EFE under Armesto made numerous news exchange agreements with foreign news agencies, adding to its old agreements with UPI, Reuters, AFP, dpa, and AP. On the one hand, this was an indication of the worldwide recognition EFE was getting for its overseas expansion achieved by Armesto's predecessor, Carlos Mendo. It, on the other hand, revealed Armesto's plan to continue to expand the scope of the EFE network. Especially notable was EFE's outreach to the national news agencies of the socialist bloc of East Europe and Cuba. Spain and its official agency EFE had come a long political way.

Mendo, a believer in the expansion of EFE's own news net, had signed exchange agreements with only 2 foreign agencies: Japanese Kyodo News Service and obscure Italian agency AGI, both in 1967. Armesto was quite active in the news exchange during his 1969–1975 tenure. He agreed on exchange with 4 European agencies: BELGA (Agence Telegraphique Belge de Presse) and APA (Austrian Presse-Agentur) in 1970; Dutch ANP (Algemeen Nederlands Persbureau) in 1971; and the Turkish AA (Anadolu Ajansi, Anatoli Agency) in 1974. Three Arabic national agencies were also signed on: APS (Algerie Presse Service) in 1973, and 2 Libyan agencies, JANA and ARNA, in 1975.

The first socialist-bloc national agency to agree on exchange was the Cuban Prensa Latina (PL) in 1970. The only socialist country in the Americas and a former Spanish colony, Cuba still had affinity with her *madre patria* (mother country). Franco's enmity to its communist system was mitigated by his indulgence for the former Spanish colony. That seemed to signal an opening to other socialist countries. Throughout 1970 Spanish newspapers increased their coverage of Soviet news. In the same year EFE agreed with the Soviet TASS (Telegrafnoje Agenstvo Sovetskovo Sojuza) to exchange correspondents. A formal EFE-TASS exchange agreement was signed a year later in 1971. That was a harbinger to the Soviet-Spanish trade agreement formalized the next year. The TASS exchange was followed by a 1973 agreement with AGERPRES of Romania with which Spain had had a formal consular-commercial protocol since 1967. Armesto ended his news-exchange spree with an agreement signed with the Czech CTK (Ceskoslovenska Tiskova Kancelar) in 1975.

In relation with EFE's news exchange agreements, there was an interesting event on 8 October 1974. The British news service Reuters held a regular annual meeting of its board of directors at the EFE Madrid headquarters at Ayala 5. It was the first time ever Reuters had held such a meeting in Spain.

Foreign-Language and Other Services

EFE also experimented with services in the foreign languages. The Moroccan news agency, Maghreb Arabe Presse (MAP), and EFE agreed on an Arab-language EFE service to be edited by Moroccan personnel in Rabat. From that Moroccan capital, it would be disseminated to other Arab countries. MAP and EFE had an exchange agreement since 1966. EFE also initiated services in English and French. On 1 March 1970, EFE started to offer French and English services to papers and radio and telvesion stations of Europe. The French service for Europe and also for the Francophone

Arab Africa had been tried in 1967 without much success. Now —3 years later— EFE edited in French and English news supplied by its Latin American bureaus and a summary of Spanish news by CIFRA. The services amounted to some 8,000 words of news and special features daily offered by teletypes. These services were also intended for marketing in Asia and Africa.

EFE under Armesto tried a third area of service. In January 1971, EFE initiated a weekly service, MEC (España-Mercado Común or Spain-Common Market).[8] MEC obviously exploited the economic and business news markets, perceived to exist for Spanish intent to gain full accession to the European Economic Communities or popularly known as the European Common Market.

All these sundry trial-and-error efforts serve to indicate the concern and impatience of EFE's top management to count up concrete results of the expensive expansion programs the agency had launched since 1965. The Sánchez–Armesto team was now reflecting on where EFE had come from and also contemplating in which direction it should be headed.

ACAN-EFE

The EFE news agency under Armesto had so far laid groundwork in technical modernization, news exchange agreements, and foreign-language and other services. These preparations would later serve as the basis for another gigantic EFE expansion in the post-Franco era. The Sánchez–Armesto duo, however, achieved a surprising feat in the tiny republics of Central America. Sánchez Bella and Armesto created a Central American news agency, combining 6 isthmian countries. ACAN-EFE has been a phenomenal success.

GENESIS OF ACAN

ACAN-EFE, "la Agencia Centro Americana de Noticias, S.A." (the Central American News Agency, Ltd.) was the showpiece to which Sánchez Bella and Armesto could point as their accomplishment. ACAN is an EFE-subsidized news agency operated as a cooperative among media companies of the 5 republics of Central America and Panama.[9] Under the Kennedy-envisioned "Alliance for Progress," 5 Central American countries —Guatemala, Costa Rica, El Salvador, Honduras, and Nicaragua— plus Panama as an associate member, had formed the Central American Common Market (MCCA). Under a similar scheme and with an enterprising imagination, newspapers, radio stations, television stations, and other entities of 6 countries of American Isthmus and the EFE agency formed a regional news agency on 30 November 1972.

The idea of a supranational Ibero-American information agency had originated from Sánchez Bella, said the ACAN-EFE director at Panama, Manuel Mora.[10] In his 1956–1969 career as ambassador to the Dominican Republic, Colombia, and Rome, plus delegation member to the UN and UNESCO, Sánchez Bella had cultivated "a great deal of friendship with the ultra right, mostly military, elements" of Latin America. Many of them were performing the "exile duties" of ambassadors or military attachés in the cities where Sánchez Bella served. They later became presidents or ministers of many Latin American governments in the 1970s. They lent a willing ear to the ideas of Sánchez Bella —by then Spain's MIT— to organize a "news common market" integrating information services of Hispano American governments.

The project was to be undertaken "under the baton of the Spanish official news agency EFE," but this Spanish government project "with its openly totalitarian and colonialist vision was aborted," affirmed Ricardo Utrilla Carlón, the EFE president/director-general since 1983.[11] Utrilla said that the EFE journalists of those days "discarded the idea as 'unrealizable and clearly injurious' to the Spanish prestige." Zoilo Gutiérrez Martínez, the EFE agency's Bogotá bureau chief, proposed the idea of a news cooperative among the mass media of the Isthmus where the Common Market (MCCA) was an operating regional system, though EFE still did not have correspondents in the region. Thus was born the idea of ACAN-EFE, an "information common market."

In January 1971 —in preparation for this plucky project— EFE established its bureau in Panama City, and also set up correspondent offices in Guatemala, San Salvador, Tegucigalpa, Managua, and San José —the capital cities of the Central American countries. EFE hooked up a permanent duplex transmission line from Madrid to the Panama bureau. The communication within the Isthmus was conducted through MCCA microwave systems already in operation. ACAN's central headquarters would be established in Panama City.

ACAN Constitution

Months of negotiations were needed to carry the project to fruition. Finally, EFE director Armesto could sit down with Panamanian lawyers to sign the "constituting document" (*pacto social*) in Panama City on 30 November 1972. Of the 31 articles of the ACAN-EFE constitution, 7 contained substantive provisions. Article 4 stipulated 70% approving votes for the dissolution of the company, while most other decisions required 50% vote. Article 5 set the initial capital of ACAN at $300,000, represented by 300 shares of $1,000 each.[12] Under Article 10 Spain's EFE news agency retained a third of 300 shares, a lion's share. It was a provision similar to the EFE structure itself, one-third of whose shares belonged to the Spanish state. ACAN had 21 founding shareholders, Spanish EFE and 20 Isthmian media outlets. These 20 local media units —Panama 5, Costa Rica 6, Nicaragua 5, Honduras 3, and Guatemala 1— paid in 120 shares (or 6 shares for each media outlet). Other companies from these countries, and also those from El Salvador, would join later to buy up the remaining 80 shares of ACAN.

The ACAN constitution gave lopsided power to EFE. Article 21 provided for a 7-member board of directors, one from each of the 6 Isthmian countries and one representing EFE. Two articles, on top of EFE's one-third share holding, guaranteed EFE control of ACAN. Per Article 25, the treasurer had to be named by EFE. The founding treasurer was Alejandro Armesto, EFE director. Article 29 said that "the designation of new General Manager 'always' shall fall on the person that Agencia EFE, S.A., may propose." To give an additional iron-clad security to EFE control of ACAN, Article 31 required a 70% vote to modify these important provisions of Articles 4, 21, 25, and 29.

"A Little Giant"

Soon 4 new local companies joined ACAN, thus raising to 25 the total number of shareholders. ACAN-EFE[13] news subscribers quickly increased to 52, finally reaching 86, "practically all the news media" of the Isthmus. ACAN-EFE was a "shining success," and the future (from 1983) EFE president Utrilla was "witness to how the colleagues of Associated Press 'pulled their hairs' [in despair] upon learning of the birth of ACAN; they had been thinking about setting their own Operation Central America then."[14] Beginning in the late 1970s, Central America became one of the hottest news spots of the world with a revolution in Nicaragua, a guerrilla war in El Salvador, and the so-called Contadora Group peace negotiations. ACAN had come to Central America at the right time, "the opportune moment," Utrilla said. ACAN's beginning also coincided with the installation at EFE's Madrid headquarters of the first computers. Computers made it possible to insert the news from ACAN in the EFE service.

By 1984 ACAN produced 70 to 80 news and features a day, which, for technical reasons, had to pass through Madrid. The EFE Madrid central desk would select about half of ACAN news for the general EFE service. But all ACAN news would "shoot right back to Central America without anybody touching them" in a system denominated "auto-rebound" in EFE jargon. By the early 1980s, ACAN had revenues of about $300,000 from its clients in Central America, Panama, and Belize. That came to a rough average of $300 monthly fees; Panamanian media paid a higher average of some $450, in that Panama had the highest cost of living in the region.

The ACAN operations cost EFE some $400,000 annually, which "is equivalent to a budget for two or at most three correspondents plus transmission costs." "For this small budget" —Utrilla emphasized— "EFE enjoys the most extensive regional news network," which gives Spain a better "penetration in the press of Central America." There is "a good dose of altruism," for ACAN operations cost money to the EFE agency and Central American media stockholders of ACAN. But "we all agree on the need to keep the tool irreplaceable now in Central America." If ACAN were to disappear, it would certainly be replaced by AFP, AP, or UPI. "To maintain ACAN alive is the cost of a Spanish news independence," Utrilla declared. "The ACAN news agency is a 'Little Giant' Spaniards can be proud of."

MID-LIFE POTPOURRI

EFE under Armesto was approaching its mid-life, becoming 35 in 1973–1974. Its mid-life was filled with sundry events. On 9 October 1971, CIFRA sent out a wire with a headline, "Homage Without Official Authorization." The story said a private citizen group headed by a Joaquín María de Ochoa Vázquez had planned to issue a postcard commemorating the 35th anniversary of the October 1936 investiture of Francisco Franco as the chief of the state and Generalissimo in the beginning months of the civil war. The De Ochoa et al. group demanded a "replication" be sent out to clarify "a few misleading" points. The "right to reply" had been stipulated by Article 58 of the 1966 Press and Print Law, and the Decree 746 of 1966 implementing that article.

The group's lengthy reply published in a 10-inch CIFRA story in the newspapers of 18 October displayed a twisted argument on the delicate issue that nobody desired to touch in Spain under Franco. If the commemorative postcard plan was "without authorization," the group disputed, "why didn't the 'authorities' confiscate the post-cards? In reality, all official organisms praised our idea." This group also stressed that it did not "pursue profits" from the project, and it was definitely not an "illicit activity." How could anyone in Spain under Franco say commemoration of the *Caudillo* was illicit? The group knew that it had CIFRA in the corner.

The EFE news agency, as a business employing hundreds of persons, had its share of labor problems even in Francoist Spain, and the Falange paper *Nuevo Diario* was after EFE. Its 30 September 1973 issue had a story with a headline, "Unrest Among the EFE Workers."[15] The story reported that "about 100 writers, assistants and substitutes of the EFE Agency have signed two letters to their union's 'Jurado de Empresa' (Jury of the Business)" —a misnomer that ought to be changed to "Jurado 'ante' la Empresa" (or "Jury 'before' the Business"). They had demanded the resignation of the jury for its disregard for their first letter, ordering a suspension of negotiations with the EFE agency.

The union members did not like the agency offer of: (1) P4,000 ($57) annual pay raise for those who made less than P8,000 ($114) a month; (2) P2,000 ($28) annual increase for those making more than P8,000 monthly; and (3) a 2-year continuation of the current labor contract. The story said those writers had been angered, for neither the jury nor the EFE agency had responded to the 2 letters from the lay members of the union. EFE ignored the story.

EFE enjoyed its state status in a very stately manner. On at least one occasion, EFE could display its influence on the top circle of Spain's ruling elite. On 17 December 1971, EFE organized a colloquium at its Ayala 5 headquarters on the 1972–1975 III Development Plan about to be launched. Laureano López Rodó, a minister without portfolio and commissioner of development, attended the colloquium himself and explained his ambitious plan to the luminaries of the Spanish press. Also significant for EFE was the presence of MIT Sánchez Bella. The MIT-EFE team had invited the cream of the Spanish press to the meeting. The directors and subdirectors of leading Madrid newspapers and 7 from Barcelona came to the colloquium. Minister López Rodó elucidated some complex issues in the new 1972–1975 quadrennial plan, which he said would involve P8 trillion ($14 billion). Moderated by EFE president Manuel Aznar, the press leaders participated with "informed" questions and comments. Ending the 3-hour meeting, López Rodó urged the journalists to "intensify the work of analysis, criticism of the III Plan." He agreed with Aznar in that the meeting had not been "convoked with semblance of 'propaganda,' to which neither you nor I would have lent ourselves, for that does not go with our own way of being."

Nobody would dare to take issue with the basic premises of the development plan, as had been done against the 1968–1971 plan with a sharp column in the weekly magazine *Actualidad Española* (*Spanish Present*) in 1967. The unsigned column had questioned the wisdom of the government which had just granted the EFE agency a monopoly on foreign news under the 1966 Press and Print Law and its accompanying rules and orders. It asked:

The Development Plan attempts to foment development of . . . the private initiative; because, if the Development Plan contemplated only the increase in level of the public, state or quasi-state enterprises, there would be no need for an indicative Plan. It would suffice with the decision of the economic Ministries or an agreement in Council of Ministers to carry it to practice. Seeing things this way, it is befitting to ask: To what point is it favorable to the information development of the country the economic assistance —with *the quantities that we would like to know*— to only one press agency? Is it fit or not to consider an assistance to other private information media? The topic is of vital interest not only for the professionals, but for all those who comprehend the importance of a freedom of press and of information, seriously lived and protected (emphasis added).[16]

As if it anticipated this questioning and skepticism in the minds of Spaniards, the 1971 memorial of the treasury ministry categorized the EFE agency as a "supereconomic" enterprise from which the state did not pursue economic benefits. The memorial said EFE was one of the 11 businesses in which the state participated with a total asset of P75.13 billion ($1.07 billion). Those businesses in 1971 produced revenues of P1.95 billion ($27.86 million), which meant an 8% net profitability. The treasury report said the state's participation in EFE was 33.3%, but it did not give the amount of state investment in EFE. (The government was always reticent about its expenditures for the EFE news agency, as was pointed out in the above magazine column.) Other "supereconomic" companies included "CineEspaña" (CineSpain) and the "Companía Española de Seguros de Crédito para la Exportación" (Spanish Export Credit Insurance Company).[17]

EFE at age 36 was finally given an accolade for its services of long years to its master. On 11 March 1975 EFE was awarded the top National Journalism Prize for 1974. It received the "Francisco Franco" prize, consisting of a silver plaque and a whopping P500,000 ($8,367). Even for a state agency like EFE, that was a considerable amount of money in Spain. It was good that EFE received, in 1975, the press award rubricated with the name "Francisco Franco," for it served to mark an epoch coming to an end. Franco became seriously ill in October. Prince Juan Carlos was appointed acting chief of state on 30 October. The 1975 National Journalism Prize was given the following year to the long-persecuted Europa Press for its "FLASH" wire on 20 November 1975, which read:

"FRANCO HAS DIED. FRANCO HAS DIED. FRANCO HAS DIED."

The 1976 prize for Europa Press no longer bore the dead dictator's name. La Agencia EFE, S.A., with the whole Spanish press, moved into a new era.

CIA "PAID" EFE

EFE was struck by lightning as it entered the post-Franco era, still under director Armesto, who would shortly be removed from his post. On 16 January 1976 the *Washington Post* reported that the EFE news agency had been involved in covert propaganda activities back in 1970, financed by the U.S. Central Intelligence Agency (CIA) against Salvador Allende, Chile's Marxist presidential candidate. The *Post* story, written by Walter Pincus, affirmed that EFE had belonged to: "a vast journalistic network that [the] Central Intelligence Agency (CIA) secretly created over 25 years and still finances . . . to carry out covert propaganda campaigns." Citing "a recent report of the Senate Intelligence Committee," Pincus wrote that on 14 September 1970, "the 'Forty Committee' of the National Security Council authorized a covert CIA propaganda operation to focus attention on 'the damage that would befall Chile' under an Allende government." Pincus made specific reference to alleged EFE involvement with the CIA:

> Twelve days after the Forty Committee action [or on 26 September 1970], the Spanish government-owned wire service, EFE, carried a report throughout Latin America from Santiago on an anti-Allende rally by a right-wing group called Patria y Libertad [Fatherland and Liberty] which was described in the story as "a growing movement."

The Pincus story followed this paragraph with another really damning paragraph:

> EFE, which transmits in Spanish, at the time received a CIA subsidy for its Latin American newswire operations, according to a former intelligence official.[18]

Leading Spanish newspapers carried a story on the *Washington Post* story, reported by their own correspondents, whom the papers had working abroad by these years, independent of the EFE service they subscribed to.[19]

EFE DENIES CHARGE

EFE would not and could not ignore the story. EFE dispatched a bristling wire to the Spanish press the next day, which all Madrid papers carried along with their own Washington wires. The EFE wire read:

> MADRID. (Cifra.)—"We can roundly affirm that it is absolutely false that the EFE agency has never [emphatic Spanish double negative] received a subsidy from the Northamerican CIA for its news operations in Latin America," the direction of the EFE agency has declared in relation with an article published yesterday by the "Washington Post," signed by Walter Pincus.

The last paragraph of the CIFRA wire alluded to the "actions" that EFE had taken and would take against the Washington newspaper.

> The director of the EFE agency has addressed, with yesterday's date, a letter to the "Washington Post" demanding the rectification of the article of Walter Pincus and reserving [the right to] the pertinent juridical actions for the damages and prejudices that could be caused to its prestige in Ibero America by the falsehoods contained in the information of the collaborator of the Northamerican newspaper.

The same CIFRA wire also cited "very real facts" that it said would refute the "falsehood in the information" of the Washington paper. These "facts" were:

> Upon election of Salvador Allende as president of Chile, it was the very Allende government that concluded a contract with EFE to distribute bulletins of the Chilean Chancellery [foreign ministry] to all its embassies in the world through the channels of the Spanish agency, to which it recognizes all credit and truthfulness and is considered an agency of great honesty and integrity in its services and function.[20]

It was a meek defense. Since EFE's establishment in the region during 1965–1967, many South American governments had been leasing the EFE teletransmission network to distribute nonsecurity messages to their foreign legations. The Allende government's use of the EFE network was nothing new or extraordinary. It might have fooled the uninformed general public as proof of trust in EFE by the Allende government. But to those familiar with the wire service business —if EFE could resort only to the Allende government contract in its defense— it made EFE all the more suspect, rather than exonerating the Spanish news service.

This probably explains the total lack of any EFE action, legal or otherwise, against the U.S. newspaper, despite EFE's blustering denial in the pages of Spanish papers. It appeared that neither EFE nor the Spanish embassy in Washington dared to write letters to the editors of the *Post*. It is a well known practice of the *Post*, —as is customary with all major U.S. newspapers— to readily air letters of protest from foreign missions and news entities, along with its own counterrebuttal to the original charges.

"IAPA ALSO INVOLVED"

Indeed, the only organization that responded to the *Post* item was the Inter American Press Association (IAPA). Its president, Raymond E. Dix, after a month-long delay, wrote a letter to the editor, published by the *Post* on 19 February 1976. The *Post*'s story on the CIA covert press activities had mentioned an anti-Allende news release by IAPA, which the story claimed had been "a CIA product," presumably written by Agustín Edwards, anti-Allende, pro-U.S. press tycoon of Chile. The IAPA letter presented a mild, pro forma denial of the Pincus charges.[21]

The Pincus story said Agustín Edwards had come to Washington in September 1970 to generate support for plans to halt Allende's election.[22] On 15 September 1970, the day after the Forty Committee approval of the propaganda campaign, Edwards had a meeting with then CIA director Richard Helms. On 22 September Edwards' *El Mercurio* (*The Mercury*) —the flagship daily in the Chilean capital, Santiago, of the Edwards newspaper chain— carried an editorial arguing that "retention of individual freedom" was the most important matter facing the Chilean people. On 26 September, 4 days after the *El Mercurio* editorial, EFE dispatched the report on the anti-Allende rally by "Patria y Libertad." The same day, a Santiago radio station carried a political commentary on the rally by "Patria y Libertad." The commentator mentioned the rally favorably, while criticizing the Christian Democratic Party, which that day offered to make an agreement with Allende.

Pincus then cited a U.S. Senate Intelligence Committee report which said "Patria y Libertad" and its rally received some money in an "indirect subsidy" from the CIA. The Santiago radio station and the commentator had also received CIA funds. But in the case of the EFE agency's "receiv[ing] CIA subsidies," Pincus did not attribute it to the senate report, but to "a[n unidentified] former CIA official," thus appearing to be less solidly founded in his allegation. The *Post*'s writer followed it up with these 2 paragraphs:

> Within a month of the Forty Committee decision, 18 journalists from outside Chile under direct or indirect Agency control had arrived in Santiago. Some were paid CIA agents working for newspapers in other countries; a few were anti-Allende and had received their transportation from CIA funds.

> Others were journalists who had been ordered to Chile by their bosses who were described by the Senate committee report as "high-level (CIA) agents . . . in managerial capacities in the media field.

It was a typical case of guilt by association, which many public figures accuse the news media of employing. Given the patently weak basis that Pincus had in saying that "EFE . . . received a CIA subsidy for its Latin American operations," it looked strange that EFE did not put up vigorous action against the *Washington Post*. Was it a case of admission by silence?

The CIFRA dispatch of 17 January 1976 mentioned that the EFE director had directed a letter to the *Washington Post* "demanding rectification" of the Pincus article.

That EFE director was Alejandro Armesto, who had been in that post since 1 December 1969. So, the sordid episode of "CIA-EFE connection" back in September 1970 was his responsibility. Yet, while he dawdled without taking precise actions with dispatch, a bigger political train hit Armesto, and he never got to act on the allegations of the "CIA-EFE nexus." Premier Arias Navarro's new post-Franco government —in power since 10 December 1975— dismissed him from the EFE director's post on 12 February 1976, less than a month after the *Washington Post* story.

Prominent in the new Arias Navarro government was Manuel Fraga Iribarne, the all-powerful interior minister and also vice premier on domestic affairs. Fraga, the former (1962–1969) "liberal" MIT, had thus staged a fast political come-back in the post-Franco era. Only 2 months in power, Fraga had Carlos Mendo, his "liberal" protégé, brought back into his former EFE directorship, replacing Armesto. It appeared that the 2 "liberal formers" had forged a new duo and would now bring in an era of liberal press.

Chapter 7

Searching the World
(1976–1982)

The decade 1976–1985 was a momentous period for Spain. After the death of Franco in late November 1975, the country went through an eventful process of domestic democratization, steadily dismantling the apparatus of the 40-year dictatorship. In the diplomatic field, Spain, erstwhile pariah state, became a full-fledged member of international society, and joined the European Communities (EC) and the NATO.[1] These domestic and foreign metamorphoses naturally affected Spain's state news agency EFE. In this period of changes, EFE contributed to the domestic democratization, as it became definitely number 5 among the Western news agencies, only after the "Big 4": AP, UPI, Reuters, and AFP.

METAMORPHOSES

Francisco Franco died on 20 November 1975. Spain became a monrchy on 22 November under King Juan Carlos I, who had been picked personally by Franco as his successor. Carlos Arias Navarro, who had been appointed premier by Franco 2 years earlier, made some cabinet changes on 10 December and brought in, among other liberals, Manuel Fraga Iribarne, the former (1962–1969) minister of information and tourism (MIT), as the powerful interior minister and vice premier on domestic affairs. In 1976 bans on politicial activity were lifted, but the country became impatient with the slow progress of the reforms under the government led by Arias Navarro. Widespread demonstrations resulted and Arias Navarro resigned in July at the king's request.

Adolfo Suárez González succeeded him as the new premier on 3 July 1976. Fraga Iribarne and 4 other liberal cabinet members refused to serve under Suárez, the former secretary-general of the National Falange movement. (Important for this book on EFE was the short, 7-month tenure of Fraga Iribarne in the first post-Franco government. Fraga, only 2 months after his accession to power, had his protégé, Carlos Mendo, appointed as the new EFE director on 10 February 1976, the position Mendo could keep for 8 months only, as will be seen later in this chapter.)

Suárez, despite his past ties with the Falange or probably because of these connections, could proceed rapidly with the introduction of democratic measures. The new Political Reform Law, which included an elected bicameral Cortes, was approved by an overwhelming 94% vote in a referendum on 15 December 1976. An electoral law was passed 3 months later on 15 March 1977. The numerous political parties —recently legalized— took part in the elections for the Cortes on 15 June 1977, except for the Falange movement; it had been disbanded on 1 April 1977. A plurality (34%) victory went to the Unión de Centro Democrático (UCD), a coalition led by Premier Suárez. (The Socialists [PSOE] won 29% and the right-wing Alianza Popular [AP] under Fraga Iribarne received 8%. Fraga Iribarne will always be present on the Spanish political arena from this date on, as will be Carlos Mendo's ambition to return to the EFE agency.)

The new Cortes wrote a new constitution and had it endorsed in another national referendum —by 87% of 68% of the electorate that voted— on 6 December 1978, "Día de la Constitución" (Constitution Day). The 1 March 1979 general elections held under the new constitution reflected the same political distribution as in the previous 1977 election among the 2 main parties: UCD 34% and PSOE 29%. The Spanish Communist Party (Partido Comunista Español, PCE) won 10% of the votes. The PCE was led by Santiago Carrillo, founder of "Euro-Communism," who advocated freedom and independence of the European Communist parties from the Kremlin. The Coalición Democrática (CD), which included Fraga Iribarne, received only 4%.

The first constitutional government was again headed by Adolfo Suárez. In March 1980 Basque and Catalán regional parliaments were elected and in both the UCD was heavily defeated by the moderate regionalist parties. Confidence in Suárez's leadership diminished and the right-wing factions within UCD forced Suárez to resign, on 29 January 1981. The deputy premier, Leopoldo Calvo Sotelo y Bustelo, was nominated to succeed Suárez, but he could not muster the required Cortes votes in the first round on 10 February. As a second vote was being attempted on 23 February in the Cortes, a group of armed civil guards, led by Lt. Col. Antonio Tejero, stormed into the Cortes and took hostage all 350 deputies present. Lt. Gen. Jaime Milans del Bosch, Valencia military commander, declared a state of emergency in Valencia and sent tanks into the streets.

King Juan Carlos I immediately secured the loyalty of other military commanders and by the next morning persuaded General Milans to retreat and Colonel Tejero to surrender, releasing the deputies unharmed. More than 30 army officers were later tried and the leaders of the failed coup received heavy jail terms after zigzag trial processes that lasted until April 1983.

Two days after the failed coup, Calvo Sotelo formed a new cabinet on 25 February. The Calvo government was faced with numerous problems in 1981: the toxic cooking oil scandal, which claimed some 300 lives; the June passage of a controversial liberal divorce law; and the decision to carry out the UCD's 1980 policy to take Spain into NATO. In the October 1981 elections for the Galician regional parliament, the Alianza Popular (AP) won 2 seats more than the UCD. This regional victory was a harbinger to Fraga's ascendancy to the head-on rivalry with the socialists (PSOE) throughout the 1980s and consequently a titillating hope for Carlos Mendo to retake the EFE news agency.

The December 1981 cabinet reshuffle could not stem the tide of desertions from the UCD. The PSOE won overwhelming victories in the May 1982 election for the Andalucian regional parliament. It accelerated the UCD defections throughout the year. By August the fragmented UCD no longer commanded a working majority in the Cortes. It called for an early election. Shortly before the election, a right-wing complot to stage a military coup was uncovered. Four army colonels were arrested and Lt. Gen. Milans del Bosch had been implicated again. The 28 October 1982 general elections resulted in a landslide (46%) for the "Partido Socialista Obrero Español" (PSOE) led by Felipe González Márquez, who formed a new cabinet on 2 December 1982.

Emerging from the 1982 elections was Fraga's AP, which won 25% of the vote. It became the main opposition party to the governing PSOE, replacing the UCD as the right-wing Spanish political group. Ever since 1982, the Spanish political scene has seen 2 major figures contesting for leadership in the destiny of Spain: Felipe González Márquez of PSOE and Manuel Fraga Iribarne of AP.

The government changes during 1976–1985 directly resulted in changes in EFE command. Political reforms caused transformation in the way EFE operated. The international status of EFE ascended in tandem with Spain's accession to the European Communities (EC), its membership in NATO, and the role it played in the Helsinki Accords —whose 1980–1982 review was hosted in Madrid by Spain, with her distinguished mediating role between the West and East. All the post-Franco changes, however, did not alter the basic nature of EFE, as it remained the state-funded and -operated news agency.

COMMAND CHANGES III

In the 1976–1982 period, EFE saw many changes in its top management. These changes directly paralleled the shifts in government. EFE's president Aznar died in 1976, and the EFE director-manager, Alejandro Armesto, was swiftly dropped on 12 February 1976 by the very first post-Franco cabinet in power since 10 December 1975. This cabinet, in which the former (1962–1969) MIT Fraga Iribarne was the powerful vice premier and interior minister, appointed José María Alfaro Polanco and Carlos Mendo to the respective posts of EFE president and director-manager. When Adolfo Suárez González became the premier on 3 July 1976, Fraga refused to serve.

On 30 September 1976, the Suárez government appointed Luis María Anson Oliart as EFE president. Two weeks later on 12 October, Anson captured the EFE directorship from Carlos Mendo, who was no longer protected by his mentor, Fraga Iribarne. Anson changed the EFE structure, naming himself as president and director-general. The 6.5-year Anson era came to an end at the end of 1982, but Anson's removal from EFE did not take legal effect until 25 January 1983.

Fraga–Mendo Ephemera

Premier Arias Navarro brought into his post-Franco government Manuel Fraga Iribarne as interior minister and vice premier on domestic affairs. Deals were cut for EFE appointments by the new cabinet. Arias Navarro put up José María Alfaro Polanco as EFE president, and Fraga Iribarne pushed Carlos Mendo as EFE director-manager. Arias Navarro had been Franco's director-general of security and he would make a perfect team with Alfaro Polanco, who had been among the founders of the Falange and the director of its magazine, *Fe*. Fraga and Mendo, both with a liberal outlook, had developed an intimate mentor-protégé relationship since they worked together as an MIT-EFE duo in the late 1960s. Mendo was named EFE director on 12 February 1976. It was a compromise quartet, when the Arias–Fraga government made the Alfaro–Mendo appointments. But these quatrain musical chairs were quickly rearranged, when Arias was forced to resign the premiership at the request of the new king in July 1976. Suárez assumed the premiership on 3 July 1976. Fraga and 3 other Arias ministers refused to serve in the Suárez cabinet. Fraga's rise to the power circles thus lasted only 7 months.

Fraga's new political demise clearly spelled the beginning of an end to the ephemeral second EFE tenure for Mendo as its director. The Suárez government waited 2 months before it fired Alfaro Polanco as EFE president on 30 September 1976, and named to the position a constitutional monarchist, Luis María Anson Oliart, a long-time writer at the leading Madrid monarchist daily *ABC*. Anson had had a run-in with Mendo's mentor, MIT Fraga Iribarne. On 21 July 1966 Anson wrote an article, "La Monarquía de Todos" ("The Monarchy of All"), and for this editorial item, *ABC* became the first newspaper to be confiscated under Fraga's Press and Print Law of 18 March 1966. Subsequent troubles with the government compelled Anson to go into a one-year exile abroad.

Anson had excelled as a journalist. Graduated at the top of the 1957 class from Madrid's Official School of Journalism, he had worked his way up through the ranks of the newsroom of the *ABC* to be its subdirector. In that capacity, Anson had traveled to more than 50 countries around the world and covered the wars in the Congo and Viet Nam. A prolific writer, he had authored 7 books, the first of which he wrote at age 19. An ardent believer in parliamentary monarchy, 3 of his books dealt with the Spanish monarchy. He had been promoted to director of the *ABC*'s magazine, *Blanco y Negro* (*White and Black*) in 1975 and immediately before appointment as EFE president, he had been named to the board of directors of *La Vanguardia* (*The Vanguard*) of Barcelona, then the largest Spanish daily.[2] Anson's journalistic career had thus been more traditional and wider-ranging than that of Mendo whose experience consisted only of news-agency journalism. Anson, however, had as strong-willed a personality as Mendo. Anson would not regard himself a ceremonial figurehead, as Mendo envisaged EFE president to be. He and Mendo were on an unavoidable collision course.

Anson's Palace Coup

In January 1976, Spain renewed its defense treaty for 5 years with the United States in exchange for U.S. support for the Spanish bid to enter the European Economic Community (EEC). A Spain-EEC trade agreement was being drafted to replace the old 7-year treaty that expired at the end of June. King Juan Carlos and Queen Sofía played an active, if ceremonial, role in Spanish image-building endeavors. The royal couple visited the United States and the Dominican Republic in June, and France and Colombia in October. Carlos Mendo succeeded in obtaining a membership in the royal entourage. Mendo wanted to stage his own triumphal return to the New World, to which he had launched a vigorous EFE expansion 10 years earlier. Mendo thought he had an upper hand over Anson in the privilege of accompanying the king. He did, for Anson had been EFE president only 10 days. Mendo departed on a "royal" tour leaving Anson behind at EFE. But little did Mendo know that by so doing he was digging his own grave.

On Tuesday, 12 October 1976, Mendo received an urgent confidential call at the Spanish embassy in Bogotá, Colombia. The call was from Madrid. The caller was the subsecretary of the MIT, Sabino Fernández Campo, an old Mendo ally. Fernández Campo informed Mendo that EFE president Anson had convened a meeting of the EFE administrative council for the next week. Mendo expressed his surprise: The council had met 10 days before and the EFE statutes required only one council meeting a month. Fernández Campo "enlightened" Mendo that the coming "extraordinary EFE council meeting was called to reform the very statutes."[3]

In Mendo's absence, Anson was to maneuver EFE's councilors to agree to rewrite the EFE statutes: (1) to appoint several directors to different EFE departments; (2) to create the new post of "director-general" to oversee the new "directors"; (3) to eliminate the post of [Mendo's] "director-manager"; and (4) to name the EFE president also the EFE "director-general."[4]

In short, Anson dismissed Mendo, and to rally support for his actions, created several "directorships" accompanied by pay hikes. It was a superb palace coup. When Mendo returned from the Colombian tour, his dismissal, effective as of 1 November 1976, was a *fait accompli*, and Mendo did not have anybody to turn to for help. His mentor, Fraga Iribarne, was no longer in power. Mendo's second directorship at the EFE agency had lasted only 8 months. During the years 1975 and 1976, Spain started on a rocky transitory road. The short-lived glory of the Fraga–Mendo duo was indeed as transient as the ephemeral political life of Spain itself.

THE ANSON ERA

Anson was a doer. He would not sit idly by in the chair of the ceremonial EFE president. He made sure that the old Mendo subordinates would not sabotage his work individually, by teaming them as a "commission of directors," or an EFE "executive commitee." Anson named himself president of the new commission. This commission was also intended to back him up in his dealings with the EFE administrative council. Anson now wore 3 hats: that of president of the EFE administrative council, of the director-general of EFE, and of the president of the commission of directors. In short, Anson consolidated an absolute —if not dictatorial— leadership over the EFE management.

People in the know, both in and out of the news agency, always mark 2 great EFE expansion movements in the mid-1960s and -1970s, attributed respectively to Mendo and Anson. Both were dynamic men and both carried tremendous journalistic baggage. But there were 2 important differences between the 2 men who made EFE what it is today. Mendo was an idealist who placed emphasis exclusively on the journalistic side of his work; Anson was an entrepreneur who took full charge of all aspects of EFE's business. The difference in their personal traits and work style might have come from their professional backgrounds: Mendo was a 100% wire service man; Anson was an all-round newsman. At any rate, Anson's entrepreneurship did not take long to show in real actions.

Upon taking command of the agency in the fall of 1976, Anson created 7 key positions in the EFE agency: "domestic director, foreign news director, editing director, coordination director, external relations director, personnel director, and business and finance director, and a manager.

Three of these 7 directors need explanation. The coordination director's job was to coordinate the news activities among the CIFRA (Spanish news for Spanish clients), EFE-Interior (foreign news for Spanish clients), EFE-Exterior (Spanish and international news for foreign customers), ALFIL (all-sports news for Spanish as well as foreign subscribers), and CIFRA-Gráfica (Spanish photo and UPI telephoto services for Spanish clients, and some Spanish photos for foreign wire services like UPI, AP, and others). These 5 news services were not simple operations. Coordination was definitely needed.

The external relations director took care of news exchange agreements and subscriptions with foreign news agencies. When Anson took over the agency, he inherited from the previous EFE management 19 agreements with news agencies of foreign countries. Some agreements dated all the way back to 1940 (Reuters) and 1945 (UPI). Old as well as new agreements had to be renegotiated periodically, and the Anson administration by 1982 expanded the EFE exchange network to 31 foreign agencies. The external relations office had to earn its keep; it was no idle, ceremonial post.

"Editing director" was a misnomer in its English translation as well as its Spanish title, *director de editorial*. The job of the "editing" director or his *dirección* (directorate) was not that of "editing" news copies. Nor did the editing director do any "editorial" work. The duties of the editing director consisted mainly in double-edged editorial control functions. One was the control of news language, or what is known in U.S. newsrooms as the "news style," by publishing the style book or desk book and enforcing the rules therein. The second aspect of the job of editing director was copy control of EFE news wires carried by Spanish newspapers, and especially the newspapers in Latin America, where EFE was engaged in direct competition with the bigger world news agencies. Copy control kept close daily, weekly, monthly, and annual tabs on the use —and whether in front-page or inside— of EFE stories by the Spanish, and again especially Latin newspapers.

Anson, the Committee Man

All 7 directors reported directly to Luis María Anson Oliart, the "director-general." The functions of these 7 directors had always existed and were carried on by the same men as before. So, in reality, this was not the creation of new positions. It was rather a promotion or an upgrading of existing positions, giving them more pay, more prestige, and perhaps more authority and, in exchange, expecting better job performance, and more loyalty. The executive committee was under the firm grip of Anson's chairmanship. And he did not weaken his power by delegating his authority to the committee. On the contrary, the executive committee was a device to impose his decisions on the more cumbersome and less malleable administrative council.

Anson —the committee man— created another committee, again to gain better control of the power structure of the EFE news agency. The EFE administrative council (board of directors), as inherited from the previous management, had a complex structure: the president (chairman), 22 councilors (directors), all with vote, and 4 nonvoting representatives of the EFE personnel, plus a secretary. It was too cumbersome and unruly. It frequently was hard even to muster a legally binding quorum, and the voting pattern was always unpredictable. To Anson, the man of action, it was intolerable. So he used his executive committee to persuade the administrative council to elect a standing committee (*comisión permanente*), consisting of the president and only 6 of the 22 councilors. This 7-member standing committee was not unwieldy at all, and it was even smaller than Anson's executive committee, made up of the directors who had been promoted by Anson.

Anson even further weakened the EFE administrative council, by gaining approval from the 12 March 1981 general assembly of stockholders for reforms to the EFE statutes. The most important reform was to drastically reduce the council membership from 23 to 13. He also eliminated the EFE personnel representation on the administrative council. And finally, Anson cut the membership of the standing committee of the council to 5 from 7. Luis María Anson Oliart, a parliamentary monarchist and man of action, had the EFE agency in his hands completely.

Adios to the Past

Nine months into the EFE management, on 21 June 1977, president-director general Anson inaugurated the EFE headquarters in a 7-story edifice at Espronceda 32, inviting the entire high society —Spanish and international. The inauguration of the new building should never be viewed as Anson's exhibitionism. The move also signified his determination to break away from EFE's past. The previous Ayala 5 locale had been the home of EFE for 36 years, practically the whole of its history, except for one year each at the founding city of Burgos and on Espalter Street in Madrid. The speed with which Anson accomplished the move was amazing. He became EFE president on 30 September 1976, removed Carlos Mendo as director in October, and convened the extraordinary general junta of EFE stockholders on 21 December to obtain approval of all organizational changes he had made in 2 short months. At the same time, Anson realized the physical move of the by then giant EFE complex.

The new EFE locale was important for another reason. The fifth- and sixth-floor spaces were leased to foreign news agencies, correspondents of Spanish and foreign dailies, magazines, radio, and television stations, which made the Espronceda 32 building a veritable international communications center. In December 1985 the tenants included: UPI, AP, AP Photo, Reuters, Yugoslav Tanjug Agency, the "France International," *France Soir*, the *Wall Street Journal, Noroeste de España* (*Northwest of Spain*), BBC, Reuters Photo, the London *Financial Times*, Visnews, AEDE (Asociación de Editores de Diarios Españoles), Asociaciones de Informaciones Provinciales, Asociaciones Gráficas, Portuguese agency ANOP, and MAP (Moroccan news agency).

Computers and Tantrums

"An Information Odyssey," read the headlines in the early January 1978 issues of Spanish newspapers.[5] The stories dealt with "an odyssey at the speed of light" of the news stories into and out of the new computers installed on the second floor of EFE headquarters. EFE had used rudimentary computers for information storage since 1973. Installed in late December 1977, these microcomputers at first "stood the EFE journalists on their heads." Some veteran writers had problems adapting to the "mysteries of cybernetics." Having to stop the use of the familiar typewriters and sitting down in front of television-like screens was cause enough for quite a few "hues and cries" coming from some EFE journalists.

"More than one writer had temper tantrums" in the process of learning computer technology. At first, much confusion resulted. A news story about Anwar Sadat – Menachem Begin interviews came out with headlines about Jimmy Carter's European tours. A story read that the Chinese were eating rice in front of the White House. Another claimed some North Americans made "chewing-gum ceremony in the nose of [Chinese leader] Deng Xiao-Ping." It took 20 days' experimentation to learn the intricacy of "modern artifacts of video-editing" technique. EFE newsrooms started using the English term *video-editing*, as many other English computer terminologies started to float around crudely without attempts at translation. Video-editing techniques gradually spread to newspapers in Spain. By 1982 the EFE wire dispatches were fed directly into the computers of the leading Spanish dailies *El País*, *La Vanguardia*, and *Ya*.

Another innovation made possible by the progress in EFE's computer system was the automated photo. Computers were used to edit AP and UPI telephotos and locally taken photo-films could be automatically revealed, developed, and printed in both black and white and in color. Telephoto circuitry was permanently installed in 1982 to connect the Las Palmas bureau on the distant Canary Isles. The trans-Atlantic satellite connections via INTELSAT set up in 1971 were updated and increased from the original 8 to 15 hookups by 1981, connecting Madrid with Buenos Aires, Santiago, Montevideo, Rio de Janeiro, La Paz, Bogotá, Caracas, Asunción, Lima, Quito, Panama City, Mexico City, Havana, Santo Domingo, and Washington, D.C. The Panama connection was extended to 5 Central American capitals by microwave and Washington was connected to New York City, Miami, and Houston.

Anson also struck out into broadcast journalism. A radio and television studios were formally installed in 1978. First temporarily set up on the ground floor upon moving into the Espronceda 32 building, the radio studio was modernized with a new console and other audio-engineering equipment, and was moved up to the fourth floor. British correspondents transmitted news stories to BBC headquarters in London from EFE's radio studio. The television studio remained on the ground floor, and was upgraded in 1978, 1980, and 1982. For transmission to Latin America, EFE-TV had to install expensive program convertors for converting 625 PAL lines of European TV to and from 525 NTSC lines used in television in the Americas. The ambitious television journalism project Anson envisaged saw little progress, confronted with the powerful RTVE (Radio-TV Española), another state-supported communication enterprise. Staffed with a dozen or so television journalists and operators in 1985, the EFE-TV studios were utilized little, except for producing commercials and other video shoots for private clients.

Losing CIFRA, ALFIL and Monopoly

The move into the new Espronceda 32 locale was only a physical break from the past. Anson also shook loose the old image of the EFE agency by changing the way his organization dealt with the news business. He did this in 2 important aspects: (1) unifying all EFE news services under the single logo EFE; and (2) renouncing the monopoly right EFE had enjoyed since 1966 in the exclusive distribution of foreign news. Both actions were taken in 1978.

A little before 29–30 January 1978, the teletypes in the newsrooms of Spanish newspapers crackled with a CIFRA news item, which announced its own demise. The last CIFRA wire was informing the EFE subscribers that, effective Monday, 30 January 1978, all news wires of the EFE agency would be uniformly signed "EFE" only. The CIFRA, ALFIL, and CIFRA-Gráfica would all disappear. From the 1938 founding days, EFE news had been classified into EFE (foreign news), CIFRA (national news), ALFIL (sports news, Spanish and foreign), and CIFRA-Grafica (photo service).

EFE's decision in June 1978 to renounce the long-held monopoly on the distribution of foreign news was a much more serious one, and it demonstrated the audacious mindset of Anson and his executives. The 1966 Press and Print Law (LPI) had granted EFE an exclusive right to distribute international news in Spain. Now less than 2 years after assuming command of the agency, Anson decided to put EFE in open competition with private agencies and other news media. He was cockily sure that his agency could survive or even defeat the competition. Anson put these ideas through the executive committee, had them approved by the administrative council, and formally notified the minister of the presidency of government about the EFE decision to forego the exclusive privilege.

The old ministry of information and tourism (MIT) —the unit charged with censorship and other press control schemes— had been eliminated in December 1977 by the second Suárez reform government, formed after the June 1977 general elections. Now, the EFE agency and other state-run media units came under the jurisdiction of the office of the president of government (premier). Anson's letter to the government, giving up the monopoly right on foreign news read in part:

> The exclusivity of distribution of the news from the foreign agencies . . . was founded on the wish of the Legislature that Spain not be subjected to a certain form of information colonialism, since the countries that lack a great news agency can hardly avoid having other

images of the world than what the four principal international agencies transmit.

But, if in 1966 EFE did not have world organization to avoid this information colonialism, today, with its half hundred bureaus on five continents and its modern installations equipped with ultimate technological advances, the EFE agency can compete in the international market of the information, in the distribution both of foreign news to Spain and of Spanish news to the rest of the world.[6]

Barbarism and Cultural Colonialism

Anson also decided to standardize the linguistic style used by EFE writers, and, by extension, the language used by diverse groups of Spanish-speaking people. As a lifelong writer and journalist, he was keenly aware of the problems arising from the lack of standards in the use of the language. In the case of Spanish, the problem was more complex, because it is spoken in Spain, about 20 Hispanic American countries, the South and Southwest of the United States, the Philippines, and the northwestern corner of Africa. And all of these ethnic, national, and geographical groups speak diverse versions of the Spanish tongue, constantly absorbing new terms and usage, derived from science, medicine, technology, music and fine arts, and sports.

Anson and other like-minded Spaniards have long entertained a feeling that all Spanish-speaking countries have been under the assault of "the Anglo-Saxon cultural colonialism by the giant U.S. news agencies in the Hispanic mass communication media."[7] To fend against the linguistic "barbarism" that writers in the popular press commit "for haste, frivolity, irresponsibility or inculture," EFE published the "Manual de Estilo" (Manual of Style) in 1978, under the direction of Professor Fernando Lázaro Carreter, member of the Royal Spanish Academy. Though similar in origin to the AP and UPI stylebook or the stylebooks or deskbooks in the editorial departments of the English-language publications, the EFE "Style Manual" was much more than just a newsroom guide. It took on a more hefty cultural and geographical undertaking, for EFE's style manual was intended to achieve a degree of uniformity in the varied Hispanic tongues.

There was an urgent need for "Hispanicizing" new words and phrases that were being constantly coined in computer communications, radio-television, aviation and space technologies, and other fields. In 1980 Anson's EFE established the Department of Urgent Spanish (Departamento de Español Urgente) jointly with the Institute of Cooperación Iberoamericana (ICI), a state cultural agency which had taken over the old Instituto de Cultura Hispánica (ICH). As the state unit charged with unifying new usage in

Spanish, the "Urgent Spanish Department" was made up of EFE editors, members of the Royal Spanish Academy, and a member from the Academy of Language of Colombia, which represented Latin American Spanish. The department published the third edition of the EFE style manual in 1981. An ACAN reporter from Panama on study leave at the University of Complutense cited some examples of "urgent translation" of new English words he received from the department: "blue jeans" should be *pantalones vaqueros* (cowherds' pants); "soft loans" should not be literally translated but should be *préstamos favorables* or *préstamos privilegiados* (favorable loans or privileged loans); "clearing house" should be *cámara de compensación* (chamber of compensation); and other difficult "neologisms" for which he could not have come up with easy solutions.[8]

EFE's department of "urgent Spanish" has confronted many difficult problems, and it has tried to strike a balance between Spanish purism and compromise with an avalanche of neologisms gushing lately from computer language. Often the balancing efforts of learned linguists have appeared to lead them to drown in the tide of change. The Spanish public, for example, has Hispanicized the word computer into *ordenador* or *ordenadora* (or orderer). But EFE's linguists ruled that it should be *computadora*. So, in this case, the experts lightly slapped the wrist of the public for its xenophobic refusal to accept the "computer" as such. EFE, however, went the other way in the case of "software" and "hardware." It ruled that the terms should be translated into *soporte lógico* and *soporte físico*, logical support and physical support respectively. But it has lost on both counts, as the Spanish public —including EFE writers— has insisted on using "ordenador, software, and hardware," the considerate decisions of the erudite scholars notwithstanding.

EFE's Tower of Babel

Now Anson was prepared to strike out in to another new direction. He started to build an EFE Tower of Babel.

In 1977 Anson inaugurated the Tele-EFE news service, specifically for top-ranking executives in business enterprises, public and semipublic entities, and socioprofessional institutions. These elite customers would be provided with carefully selected domestic and foreign news, covering politics, society, finance, culture, and so forth, condensed for a "quick read" and instantly trassmitted by video-editing as the news happened. The increasing popularity of these services reflected its importance for these special clients and the proven need in some elite circles for rapid, concise, and instantaneous breaking news. The Tele-EFE grew into VIDEO-EFE.

VIDEO-EFE was a cable-connected Videotex news system, operated with closed-circuit video screens in public places such as airports and government and business offices. The headline news service projected short paragraphs of news on video screens in characters large enough to be legible from 5 to 6 meters (15 to 20 feet) away. It was done with technical coordination from the Companía Telefónica Nacional de España. By the end of 1982 EFE installed 36 screens, and 12 more were "contracted for an early installation." Barcelona had the 15, followed by 12 in La Coruña, 11 in Madrid, 5 in Bilbao, 2 in Valencia, and one in Valladolid.

Anson was not content with the Spanish-only service of his agency. In 1978, EFE started a Catalán service in the dialect spoken by some 6.37 million people living in Catalonia. The Catalán-speaking people represent 16.4% of Spain's population.[9] The EFE news service in Catalán —a language prohibited in the Franco era in the name of national unity— was routed through, of course, EFE's Barcelona main regional bureau. The half-hour daily Catalán service began on 1 September with a 45-minute inaugural transmission. The Catalán news service was in line with the post-Franco era politics of regional autonomy and EFE's Barcelona bureau chief, Rodger Jiménez, declared that this Catalán service would not be a mere translation but would be "directed in special ways to the Catalán ambiance" and the news would be "seen with Catalán optics."

In 1979 EFE started an English service. Originally intended to penetrate the non-Hispanic-speaking international markets for EFE's "world news agency," Anson admitted in a 1985 interview[10] to having "committed the error of mounting the English service in Spain, and it was not good in quality, even in the language, despite the Britishers we employed." Two years later in 1981, Anson moved the English news service to London, which produced 100 news stories in a 20-hour daily cycle. Anson remembered that "in fact, [it] started to have subscribers, once established in London." He lamented that his management "did not work sufficiently on this English service, for the agency had a big probability of penetration in the Arab world, if [EFE] had had an English service sufficiently good."

Anson rejected the idea of employing the Arabic language for the Arab world for "the difficulty of adaptation of computer and transmission systems into the Arabic." Anson said: "An Arabic service would have to 'presuppose' technical efforts of such a caliber that I think there is not a single agency that transmits in Arabic." Besides, "an Arab-language news service cannot be marketed in other regions as an English service can be." He was repudiating the earlier efforts by his predecessors, Mendo and Armesto, to attempt to mount Arabic service with the Maghreb Arab Presse (MAP) of Morocco.

Anson also explained his reason for not setting up an English news service in Washington, D.C., because the Arabs "appreciate the English of England much more than the North American English." Anson supported his estimation of the difference between the British and North American versions of English, saying "we have precisely the same problem with the Hispanic American Spanish which is not exactly same as our Spanish." Anson insisted that "the English service to market in the United States will have to be retranslated by North Americans." But, "the English language service that can be sold in Africa, in the Middle East, and in Asia like Hong Kong and Singapore, etc., must be the service in the English of England."

He made disparaging remarks on the French service of which he had so highly spoken in EFE's promotional booklets in 1980, 1981, and 1982, and also in his own 1981 annual memorial. Those EFE documents had said that the French service set up at the EFE Paris bureau sent out 12,000 words a day on a 20-hour cycle. The negative notes he sounded on the French service blamed it on his predecessors: "When I arrived at the EFE agency [in 1976] there was only one foreign-language service —in French. It was 'an absurd thing,' for the French is a language now almost nonexistent in the world." Anson's EFE still held onto the French service in its Babel-like collection of news services. He was not one to shrink in his news endeavors.

Anson's EFE marched into another field in his search for newer and bigger dimensions. Anson instituted a club of world-class Great Writers ("Grandes Firmas," "Great Signatures" in direct translation) in 1979. EFE contracted the services of 12 prominent Hispanic-world writers: such as Jorge Luis Borges, Gabriel García Marquez, Carlos Fuentes Alejo Carpentier, Mario Vargas Llosa, and Octavio Paz. EFE maintained an exclusive international contributor service for articles and essays written by these "Great Writers" of world fame.[11]

In 1980 and subsequent years, EFE added more writers from outside of the Hispanic communities, as well as within the Hispanic nations, to the "Great Writers" membership. Among the non-Hispanic notables were Alexander Solzhenitsyn, and Maurice Duverger, Raymond Aron, Jean Francois Revel, and Bernard Henri Levy. Later more Hispanics were also added to the "Great Writers" club.[12]

In 1980 Anson set up a subsidiary news distribution company in the United States, the ACHA-EFE news agency "in cooperation with a major U.S. firm to transmit the EFE services to the Spanish-speaking media" in the United States. ACHA stood for the "Agencia de Comunicaciones Hispano-Americana" (Hispanic-American Communications Agency). The ACHA-EFE offices were established in 1981 at Houston in a building purchased by EFE. Direct Madrid–Houston telecommunication lines were set up, which branched into a Houston–Los Angeles–Miami–New York network. The

ACHA-EFE received EFE news, especially on the regions, from which came
the majority of Hispanic residents of the United States, like Mexico, Central
America, Puerto Rico, Cuba, and the Dominican Republic. The news from
the Caribbean Basin was complemented by that of the United States,
supplied by EFE bureaus in Miami, Los Angeles, Albubuquerque, New
York, Washington, and other U.S. cities. Anson projected originally that
ACHA-EFE could supply EFE news services to 4 dailies, 50 weeklies, 278
radio stations, and 3 television chains, which he claimed "some 30 million
Hispanics read and follow"[13] in the United States.

A development of major significance, yet little noted by EFE itself, took
place in the "Comercial Telegráfica, S.A. (COMTELSA)," which had been
a financial-economic news service for 36 years, in joint venture with the
British Reuters since 22 July 1946. In 1982 Reuters withdrew its 50%
interest, and EFE became the total owner-operator. To take effect on 1
January 1983, the dissolution of the Reuters-EFE partnership was negotiated
in 1982. The disengagement of Reuters caused the disappearance from Spain
of Reuters' services of the COMEURO (European commodities markets),
video economic news, WSP (Wall Street Press), and RMR (Reuters Money
Report). They were mostly taken over by Comtelsa now totally owned by
EFE. The dimensions of Reuters' and EFE's investments were never
revealed. Yet it could be deduced that Comtelsa was a sizable operation. Its
nominal capital in 1978 was P5 million (US$67,450), half of which was the
EFE agency's share. In the same year, Comtelsa reported a profit of P1.24
million ($16,754). (The Comtelsa capital was 1-40th of EFE's 1978 nominal
capital, P200 million [$2.7 million], and it rendered a profit that amounted
to about 1-43rd of the total EFE profit of P53.2 million [$717,658].[14]

ANSON'S EXPANSIONS

Anson quickly gained firm control of the EFE power structure through
several fundamental reforms. He now sprang full steam ahead into
tremendous expansions from the new EFE headquarters at Espronceda 32.
During his 6.5-year tenure, EFE built itself up to be the fifth-largest Western
news agency, the third biggest Latin American news service, and the leading
Spanish-language agency.

EFE News Bureaus

Anson transformed the Spanish news agency into a giant worldwide news
service by both solidifying the existing network and blazing new paths in the

yet unexplored corners of the world. From 1976 through 1982, he expanded EFE's news network to 89 offices all over the world, 15 in Spain and 76 overseas. (Table 7.1 gives an overall picture of the EFE news network in the pre-Anson and Anson eras by geographical regions.)

Table 7.1
EFE News Network in the Anson Era

EFE NEWS OFFICES			
Regions/Categories	Before Anson	Anson Era	Growth %
FOREIGN POSTS:			
South America	11	13	18 %
Central America	6	7	17
The Caribbean	3	9	200
Western Europe	9	16	78
Eastern Europe	0	3	~ ~
North America	2	7	250
Far East	1	7	600
Middle East	1	6	500
Black Africa	0	6	~ ~
South Pacific	0	2	~ ~
Foreign Total	33	76	130 %
DOMESTIC POSTS:			
EFE Headquarters	1	1	0
Madrid Central	1	1	0
Main Bureau	4	5	25
Regional Bureau	1	1	0
City Bureau	0	7	~ ~
Domestic Total	7	15	114 %
GRAND TOTAL	40	91	128 %

~ ~ indicates infinite % as the growth started from zero.

EFE under Anson ventured into 3 new ethnic, geopolitical areas that EFE had not dared to go during the Franco years: Eastern Europe, sub-Saharan Africa, and the South Pacific. EFE opened offices in 3 socialiast-block cities: Moscow, Warsaw, and Belgrade, Yugoslavia; 6 sub-Saharan countries (cities) in Africa: Senegal (Dakar), Uganda (Khartoum), Equatorial Guinea (Malabo), Zaire (Lumumbashi), Zimbabwe (Harare), and South Africa (Johannesburg); and 2 South Pacific countries (cities): Australia (Canberra) and New Zealand (Auckland). Even at the height of the Viet Nam War, the EFE news agency had only one Far Eastern bureau at Manila, through which it channeled news from 6 cities: Beijing, Tokyo, New Delhi, Seoul, Jakarta, and Hongkong.

Arabic Middle Eastern countries —including those in northern Africa— and Israel were strengthened in news coverage by 5 new offices in Jerusalem, Cairo, Beirut, Algiers, and Tunis, in addition to the sole Arabic city previously covered, Rabat, Morocco. EFE's presence in North America included offices in Washington, New York City, Miami, Los Angeles, Houston, the UN, and Ottawa, Canada. Western Europe was not neglected, where Anson opened offices at 7 new locations: West Berlin, Copenhagen, Helsinki, Oslo, Athens, Dublin, and Strasbourg (France), on top of 9 former offices at Lisbon, Paris, London, Rome, the Vatican, Geneva, Bonn, Brussels, and Vienna. The Caribbean countries received a hefty uplifting in EFE strength by 6 new offices at Barbados, Guadeloupe, Martinique, Trinidad, Port-au-Prince, and Jamaica, an increase of 200% from 3 offices at Havana, Santo Domingo, and San Juan (Puerto Rico).

The geographical Central America was given one new EFE office at Belize (British Honduras), added to the 6 ACAN bureaus existing already. The rest of Latin America received 2 more Brazilian bureaus at Sao Paulo and Brasilia (new capital city). Those were additions to 11 traditional Latin American bureaus.[15]

EFE's domestic bureaus underwent considerable (114%) expansion and upgrading too. The Catalán regional main bureau at Barcelona had been created at the end of the civil war, even before EFE headquarters moved to Madrid from Burgos. Through the years of its domestic phase, EFE had set up 3 more main bureaus at the Basque city of Alava, the Galician capital of Santiago de Compostela, and at Las Palmas on the Canary Isles in the Atlantic Ocean off northwest Africa.

Aside from this distant Canary Island main bureau, EFE's 3 main bureaus, and Madrid Central Regional bureau and Madrid's EFE headquarters —both at the same Espronceda 32 locale— tended to be "north-heavy" and "south-weak." Anson took care to correct this imbalance by adding an Andalucian regional office at Sevilla, thus completing the network of 5 main bureaus —at Barcelona, Alava, Santiago, Sevilla, and Las Palmas. The Valencia bureau was upgraded to Valencia-Murcia regional bureau to improve the coverage of the weakest southwestern Mediterranean flank of the Spanish peninsula.

EFE'S domestic coverage was still weak. Anson corrected the deficiency by setting up 7 new bureaus in Asturias, Oviedo, the Mediterranean Balearic Islands (Palma de Mallorca), and Costa del Sol (Málaga), Guipuzcoa (San Sebastián), Navarra (Pamplona), Vizcaya (Bilbao), and the Canary Islands (Tenerife). The 15-point EFE domestic network was now complete. In addition, EFE used a fleet of radio-equipped vans —*Equipo Móvil* (Mobile Unit)— to supplement the EFE domestic network.

How does the EFE agency fare when it is contrasted with other international news agencies in the domestic and foreign bureaus? For comparison purposes, the early 1980s figures, reported to the International Organization of Journalists (IOJ) are used.[16] Along with the comparative data on the news agencies, the populations of their countries of origin are presented in Table 7.2.[17]

Placed side by side with other news agencies, EFE's 95 bureaus do not compare poorly at all. The "Big 5" —TASS, AP, UPI, AFP, and Reuters— have more bureaus than EFE. But they are from much more potent nations, both in population size and geopolitical influence. West Germany and Italy are "bigger" countries than Spain, and their ANSA and dpa respectively are "neck and neck" with EFE. Compared to Poland with a similar population, EFE far exceeds PAP in the number of bureaus.

Table 7.2
Comparison of Agency Bureaus

NUMBER OF AGENCY BUREAUS								
EFE	AP	UPI	Reuters	AFP	ANSA	dpa	PAP	TASS
Country								
Spain	USA	USA	UK	France	Italy	Germany	Poland	USSR
National Population (millions *)								
39	241	241	57	56	57	61	38	280
Domestic Bureaus								
19	132	173	0	12	17	46	49	17
Foreign Bureaus								
76	81	92	92	88	89	44	26	98
TOTAL BUREAUS								
95	213	265	92	100	106	90	75	115

*Population figures are rounded off to the nearest million.

EFE, a Real Estate Agency? In October 1981 the budget committee of the Spanish Cortes was holding hearings for the 1982 budget.[18] The committee called on the carpet the state news agency EFE on 26 October. When his turn came, socialist deputy Enrique Barón Crespo directed hostile questions at Anson and accused him of running an "international real estate agency," not a news agency. The EFE news agency had purchased, intoned Deputy Barón, "neoclassical palaces" in Quito, Ecuador, and Lisbon. Anson answered that EFE had a building policy which economized on "expensive rents" and "built up EFE's equity." Anson's building policy was carried out in this manner.

In 1978 EFE bought buildings for bureaus in Las Palmas, Canary Islands; Santiago de Compostela, Galicia; and Bilbao, Basque Country. EFE also purchased 6 houses in Panama City, Mexico City, Lisbon, Lima, Santiago de Chile, and Caracas. In the same year, EFE moved its London and Paris bureaus to new and bigger offices. The year 1979 saw EFE acquire buildings in Barcelona and Bogotá, Colombia, and it installed its Quito bureau in new offices. In 1980 EFE installed a modern security system in Madrid headquarters, inaugurated its Barcelona bureau at a building purchased the previous year, moved its San Juan and Santo Domingo bureaus to new buildings, bought houses for its bureaus in Montevideo, Uruguay, and also for domestic bureaus at Vitoria, Pamplona, and San Sebastián.

In 1981, EFE's Basque general bureau moved into its Vitoria, Alava, office building. In 1982, his last year at the helm of EFE, Anson purchased buildings for the bureaus at Managua, Buenos Aires, and Washington, D.C. EFE moved into new buildings at Asunción and Santo Domingo —this last one with the presence of Domonican President Antonio Guzmán at its inaugural.

In all, the Anson administration purchased 15 new buildings and inaugurated 5 foreign bureau sites, plus the EFE headquarters building. That adds up to a total of 21 "property movements." Anson built up a 91-post EFE network from the 40 EFE posts he had inherited. The 21 "realty movements" came to 23% —almost a quarter— of EFE's 91 bureaus. None could accuse Anson of inaction. Moreover, his real-estate interests represented exactly the financial and operational interests of the EFE news agency. Those purchases were not a "shopping spree," and were not made in a surreptitious manner. These EFE properties received due publicity in EFE publications.[19]

THE KREMLIN AND "SAD SAM"

The Kremlin summoned the EFE Moscow correspondent to deliver a warning on 30 May 1979. Ramón Pedros, also stringing for the Televisión Española, was called from the Western correspondents' barracks on a Moscow street named *Sadovo-Sam*otiochnaya.[20] The Western news correspondents housed there called the street "Sad Sam" for humor and also because of the difficulty of pronouncing the words in Russian —of which they did not have a sufficient command. Alexander Vasnikov, the first secretary of the press department of the foreign ministry, read to Pedros the second warning since February and advised him that the third would mean his expulsion from the Soviet Union. Vasnikov read and spoke to the EFE correspondent in Russian, "despite his perfect mastery of Spanish."[21]

The Kremlin's wrath emanated from an EFE story which had been sent exclusively to Venezuela. The EFE report said that the Soviet authorities had retained for more than 10 months luggage of the Venezuelan ambassador to Moscow, which he wanted to take with him to Caracas. The Soviets sternly reprimanded the EFE agency for diffusing news stories that "disturb the relations of the USSR with other States." Another Spanish journalist of *El País* (*The Country*) had also been warned in February. The leading Madrid newspaper had run a story about EFE's run-in with the Soviet government and said that the case of the Venezuelan ambassador had increased the pressures on foreign correspondents. The *El País* story added that 2 West Germans had "been expelled and the same threat weighs over another North American journalist."

The hardening attitude of the Kremlin obviously was related to the spate of dissident protests led by the so-called Helsinki [monitoring] Group and the ongoing negotiations over the SALT II treaty which eventually was signed in Vienna in June of the same year. The events must have perplexed EFE president Anson, who had signed only 2.5 months before (on 12 March) a renewal of the exchange agreement with the Soviet TASS agency at EFE headquarters. Indeed, it was much more than a simple news exchange agreement. The "new contract for information and technical cooperations" stipulated a transmission agreement: EFE's Moscow bureau would use TASS's English service to transmit news to Madrid, and the TASS Madrid bureau would use EFE's channels for its transmission to the Soviet capital.

One way or another, Anson was not one to be fazed by some small mishaps like an expulsion menace to one of his hundreds of correspondents spread all over the world. Anson himself had spent a year of foreign exile during the Franco era. So Anson forged ahead with the second phase of his expansion plan. In the first phase, he more than doubled the EFE foreign bureaus from 33 to 76 (a 130% increase). But he knew that his network was lopsidedly heavy in Latin America, Western Europe, and North America; probably thinly spread in the Middle East; and definitely deficient in Eastern Europe and the Far East. In the second phase, he strengthened the weak links in EFE's world network by expanding on exchange agreements with his foreign colleagues. It cost an enormous amount to establish even a simple correspondent's office abroad, let alone bureaus. So, news exchange agreements were an acceptable substitute for expensive EFE bureaus overseas.

News Exchanges III

Anson inherited in 1976 from his predecessors 19 news exchange agreements of various dimensions with assorted agencies, including the "Big-4" world news agencies, AP, UPI, Reuters, and AFP. During his 1977–1982 activity-laden years, he signed 13 more news agreements with foreign agencies, for a total of 32 exchanges, an increase of 68%. (Table 7.3 gives a numerical overview of Anson's expanding exchange network.)

As was the case in the 600% increase of EFE's own bureaus, Anson placed major emphases (300% hike) in news exchanges also in the Far East, the weakest link in the EFE news network. EFE had signed only one agreement in the vast Pacific Basin, with Japan's Kyodo News Service in 1967. Anson added 3 more. In December 1977 Anson traveled to the People's Republic of China and inked an exchange accord with President Zeng Tao of the XINHUA, New China News Agency. Since the restoration to power in July 1977 of Deng Xiao-Ping, China had opened up to the West and Anson took advantage of the trend to gain an entry into the giant country where almost a quarter of humanity resided. A month later on 9 January 1978, Anson initiated the application process to set up an EFE bureau in Beijing. The other 2 news exchange agreements in Asia were signed with the Indonesian ANTARA News Agency in 1980 and with the South Korean YONHAP in 1981.

Table 7.3
Growth of EFE News Exchanges in the Anson Era

GROWTH IN EFE NEWS EXCHANGE AGREEMENTS			
Regions	Before Anson	Anson Era	Growth %
The Caribbean	1	1	0 %
Western Europe	9	11	22
Eastern Europe	3	9	200
North America	2	2	0
Far East	1	4	300
Middle East*	3	5	67
Total	**19**	**32**	**68 %**
Socialist Bloc+	5	11	120 %

* Middle East includes the Arab countries in North Africa.

+ This bloc comprises East Europe and Cuba.

The next biggest boost was given to Eastern Europe where Anson set up 6 new exchanges and added to 3 existing ones, for an increase of 200%. The 6 new agreements were with NOVOSTI (Soviet domestic news service as opposed to the international TASS), East Germany's ADN (Allgemeiner Deutscher Nachrichtendienst), MTI (Magyar Tavirati Iroda) of Hungary, the Bulgarian BTA (Bulgarski Telegrafitscheka Agentzia), TANJUG of Yugoslavia, and the Polish PAP (Polska Agencja Prasowa). The Socialist-bloc countries had 11 exchange agreements with EFE, includng the Chinese Xinhua, Cuba's Prensa Latina (PL), TASS, CTK (Czechoslovenska Tiskova Kancelar), and Romania's AGERPRES, in addition to the 6 new ones above. Four more exchange agreements were signed with Portugal's ANOP (Agencia Noticiosa Portuguesa) and ATS (Agence Telegraphique Suisse) of Switzerland in Western Europe; and Iraqi News Agency (INA) and Tunisia's TAP (Tunis Afrique Presse) of the Arab Mideast.

Again how does EFE fare when it is contrasted with other international news agencies in the number of news exchange agreements? For comparative purposes, the early 1980s IOJ figures are. again used here.[22] This time, however, each agency's exchange agreements are compared to the number of its own news bureaus, rather than the national populations (see Table 7.4.) The ratios between the exchange agreements and the agencies' own foreign bureaus range from the low 42% of EFE, to AP's 51%, and ANSA's 73% to the high of 79% of TASS. It can be said that EFE was relatively the least dependent on news exchanges. The cases of the German dpa and Polish PAP, in which the news exchanges exceed their own foreign bureaus, seem to be aberrations.

Table 7.4
Comparison of News Exchanges

COMPARISON OF EXCHANGE AGREEMENTS								
EFE	AP	UPI	Reuters	AFP	ANSA	dpa	PAP	TASS
Country								
Spain	USA	USA	UK	France	Italy	Germany	Poland	USSR
Exchange Agreements								
32	41	n/a	n/a	n/a	65	55	40	77
Own Foreign Bureaus								
76	81	92	92	88	89	44	26	98

n/a = not available; 3 agencies did not report these figures to IOJ.

Association Activities

EFE also broadened its foreign horizons by actively participating in international press organizations of varied dimensions and areas. EFE was definitely a Hispanic American news agency with most of its news sources and clients in that continent. It was only natural that EFE would be attracted to the Inter American Press Association (IAPA), or Sociedad Interamericana de Prensa (SIP), the premier association of press-related entities, professionals, and academics of the Western Hemispheric countries. The IAPA-SIP covered North America (USA and Canada), Latin America (Mexico, Central America, Panama, Spanish-speaking South America, and Portuguese-speaking Brazil) and the Caribbean isles. After behind-the-scenes negotiations, EFE and ACAN were admitted to the IAPA-SIP as full-fledged corporate members in October 1979 during the annual convention in Toronto, Canada.

For Anson, it was a glorious moment, as the 45-member board of directors of the IAPA-SIP welcomed the new member unanimously with loud applause. Anson joined the inter-American association and its ruling board as the president of EFE, ACAN, and the Press Association of Madrid and also as the director of the *Hoja del Lunes* (*Monday Sheet*) of Madrid. The occasion also marked international acceptance of the press of Spain, which, up until 4 short years before, IAPA-SIP had shunned as the organ of a dictator state.

The post-Franco EFE was not only accepted by the mainstream press entities of the Americas but was actively solicited by the Latin Amrican press units for leadership. In 1978 Anson initiated gestures to create a news agency for Venezuela, as the first step toward the constitution of a multination project, with a vaguely denominated idea of an Agencia Bolivariana de Noticias (a Bolivarian news agency). He was formulating a news agency for the "Bolivarian-area" nations of the northern part of South America, patterned after the Central American subsidiary ACAN-EFE.[23]

Anson's restless ambition led to yet another Iberoamerican project. In 1982 several news agencies of Latin America entrusted EFE with a project to set up an Alianza Ibero Americana de Agencias de Noticias (ALIAN) (Iberoamerican Alliance of News Agencies). An EFE-drafted statute was approved in a September 1982 meeting in Madrid. ALIAN integrated —besides EFE— these national news agencies: the Argentine DYN, Bolivian FIDES, Colombian COLPRENSA, Ecuadorean AEP, Peruvian ANDINA, Paraguyaan APN, and "Panamanian" ACAN. The director of the Argentine DYN was elected ALIAN's president and the Colombian director the secretary. The ALIAN was actually a coup for Anson's EFE. The ALIAN constitution stipulated "free news cooperation" among the members.

It meant that EFE could use news gathered by the member Latin American agencies, and vice versa. But the national agencies could not sell EFE news to any national clients of their own, for most of them were already EFE's clients. Besides, the Alliance gave EFE a chance to watch over these national agencies for possible formation of an anti-EFE Latin American alliance. For these and other reasons, neither the Agencia Bolivariana nor ALIAN has become much of a news organization.

Outside of the Americas, Anson's EFE agency also sent a representative to the annual assembly in March 1981 at Nairobi, Kenya, of the Zurich-based International Press Institute (IPI), a press entity of the entire Western world, much wider in scope than the IAPA-SIP. The IPI gave its belated recognition to the now-liberated Spanish press, by celebrating its 1982 meeting in Madrid, to which EFE and other press units of Spain provided facilities as the host nation.

In these wide-ranging international involvements, Anson never lost sight of the business side of EFE. As in all wire agencies, EFE's transmission circuits were spotty in occupation; there were rush hours and less busy times as the early morning hours. As do all wire services, EFE sold those hours to any clients in need of message transmission. In 1982 —his last year as its president— Anson's EFE signed a transmission contract with the Organization of Petroleum Exporting Countries' News Agency (OPECNA) at Geneva and the Venezuelan news agency VENPRES. The EFE transmission service was also contracted by the foreign ministries of Spain, Argentina, Mexico, and Venezuela for nonsensitive bulletins to diplomatic posts the world over. EFE was particularly fit for that kind of service because of its natural language affinities.

LUXURIANT HOUSEKEEPING

Amidst all the dynamic expansion activities, the EFE household under Anson of course had its share of miscellanenous housekeeping chores to perform. But such tasks were discharged with style. Even in sundry duties, Anson exhibited political shrewdness.

Prizes and Awards

Journalists are a proud and to a degree egocentric intellectual lot. Their profession is not highly rewarding monetarily. They are occasionally compensated for the honest poverty by usually ceremonial peer recognition in the form of awards.

Shortly after he assumed the presidency of the EFE agency in October 1976, Anson established a journalism award with the name of his predecessor, Manuel Aznar Zubigaray, who had been the short-time EFE director in the late 1950s and the EFE president from 1968 through 1975. The Aznar Journalism Award of half a million pesetas —a sizable amount in Spain or anywhere else (US$7,372 at the 1976 exchange rate of $1 = P67.8)— was given to the author of the best Spanish article published in a Spanish newspaper every year. For the prize amount and its prestige, the Aznar Journalism Award has been highly coveted among Spanish journalists, which gave a certain "power" to the EFE agency and its president, who presided over the award's jury.

Conspicuous among the 7 winners of the coveted award from 1976 to 1982 (Anson's last year at EFE) was the 1981 recipient, José María Alfaro y Polanco, poet, journalist, and ambassador, who had been EFE president for 6 months from February to August 1976 —just before Anson took over. With the Aznar Award, Anson covered all politically touchy points in Spanish press circles.

Anson's ceremonious coverage with prizes was not limited to Spain and Spanish journalists. He reached out to the imaginable extremes of the Iberian heritage. In 1977 he created the EFE International Journalism Awards. Prizes of $8,000 each were awarded to the "Best Reporting Work, Best News Chronicle, Best Photography, and Best Reportage" of each year. Its coverage revealed typical Ansonian outreach. The prize aspirants could be "all journalists of the nationality corresponding to countries in some form of 'Iberic' origin." This criterion encompassed Angola, Cape Verde, the Philippines, Ecuatorial Guinea, (Sephardic) Israel, Mozambique, Guinea-Bissau, and the United States, in addition to the traditional Hispanic world.

Flaunted as the "Iberian Pulitzer," the 1977 prize for the best news chronicle was given to Colombian journalist Enrique Pulido, at the San Carlos presidential palace in Bogotá by Colombian President Alfonso López Michelsen. The 1979 prize for the best news chronicle was conferred on Sephardic journalist Camelia Shajar by Israeli President Isaac Navon in a ceremony conducted at the presidential palace in Jerusalem.

Notable among the 1980 prizes was the best news chronicle for a television chronicle by Salvadorean journalist Carlos Rosas Gaitán entitled *El Salvador 80*, about the big funerals of the archbishop of San Salvador, Oscar Arnulfo Romero y Galdamas, victim of a 24 March assassination thought to be the work of right-wing factions in the civil war in El Salvador. The prize conferral was conducted on 3 April 1981 at San Juan, Puerto Rico, attended by 300 guests and presided by San Juan mayor Hernán Padilla. The prize for Portuguese journalist María Joao Avillez for the best reportage was given at a separate ceremony on 17 June at EFE's Lisbon bureau, presided by

Portuguese Premier Pinto Balsemao. The 1981 prizes were handed out on 29 May 1982 at Santo Domingo of the Dominican Republic for the best works selected from among 300 plus contestants from 26 countries. Among the plethora of names of the contestants, judges, and winners, one name alone always stood out all over the Iberian world —that of Anson.

Employee Relations

Anson inherited a 500-person staff at the Madrid headquarters of EFE, which increased to 735 employees by the time of his departure in January 1983. He not only held firm control of the staff through the commission of directors (executive committee) but treated the EFE staff luxuriantly. For his employees, he augmented medical and legal services and acceded to collective labor contract.

Yet all was not always rosy. The 1980-1981 collective bargaining was held between the EFE agency and the negotiating commission of EFE employees. The "slow" negotiations for a union contract were interrupted at the request of the employee commission for a "definitive suspension" on 13 March. As a "definitve solution" was legally required, the EFE agency filed a document with the directorate general of labor, submitting the collective contract to obligatory arbitration on 15 March. Some 10 days later, on 26 March, the Labor office summoned both parties to a preliminary conciliation meeting. EFE reiterated its willingness to accept all provisions of the previous arbitration decision handed down at a 31 October 1979 meeting. In addition, the news agency offered to set up a P3 million (US$45,440) fund for the widows and orphans of EFE employees and to set a P10,000 ($151) minimum monthly pension for the retirees. The union representatives, however, insisted that the pay hike be 13% rather than 11% as offered by the agency. The 2 sides did not agree to the each other's proposal, so the official arbitration was deadlocked.[24]

Anson and employees of the EFE agency performed much better in their next biennial collective bargaining for 1982-1983 contract. By 24 February 1982 they agreed upon a contract and on 11 March presented it to the Labor office. The 52-article contract was very progressive because of a visible ascendancy of socialist elements in Spanish politics, which later led to the landslide victory of the PSOE in the October 1982 elections. The contract provided for, among other things:

> 1. EFE workers were on 33-hour, 6-day workweek, 6 hours on duty daily and with alternate Saturdays off. Any number of hours in excess of the 33-hour workweek would be paid a 50% extra.

2. All employees had a 30-day paid vacation a year, plus 15 days of holidays. In addition to 90-day paid maternity leave decreed by the general labor law of Spain, all employees —female and male too— received a "premium" for birth of each child.

3. The EFE agency could not obligate its writers to sign the news stories which may go against their moral and ideological principles and EFE could not give "by-line" for the stories with which writers did not agree.

4. All employees would be compensated for matriculation and monthly fees incurred for the "courses of study" they pursue.

5. Retirees at age 65 with a minimum of 10-year service would receive pensions equivalent to 100% of their highest salaries, and those retiring at 60 with 20-year service would also receive 100% pension.

6. The EFE agency's medical service was supplementary to the health insurance under the Social Security system. EFE had for all its employees group life and accident insurance policies.[25]

EFE 1981–1982 STATUS

President-Director General Luis María Anson, by his political acumen and entrepreneurial leadership, built the EFE agency up to the number 5 Western, number 3 Latin American, and number one Spanish language "world" news agency during his 6.5 years at the helm. Toward the end of his tenure in 1982, EFE had grown to show an unprecedented scale of operation in news network, technology, production, and finance. Anson was keenly aware of the need to "sell" and promote the EFE agency, now that the state news agency was no longer operating under the privileged status it had once enjoyed in the Franco autocracy. It now had to prove its worth in the highly politicized "democracy" of the post-Franco era.

The EFE news staff at the Madrid headquarters had increased to 735 persons from the 500 of the Mendro and Armesto eras. EFE increased its domestic bureaus from 5 to 13, and its foreign bureaus from 33 to 76 located in 68 countries. About 1,640 journalists toiled at these 86 domestic and overseas bureaus. In all, some 2,200 journalists were gathering news from 5 continents. These EFE news people, in Spain and abroad, provided verbal and photographic news. The total annual wordage went from 135.13 million to 342 million (a 153% boost), which broke down to: 112 million for foreign clients, including 12 million in English and 10 million in French; 30 million words of foreign news to Spanish clients; 63 million words of domestic news to Spanish clients; 47 million words of sport news (both domestic and foreign); 65 million for radio news; and 25 million for television news.

Photo service went from 109,500 photographs processed annually in the late 1960s to 742,800 under Anson (a whopping 578% increase) of which 50,790 were telephotos, supplied through EFE photo and AP and UPI radio photos. EFE's subscribers went from 446 to 1,984 —840 Spanish and 1,144 foreign— clients, which represented an almost 350% increase.

EFE's 1982 Finances

EFE's annual total expenses jumped from P175.46 million (about $2.5 million at 1968 $1 = P70 rate) to P3287.7 million ($29.25 million at 1982 $1 = P112 rate). That was almost 19 times the expenditures of 1968. EFE's annual total revenues went from P168.8 million ($2.41 million) to P2894.6 million ($25.75 million), more than 17 times the pre-Anson revenues. Of these 1982 incomes, nongovernment EFE subscribers paid some P1040.6 million ($9.25 million) —Spanish clients P789.4 million ($7.02 million) and overseas clients a mere P251.2 million ($2.23 million). The agency had sundry non-news revenues of P123.3 million ($1.09 million).

The rest of the 1982 service revenue, some P1730.7 million ($15.4 million), accrued from the "services to the Spanish government." That meant that EFE received almost 60% of its total service revenues from the government. In addition to lopsided service fees it was paid by the government, EFE received a direct government subsidy of P817.2 million ($7.273 million) in 1982. The 1982 receipts from the Spanish government amounted to P2547.9 million ($22.67 million), or some 88% of the aggregate revenues of the agency in 1982!

There was one constant in EFE's economic situation, though. Its balance sheet was always in the minus. Expenses outstripped revenues, but in markedly different scales from the Franco days to the Anson era. The negative balance in 1968 came to only P6.6 million ($94,286), which jumped to P63.1 million ($744,417) in 1977 to P393.1 million ($3.5 million). Of course, the government subsidy of P817.2 million more than covered the loss.

The agency's nominal capital also leaped astronomically during the Anson years. At its 1939 founding, EFE had begun with a meager P10 million ($1.11 million). The capital was doubled by the Fraga–Mendo team to P20 million ($333,333) in 1966. The Sánchez–Armesto duo boosted it to P50 million ($714,286) in 1970. Anson increased it in quick succession to P200 million, P400 million, and P800 million, respectively in 1978, 1979, and 1981 —US$2.70 million, $6.06 million, and $8.69 million at each year's prevailing exchange rate. Anson's capital increase —from P50 million to P800 million— was a whopping 1,500%! Since more than two-thirds of EFE capital belonged to the government and semigovernment entities, these huge increases in capital meant another government outlay for EFE.

Two comments should be made concerning the colossal amounts of government money the agency was getting in the Anson era. First, without an iota of doubt, EFE was a "government" news agency, not only legally but financially, even though, throughout its existence, successive managers claimed EFE was a financially feasible enterprise, with the exception of the Anson management.

Second, Anson did not try to live the fiction of the EFE agency as a nongovernment agency. He was completely open —or the post-Franco era democracy forced him to be open— about the governmental sustenance of the EFE agency. Anson's EFE presidency was the first one to render in its annual memorials (reports) an audited, formal accounting of finances, with a balance sheet and a profit-and-loss statement. In the murky Franco era, there was no such formal accounting of EFE's finances; at least they did not appear in the annual reports. The annual memorials of the Franco era (1939–1975) made spotty and passing references to finances, but never gave audited accounting. This was another indication of Spanish democracy: a change away from secretiveness to openness in the use of the government money.

Table 7.5
EFE Finances, 1982 (in P millions)

CONCEPT	Pre-Anson		Anson Era		Growth %
CAPITAL	50		800		1500
EXPENSES	175.4		3287.7		1774
TOTAL REVENUES	168.8		2894.6		1615
From Services		157.7		2771.3	1657
- Spanish		86.3		789.4	815
- Foreign		71.4		251.2	252
- Government		secret		1730.7	????
Sundry Incomes		11.1		123.3	1011
BALANCE (minus)	(6.6)		(393.1)		5856
GOVT SUBSIDIES	secret		817.2		????

Table 7.5 focuses attention on the scanty gain in revenues from foreign clients, only 252% in a sea of the stupendous increases in all other areas. Only one interpretation emanates from this fact: the EFE news agency was an enterprise of "national" interests, not only of the Spanish government but of the 840 private Spanish media businesses. Spanish newspapers bore a big 815% increase in payment for the EFE news services, which amounted to more than 3 times as much as the burden borne by their 1,144 Latin American colleagues.

Inter-Agency Comparison

How does EFE compare with other international news agencies in the scope of its operations? Comparison is possible with 2 of the "Big 4" (AP

Table 7.6
Interagency Comparison

EFE COMPARED TO OTHER AGENCIES			
Agency	EFE	AP	Reuters	ANSA
Country	Spain	USA	Britain	Italy
Founded in	1939	1848	1851	1853
Nat'l Population	39m	241m	56m	57m
# As of	Dec. 81	Dec. 83	Dec. 83	Dec. 84
Employees	2,200	2,850	3,600	830
Bureaus	95	212	92	106
Domestic	19	132	0	17
Foreign	76	80	92	89
(in # of nations)	(68)	(63)	(64)	(84)
Exchanges	31	41	n/a	65
Subscribers	1,984	15,700	15,000+	957
Domestic	840	7200	0	628
Foreign	1,144	8,500	15,000+	329
(in # of nations)	(30)	(114)	(158)	n/a
Languages Used	3	6	5	4
Wordage	342m	803m	548m	89m
Revenues $	$33m	$188m	$366m	$31m
From Govt $	$18.9m	n/a *	n/a *	$1.16m

m   represents million.
+   Reuters' 15,000+ clients include branches counted separately.
*   AP and Reuters —especially AP— may allege that they do not receive any revenue from the U.S. and U.K. governments. It does not, however, represent reality. They certainly get paid for the news services provided the government agencies at least, which EFE and ANSA openly include in their accounting.

and Reuters) and the Italian ANSA. The data of only these 4 agencies are available to the present author.[26]

EFE compares well with other agencies. Statistical comparisons should be made in relative terms rather than in absolute volumes. EFE was founded in 1939, and is now (in 1989) only 50 years old; AP is 141 years old, Reuters 138 years of age, and ANSA —the successor of Stefani set up in 1853— counts 136 years of history. The 3 other agencies have on an average almost 3 times as long a tradition as EFE. Looked at from that historical angle, EFE was not performing poorly at all. National strength emanates from the national population. The United States, AP's home country, is populated by 6.18 times as many people as Spain, EFE's home. AP in 1983 produced only 2.4 times the 1981 wordage of EFE (803 million versus 342 million). And AP's revenues were only 5.7 times of EFE's ($188 million as opposed to $33 million). Compared to another "national" agency, Spain's EFE outstrips Italy's ANSA in most categories.

MONARCHIST SPRINGTIME

What does the Anson era signify in the overall context of the Spanish press and democracy? He headed the EFE news agency for 6.5 years in the post-Franco "springtime of the Spanish press."[27] The Ansonian tenure at EFE was more an enlightened monarchy than management. He "ruled" the Spanish national news agency with style, a royal splurge. And through his "royal" rule at EFE and his leadership as the president of the Federation of Press Associations of Spain, Anson greatly influenced the way the Spanish press in general shaped itself in post-Franco Spain. Anson made EFE the number 5 Western, number 3 Latin American, and number one Hispanic agency. He played key roles also in cementing the foundation for a democratic Spanish press. The Spaniards, with Anson as a leader in journalism, took on the task of reestablishing a free press in the post-Franco era. For that they took numerous politico-legal steps.

Liberty of Expression Decree

The national referendum of 15 December 1976 approved, by 94%, the Law of Political Reforms and the 15 June 1977 elections opened the door to the liberal monarchy. Among the early reform acts was the Royal Decree

Law of 1 April 1977, which set the tone for a free press. This law on the "Liberty of Expression" was a transitory legal device from the 1966 Fraga Law of Press and Print (LPI) to the 1978 constitution. It freed the Spanish press from Francoist restrictions, but it also put limits on freedom of the press. The new law repealed Article 2 of the 1966 Press Law which had severely limited freedom of expression, enunciated by its Article 1 making it a sham liberty. The decree on "Liberty of Expression" also revoked Article 165b of the 1973 Penal Code, which supplemented the punitive sanctions outlined in the 1966 LPI. The "Liberty of Expression by print and sonorous (radio and television) media" could, however, be limited for such "bigger evils" as attack on public morals and personal honor and reputation.

MCSE (State's Social Communication Media)

The Falange movement press system (*Prensa del Movimiento*) in its heyday operated 37 daily papers, 5 "Monday sheets," 8 weekly and 7 monthly publications, a radio network, and the PYRESA news agency. At Franco's death in 1975, it still showed vestiges of "the most important press complex in Spain, and one of the first of Europe."[28] The democratic Spanish state had to assume reponsibilities for this gigantic press complex. On 15 April 1977 the government decreed into existence an autonomous organism, "Media of Social Communication of the State" (MCSE, *Medios de Comunicación Social del Estado*) for this purpose. Two years later in July 1979 the government closed 6 Movement dailies that were not self-supporting, including Madrid's *Arriba*, Barcelona's *La Prensa* and *Solidaridad Nacional*, and the PYRESA agency.[29] After these actions, the government was still operating the MCSE press, the national television system, 2 radio networks, and the EFE news agency.

New Constitution

The new Spanish constitution was passed by another referendum on 6 December 1978 ("Constitution Day"). Its Article 20 recognizes and protects press, academic, and communication freedoms, and prohibits all prior censorships. This article, however, sets limits (only by law) on these freedoms for the right "to the honor, the intimacy, the [persons'] own image, and the protection of the youth and the infancy" (Article 20.4). It also stipulates that the seizure of any information media can be authorized only by judiciary resolutions or court warrants (Article 20.5).

Directly relevant to the EFE news agency is Article 20.3, for it provides for future legislation on "the organization and parliamentary control" of the MCSE or any other public communication entity, access to which would be guaranteed to the "pluralism" of the social and linguistic groups of Spain. To this date (April 1989), however, no legislation has been realized either by the center-right or by the socialist government to give constitutional basis to the EFE news agency or any other state communication media and they are all still operating under their individual mercantile statutes.

A Draft Press Law

After the promulgation of the 1978 constitution, Spanish journalists were divided over whether or not it was in the interest of a free press to legislate a press law, thus detailing the rights and responsibilities broadly stated in the new constitution. EFE president Anson, who was also head of the Federation of Press Associations of Spain, supported such legislation. A draft press law was worked out. Two provisions in the draft law caused controversy. First, it would maintain the old press accreditation system by means of enrollment in the Registry of Professional Journalists. Second, it would allow accreditation only to the graduates of recognized journalism schools (Journalism Division of the Faculty of Information Sciences, which had replaced the old Official Schools of Journalism in 1976).

This was in keeping with the centuries-old Spanish custom, which dated back further than the Francoist dictatorship. The idea behind this tradition was that journalists should be licensed and respected —and their incomes guaranteed accordingly— just like physicians, lawyers, architects, dentists, accountants, auditors, pharmacists, engineers, and other professionals. Some argued that journalists' responsibilities were greater than those of other professions, for journalists deal with the much wider interests of society as a whole, as opposed to other professionals whose focus is more on individual, private interests. This idea above all was consonant with the monarchist hierarchical world view of EFE president Anson, that is, all human endeavors should be systematized clearly by legal dispositions.

Spain was going through great democratic changes and divergent interest groups were willing and getting accustomed to compromise and reconciliation. To resolve the devastating crisis caused by an inflationary economy, for example, the government, the opposition parties, and the trade unions had signed at the Moncloa Palace the Moncloa Pact on economic austerity measures in October 1977. A journalistic version of the compromise pact, similar in spirit to the economic Moncloa Pact, was signed on 16 October 1980 among the national press federation led by Anson, the Union of Journalists (UDP, or Unión de Periodistas), the media component of the ultra-left Workers' Commissions (CC.OO.=Comisiones Obreras), and the media branch of the center-left General Union of Workers (UGT, Unión General de Trabajadores). These unions agreed to 2-track access to press professions —by work experience or accredited college degree. All 4 parties supported the idea of limiting media ownership to Spaniards —both natural and legal persons— and civil-law trial of all offenses dealing with press, as opposed to military tribunals of the Franco years.

The agreement specified 3 additional provisions. All parties would attempt to give priority in hiring to unemployed journalists; would give press workers a voice in important editorial decisions; and would spell out the rights to secrecy as provided for in the constitution.

A Law on Limits of Freedom

Two years after the agreement on the Anson draft press law, the government turned to implementing Article 20.4 of the constitution on the limits to liberty of expression. The 1982 Organic Law on the Limitations to the Liberty of Expression spelled out in minutest detail that the freedom of people could only be limited for the reasons of "the honor, intimacy, [person's] own image, and protection of the youth and infancy." The law was not only meticulously crafted by its lengthy 9 articles —each had numerous subparagraphs— but it was also given the category of the Organic Laws of Spain, meaning they are "fundamental" laws, lower in effects only to the constitution.[30] Post-Franco Spain would not dispose lightly with the limitations of press freedom. The old Francoist 1966 LPI had limited the freedom given in its Article 1 immediately in Article 2. Spaniards had come to cherish their basic freedoms, and had made certain to guarantee them for their own good.

A Decree on Foreign Correspondents

Finally, the government did away with various legal means that the old Francoist regime had devised to control the foreign correspondents assigned to Spain. A royal decree of 29 December 1982 accorded almost complete freedoms, as much as given to the Spanish press, to foreign journalists assigned to Spain. But, at the same time, the decree cancelled all former privileges that had been granted to foreign journalists, such as reduced public transportation fares, free or discount-rate accommodation in national tourism hotels, gasoline ration coupons, and many other amenities, which had been utilized "by the dictatorship as incentive or bribe."[31]

The parliamentary democracy prevailing in the post-Franco era was also applied to the way EFE was run by Anson. His rule at EFE was always based on the democratic processes —never a spontaneous dictate that his predecessors could afford under the "bigger" dictatorship of the Franco regime. Anson had the statutes of the EFE agency reformed 4 times, principally to boost the amount of the EFE agency's social capital (from P50 million to P200 million to P400 million to P800 million). But to achieve these and other basic reforms in EFE, Anson went by the democratic game plans to the hilt. Anson formed the standing committee within the administrative council and also established the executive committee of directors.

He also instituted an EFE employee referendum to solicit rank-and-file participation in the major changes. Anson was not legally required to do this; he only needed authorization by an extraordinary general assembly (junta) of EFE stockholders. But he knew that almost 70% of EFE stocks were controlled by the state and semistate entities, and the remaining stocks were fragmented among 376 stockholders who did not have any real power. So, the general junta of EFE stockholders was not a fundamentally democratic institution. The EFE referendum accorded the statutes of November 1977 overwhelming approval. After the "democratic ceremony," the "employee-subjects" could not claim their "monarchist leader was ruling" them without their consent.

By the referendum, EFE employees endorsed the 1977 statutes which contained important reforms besides quadrupling the EFE capital from P50 million to P200 million. The reform measures claimed to pursue "the maximum professionalization" of the EFE news agency. Its president and/or director-general "must be professional journalists with a minimum of 10 years of experience and with no political affiliation in the three years prior to their appointment" to their EFE positions. Also future department heads "will be selected from professionals with at least 2-year experiences in the Agency." These measures purported to shield the EFE agency against political intrusion under the volatile environment of post-Franco Spain.

In the bigger context of the Spanish press in general —and in the narrower perspective of the EFE agency in particular— the Anson years (1976 – 1982) represented a real springtime of gigantic strides. In the opinion of Juan Luis Cebrián,[32] director of *El País*, the new (from 1976) leading Spanish daily, the Anson era signified 3 things for the EFE agency —and by extension, for the Spanish press also: "(1) tremendous expansions, (2) technological renovations, and (3) financial crises." Anson showed prowess in all 3 areas.

And even in the financial crises, with which the EFE agency was confronted for the needs of geographical expansion and technological renovations, he proved his political clout. Anson wrenched away from the impoverished Spanish government astronomical sums in payment of EFE services and direct subsidies: in 1980 EFE received P1.12 billion ($15.5 million), in 1981 P1.74 billion ($18.9 million), and finally, in 1982 P2.55 billion ($22.7 million).[33] Anson was a doer.

MUDSLINGING

A "dictatorless" democratic Spain from 1976 was fraught with infighting; any politician was fair game, any accomplishment subject to criticism, and any enterprise a target of scrutiny. Anson was no exception, and his successful management of EFE was not spared. From the very beginning of his tenure at EFE, Anson was plagued by attacks from many hostile groups. Throughout his tenure at EFE, Anson successfully fended off the assaults that never ceased coming from divergent quarters.

Anson's Salary

The first offensive came from the first enemy Anson had disposed of during the very first month of his EFE tenure, Carlos Mendo, who had been renamed the EFE director on 12 February 1976. Anson had staged a "palace coup" and fired EFE director Mendo in October 1976, when Mendo was away on a royal tour with King Juan Carlos I in Colombia. Anson then became the EFE president and director-general. Since his mentor, Manuel Fraga, had resigned from the government in July 1976, Mendo did not have any governmental backing. So, Mendo turned to Anson's perceived enemies. An October 1976 issue of the news magazine, *Cambio 16* (*Change 16*), carried a story, which, citing Mendo with his picture in the story, accused Anson of "paying himself" a fabulous monthly salary of P300,000 (US$4,423).[34] The magazine was published by a group of 16 persons of liberal and definitely antimonarchist tendencies who had formed the "Grupo 16" in 1970. The group had anticipated changes that would result when Franco disappeared from the scene.

Anson rebutted the magazine story and had an EFE spokesman give lie to the version. The spokesman affirmed that Anson's salary was only P30,000 ($442) monthly —"exactly half of what his predecessor collected," that is, as his allowance as the president of EFE. The EFE man further confirmed that Anson also received an amount as the EFE director-general, "which will be exactly the same as the amount for his predecessor [Mendo] —minus the pay the latter [Mendo] got as the EFE manager." It should be recalled that EFE's director had also been the manager until Anson eliminated the "director-manager" position, and created for himself the position of director-general. Anson's spokesman added that Mendo had received a severance pay amounting to a half of his annual salary, and would continue as an advisor for "exterior actions" of the EFE agency.

At any rate it was not an elegant scene that resulted from the flak, exposing the private salary matters in the extremely status-sensitive Spanish society. It resulted, however, in a draw between Anson and his adversaries. Anson escaped the first hassle without much injury.

EFE Board Reshuffle En Masse

Over the years the membership of the EFE administrative council (board of directors) had grown to an unwieldy size: 23 voting directors, 4 nonvoting personnel representatives, and a nonvoting secretary. In 1979 Anson chose 7 out of 23 to form a standing committee, including himself as president. The decision-making process was thus streamlined was transformed into an Anson machinery. Most of the 16 directors excluded from this Anson inner circle represented the Spanish press, some of them continuously on the EFE board, going back to the late 1960s, when Mendo would boast that more than half of the EFE board was from the press. They naturally did not take kindly to the Anson maneuver. In mid-June 1980, these press-component members resigned from the board, half in protest and also half prodded by the Anson force; they could not see any meaning in their ceremonial board positions. The incident seemed to shake the EFE agency at its legal foundation. If 16 of 23 board members —almost 70%— resigned, was this not a repudiation of the current EFE management? Some critics found it to be "fundamentally bound to the conflicts and polemics surrounding the future organization and structure of the journalism profession in Spain."[35]

Anson survived this storm, and came out of the shakeup with his power base even more firmly solidified. He went on to appoint 6 new board members, bringing the total membership to a more manageable 13. He also trimmed the standing committee membership from 7 to 5 and eliminated the 4-member Labor representation on the board. He no longer needed it to counterbalance the EFE board, whose composition had been lopsidedly pro-press. Anson had all the fundamental changes to the EFE power structure quickly ratified by the next ordinary annual stockholders' assembly.

The assembly gave Anson authority to have the EFE statutes reformed by extraordinary general assemblies of EFE stockholders. Thus, Anson gained a monarchistic omnipotence in EFE without doing serious damage to its democratic facade. Anson won this one.

Europa Press Fracas

The next controversy was provoked by EFE itself and Anson came out of it with a black eye. An EFE story in mid-October 1981 suggested that the Europa Press, a private agency, "has stood out in the past months by 'filtering' (leaking) news and declarations of the defense attorneys" of the military officers implicated in the coup attempt at the Spanish Cortes on 23 February. The Europa Press shot back with a sharp 4-point rebuttal. Two out of the 4 points hit particularly hard:

> 1. EUROPA PRESS . . . revealed —not filtered— the text of the conclusions of the prosecution report and the part of the indictment . . . that it considered more important, . . . and when the indictment already was in the phase of plenary court and, therefore, had ceased to be secret. . . . [The] complete information obtained and facilitated by EUROPA PRESS has served . . . to impede any manipulation based on partial information or half truths.

> 3. EUROPA PRESS has never figured in classified reports as coup conspirators, . . . nor been obliged to rectify laudatory declarations in favor of those implicated in coups d'etat, . . . nor had to resort to such poor procedures as *copying in systematic manner the news of others* (emphasis added).

The implication was that EFE, when scooped by its much smaller competitors like Europa Press, would plagiarize others' stories in the form of commentary, as it had done in this particular case. Europa Press was joined in this fight by the *Diario 16* and the communist parliamentary group. The daily carried the news on the EFE-Europa Press spat by describing how the communist congress deputies had formulated an accusatory question to the government on "the [plagiarizing] posture the state news agency EFE had adopted." The *Diario 16* headlined the front-page news, "Bruising Responses of EUROPA PRESS to EFE,"[36] thus adding salt to EFE's wounds.

Parliamentary Attacks

As exemplified in the Europa Press case above, the opposition left groups in the Spanish Congress were ever watchful of real or imagined missteps of EFE and the administration in power, which they perceived to be exploiting EFE for its partisan interests. On 23 October 1981 the PCE (Spanish Communist Party) group in the Cortes presented a motion in the lower house, demanding that the government send up a bill to "regulate the EFE agency in accord with the Constitutional requirements" and also to "appoint new EFE president of the state entity, subject to approval by the Congress." The PCE motion gave the government 3 months to satisfy Article 20.3 of the constitution, which stipulated that all MCSE outlets (Medios de Comunicación Social del Estado), including the EFE agency, should and must come under "the parliamentary control."

The acerbic text of the PCE motion pointed out that 3 lengthy years had passed since the promulgation of the constitution, during which the administration had not taken legislative initiative to bring the EFE agency under the parliamentary control as required by Article 20.3 of the constitution. Thus, the PCE motion added, the EFE agency had come "acting until our days as a mere administrative organism under government dependence" which compromised the principles of "objectivity, truthfulness, and impartiality of information, with respect to political, religious, social, cultural, and linguistic pluralism." In other words, the PCE deputies were accusing the administration of legislative foot dragging on the EFE news agency, because the state-funded news service favored the party in power in its news coverage and distribution. They specifically demanded "the immediate removal of the current president of EFE Luis María Anson" for the "lack of 'professionality' in his appointments of the directive personnel" of the state news agency.

Anson's enemies in Spanish press circles joined the PCE assault, giving the communist motion a prominent play in their news coverage, which they usually did not accord the party (PCE) of Santiago Carrillo. "Anson's paper," *ABC*, tried to ignore the news, but the other 2 new and leading dailies, *El País* and *Diario 16*, gave it a big play,[37] though the general Spanish public did not have a keen interest or a ready comprehension of the affair. The Spanish press was making news about itself in an orchestrated attack on EFE under Anson. (To this date —April 1989— the PSOE government in power since late 1982 has yet to implement Article 20.3 of the constitution. The *ABC*, now under the editorship of Anson, has been turning on the socialists with the same club that they used to wield on "the Centrist group's inertia" in the MCSE legislation.)

ANSON DENOUEMENT

As 1982 rolled around, Anson, though besieged by internal politics, was actively engaged in external expansion and technological innovations. The year 1982 provided Anson's EFE with transcendental events.

Malvinas/Falklands War

Argentina was crying for solutions to its worsening domestic crises in early 1982.[38] Lt. Gen. Leopoldo Galtieri had assumed power in the Argentine junta on 22 December 1981. He faced increasing popular resistance to military rule during the first months of 1982. The reasons were twofold: The national economy was worsening, and there was that horrendous "dirty war on the Reds" —"disappearance" by death squads of thousands of dissidents.

To divert internal and external attentions away from the deteriorating situation, Argentina's armed forces invaded the British-occupied Falklands Islands (called Islas Malvinas by Hispanic America) on 2 April 1982. Sovereignty over the south Atlantic islands had long been in dispute between Argentina and the United Kingdom. The British government astonished the world and dealt a deadly blow to the Argentine military invaders with counterattacks originating from halfway around the world. The Hispanic nations and the Third World in general, although condemning the military atrocities in Argentina, turned out clearly against the vestiges of British imperialism.

Anson's EFE, the Hispanic American news agency, naturally took the Argentine side, against the old "enemy" Britain, which held on to Gibraltar. EFE offered its Iberoamerican subscribers "the point of view and the focus [which were] more 'objective and independent' of Anglo-Saxon news agencies."[39] EFE's Latin American clients could present "balanced" coverage of the war's progress "thanks to EFE's efforts." EFE distributed with efficiency news on such spectacular battle operations as the sinking of the Argentine cruiser *General Belgrano*, on 2 May, and of the British frigate, HMS *Sheffield* by an Exocet missile on 4 May.

EFE's bureaus in Europe and the Americas supplied the Hispanic version of multi-point events throughout the war: actions at the UN Security Council, trade sanctions imposed by the European Common Market (EC) on Argentina, mediation attempts by President Fernando Belaunde Terry of Peru and U.S. Secretary of State Alexander Haig, and a condemnation of the British posture by the Organization of American States (OAS). This was the first time, in anyone's memory, that a major international wire service [EFE] "covered with balanced eyes" an Anglo-Hispanoamerican conflict, and EFE's Latin clients were appreciative of the the Ibero-American news agency.[40]

World-Cup Soccer

Hot on the heels of the Malvinas/Falklands War, there opened in Madrid the 1982 Association Football (Soccer) World Cup championship, which lasted from 13 June through 11 July. Teams from 24 nations vied at 17 centers in Spain for the coveted World Cup of the most popular sport of the world. EFE pulled out all the plugs on these quadrennial premier sport events, taking place in Spain for the first time since the 1930 founding of the World Cup. EFE's coverage had begun months before the actual games, with more than 150 stories a day to Spanish and Hispanic American clients, "without disregarding other important news such as the Malvinas War." Seven Latin American national teams were among the 24 finalists. During the games, EFE-Sports sent out more than 350 dispatches daily. EFE's new radio-television distributed 225 feeds to 13 broadcast channels before the matches, with weekly "Pre-World Cup 82, Date in Spain," and during the games, with a daily program called, "World Cup 82, Match in Spain" EFE-TV helped the national Televisión Española (TVE) in its game coverage and facilities provided for foreign broadcasters. Through these "impressive achievements" by the Spanish national television in the "most important international broadcasting event of the year," more than 1 billion people around the world viewed the World Cup finals.[41] (Italy won the 1982 Cup by defeating West Germany 3-1.)

Socialist Landslide and Papal Visit

The center-right coalition under the umbrella of the Unión de Centro Democrático (UCD) —which had governed Spain since July 1976— disintegrated in late 1981 and in 1982. Three coalition components splintered away: the Democratic Action Party (PAD), Popular Democratic Party (PDP) and Liberal Democratic Party (PDL). No longer holding the governing majority, the UCD administration had to dissolve the Cortes on 27 August and call elections scheduled for 28 October. In the race were the UCD, socialist PSOE, social-democrat CDS, communist PCE, and Alianza Popular (AP) led by Fraga Iribarne, former (1962–1969) minister of information and tourism, and short-term (1975–1977) interior minister.

EFE assigned a writer-photographer team to each of the parties in the race. These teams accompanied the candidates throughout Spain, covering their campaign speeches and the human-interest side of their actions. EFE's 13 regional bureaus transmitted to the Madrid Central the campaign news and photographs. On election day (28 October), EFE mounted a special ballot news center at the Palace of Congresses and Expositions with 3 VDT terminals, for a 24-hour transmission of verbal and photographic news. EFE bureaus in the Americas offered ballot-counts through the night of 28–29 October. Spanish communities in the Americas, Spanish diplomatic and consular legations around the world, and politicians and pundits of Latin America followed the election results through the EFE bureaus. The elections resulted in a landslide for the PSOE, which garnered some 46% of the popular votes versus the 25% received by the AP.

In the middle of the election campaigns, the Vatican announced on 7 September its decision to postpone the papal visit to Spain on the advice of the Spanish bishops. Pope John Paul II had scheduled a mid-October tour of Spain, which he now was delaying until early November. The major left-wing opposition parties had expressed the view that the pope's visit would bolster conservative voting in the elections. When the pope finally came after the elections, EFE gave the visit a "studied" extent of coverage, definitely less expansive than its live broadcast of the election-victory speech and interview to the Americas of socialist prime minister-elect Felipe González Márquez.

With the victory of the socialists, monarchist Anson's fate as president of EFE was doomed; no amount of papal blessing or of catering to the future premier could save Anson. And Anson knew it, for he himself had been a "political appointee" of the UCD premier, Adolfo Suárez. But Anson still tried to save "his" EFE agency in 2 transparent moves.

On 29 October, the day after the general elections, Anson tendered resignation as the director-general —but not as the president— of the EFE agency at the monthly meeting of the EFE administrative council. Anson had held off this required monthly meeting until the last possible day —Friday the 29th— hoping against hope that the UCD might still hold on to some political sway. By taking off one hat, Anson would be only the president. The job of director-general could be given to someone else. It was Anson's way of indicating to the incoming PSOE government that he was flexible and ready to negotiate.

Anson mounted a campaign in December 1982 to dissociate the EFE news agency from the Franco dictatorship, which had founded it in 1938. By this campaign, Anson was beating on the drum that the EFE news agency was a "national" enterprise, not belonging to any particular government. The campaign attempted to persuade the public, and especially the incoming PSOE administration, that the title *EFE* was unrelated to *F-efe* in the Spanish alphabet for the "*F*-alange" and its magazine *Fe* (*Faith*) or the name "*F*-ranco."

All this mattered little. The PSOE government assumed power on 2 December. When the new administration turned to the business of the state news agency EFE, Luis María Anson Oliart was summarily dismissed also as the president of EFE on 25 January 1983. For Anson, the doer, the last hurrahs had been the Malvinas War, the World Cup Soccer Championship, and, ironically, the 1982 general elections which his EFE could cover so efficiently, thanks to the expansion and technological advances he had accomplished during his 6.5-year EFE tenure. Anson went back to his monarchist newspaper, *ABC*, as director.

The Anson Transition

Anson, the *parliamentary monarchist*, had assumed the top posts of Spain's national news agency created by the *Francoist autocracy*. Through his many-splendored management, Anson carried the EFE agency to a leadership position in the democratizing process of the post-Franco Spain. Now the *socialists* were taking over the destiny of the new Spain. They would also lead the EFE news agency in their own way.

Chapter 8

On U.S. Wavelength
(1983-1986)

The victorious Spanish Socialist Workers Party (PSOE) formed the government led by Felipe González Márquez, and it formally assumed power on 2 December 1982. There took place many political appointents in the state-run entities. EFE's turn arrived in less than 2 months. As in all other political moves, the socialists effected radical changes inthe EFE news agency.

COMMAND CHANGES IV

The new PSOE administration restructured the EFE agency into an outright government news organization. First, it dismissed all 10 members of the EFE administrative council, including president Anson, on 25 January 1983. An extraordinary session of the general junta of EFE stockholders, convened on that day, appointed the new council, with Ricardo Utrilla Carlón at its head as the new president. Since the government and various public entities owned some 98% of EFE stock, the PSOE made all the decisions concerning the organization of the government news agency. The new EFE council included 7 members related to the government, and the "independent" councilors were soon removed.[1]

The socialist administration did not even pretend to present a facade of "independent and autonomous" EFE agency, which the previous Franco and monarchist regimes had feigned. And EFE's new president, Ricardo Utrilla, formulated and carried out that PSOE policy throughout his 4-year tenure at the state news agency.

In the late fall of 1984, EFE president Utrilla was winding up his periodic tour of the Americas with a visit to the EFE bureau in Washington, D.C. He was having lunch with a young —age 29— bureau member, Georgina Rosa Higueras (and an invited U.S. academic). They were engaged in shop-talk such as: his explanation to the young reporter of the difference between currency devaluation and revaluation, and how they both got their EFE jobs. Utrilla casually mentioned that he had obtained the job of EFE president "because I had a good friend." Extremely intrigued by his candidly humble remark before his subordinate, the U.S. academic inquired some months later with Utrilla who that "good friend" had been. Utrilla replied that Felipe González Márquez had been that friend and that the PSOE premier had picked him as EFE president "because I am the best news-agency journalist of Spain." The apparent arrogance in his response not only sharply contrasted with his earlier humility but correctly reflected his condescending attitude.[2]

Ricardo Utrilla Carlón was born in 1935 —as was his immediate EFE predecessor Luis María Anson— the year before the outbreak of the Spanish civil war. Both men came of age under the Franco rule. Like virtually all Spanish journalists, both were graduates of the "Escuela Oficial de Periodismo" (EOP) —Official School of Journalism. Each then went different ways in the profession. Anson became a print journalist, while Utrilla —like both men's EFE predecessor Carlos Mendo— went into news-agency journalism. Upon graduation from the EOP, Utrilla worked for 3 years at the EFE international desk. In 1960 he was hired by AFP as an associate editor in the Spanish service at its Paris headquarters. In 1969, the French wire service dispatched Utrilla as correspondent at its Washington, D.C., bureau, where in a 3-year sojourn, he learned the intricacies of news business in the world news capital.

This exposure to Washington journalism later led Utrilla to emphasize U.S. capital much more readily than his 2 predecessors, who were more "Ibero-American" in outlook. In 1972 Utrilla came home to Spain to assume the editorship of the weekly magazine, *Cambio16* (*Change 16*), established in 1970 by the "Grupo 16" (Group 16), comprised of 16 reform-minded Spaniards. While he was in Washington as AFP correspondent, Utrilla also moonlighted for the new Spanish magazine. Grupo 16, in 1976, launched a new Madrid paper, *Diario 16* (*Daily 16*), with Utrilla as director (editor), during the post-Franco "avalanche" of new publications. A year later, in March 1977, Utrilla left the editorship of the now number 3 capital daily to younger journalists, but he continued as director of the publishing house Cambio 16, until he was picked as the new EFE president in January 1983.[3]

THE UTRILLA ERA

Utrilla's claim to be "Spain's best news-agency journalist" is largely based on his 16-year wire serive (mostly AFP) experience. His management style contrasted that of his predecessor Anson, a print-media journalist. The difference was dramatized by a deeply held mutual enmity.

Belt-Tightening Adjustments

The wire-service man Utrilla has been a nitty-gritty EFE president, unlike Anson who sought glory in EFE's grandiose expansionist schemes. As his first task as EFE president, Utrilla took belt-tightening measures on the bloated EFE finances and reined in the overextended structure of EFE, all the while blaming the alleged "excesses of the Anson administration."

One of the first austerity measures —"rationalization" of EFE services— was dissolution of the ACHA news service (Agencia de Comunicaciones Hispano-Americana) headquartered in Houston. Utrilla conspicuously placed this "readjustment" of "inoperative and redundant" services in the very first page of EFE's 1983 annual memorial. The obvious political implication was that Anson had squandered scarce resources in this luxurious operation. ACHA news subscribers would now be provided regular EFE news through normal channels.

Anson had purchased 15 buildings to house 12 foreign and 3 domestic bureaus, plus 4 flats for 4 other domestic bureaus. "With the view to profitable operations," Utrilla quickly initiated the liquidation process on some of the properties that were "little or not fit for the activity" of EFE. He indicated that some buildings had been "overvalued at their purchase." Anson did not stay silent to the charges of having made bad buys of "palaces at overvalued prices." Even finance ministry auditors acknowledged the current values of the real estate came to at least P587 million ($3.86 million), a whopping 71% increment over and beyond the original investments.[4]

Anson's director-committee apparatus also got Utrilla's retrenchment axe. He demoted all 12 [5] to simple "chiefs" (*jefes*), not only in title but in salary and perks. He accused Anson of having hiked the salaries of these directors 20 to 28%, much above the 13.42%, as determined by the collective labor contract without authorization from the EFE administrative council, "necessary to establish these increases."[6] Utrilla readily acknowledged there was a certain malaise among EFE workers. His cuts were applied not only to these "directors" but to all employees. Utrilla did not make any excuses; he insisted that these measures were unavoidable in order to "rectify the excesses" inherited from Anson. Utrilla "reined in" severely on EFE expenditures too. His retrenchment measures naturally exposed Anson but they also exposed Utrilla to counterattacks. There followed acrimonious charges and countercharges between the 2 men, who used the news media at their disposal to engage in the brawl.

MUDSLINGING II

Anson's monarchistic reign over the EFE news agency had been the target of constant attacks from the Spanish liberal clusters, such as 2 new Madrid newspapers *El País* and *Diario 16*, and the private agency Europa Press which resented a David-Goliath advantage of the state agency EFE. In post-Franco Spain, EFE was fair game for bitter personal criticism from all sectors. During Anson's EFE tenure, the ever-watchful press and political circles had accused him of many "excesses" in management. After his departure, reproaches continued over Anson's alleged wrongdoings at EFE, which he denied —and also counterattacked Utrilla's work— now through the columns of the powerful monarchist daily, *ABC*, to which Anson had returned as director.

Anson's "News Piracy"

In mid-October 1981 Europa Press had ridiculed Anson's EFE for "the process of copying other people's news scoops" in disguise of commenting on news EFE had missed. In February 1983, the very first month of the Utrilla era, "the new EFE team stopped 'flagrant journalistic piracies' practiced by the state agency during the days of Luis María Anson." This was carried as big news on 16 March 1983 in *Diario 16*, Utrilla's former daily, which greatly expanded on "a communique diffused by EUROPA PRESS" the previous day.[7] The old anti-Anson alliance was now out to "get" Anson. The story depicted the alleged Ansonian mischief as much more malign than the mere "procedure of copying other people's scoops by commenting on them." The story affirmed that Anson had been engaged in "such a sultry disloyal competition" as paying a third-party reporter to subscribe to Europa Press (EP) service, whose news then was plagiarized outright. The "expose story on Anson's piracy" said that, on several occasions, EP addressed the "high EFE executives," requesting them to terminate "these anomalies" without satisfactory results.[8]

Utrilla's Sellout to UPI

When Utrilla became its president in 1983, EFE had had almost a 40-year relationship with UPI. Since 1945, EFE exclusively distributed the UP and later UPI verbal and photo services to Spanish subscribers. This, however, had always been a one-way deal. In the fall of 1983 when he moved his Washington bureau into the new UPI headquarters, Utrilla could turn the long EFE-UPI relation into "a 2-way collaboration: Now UPI broadcasts the EFE news."[9] EFE and UPI were now engaged in an experimental arrangement to feed EFE news to Spanish-language radio stations in the United States. EFE and UPI called the new program "Nuestras Noticias" (Our News, stressing 'our [Spanish] news'). It was launched "to penetrate potential markets of 500 Spanish-language stations in an area of high income."

Well accepted from the beginning, the program grew into a 45-station U.S. radio network, with 10 additional stations in Puerto Rico and one in Mexico by the end of 1985 and was also allegedly heard in Spain and South America.[10] Conservative press and parliamentary circles thrashed the deal as a sellout of Spanish interests to UPI which "sought to make the Spanish national agency its satellite in the Hispanoamerican area."[11] Former EFE president Anson, who had taken both EFE and ACAN-EFE into the U.S.-dominated IAPA-SIP (Inter American Press Association) in his days, pointed out that the UPI-EFE program "would damage the Spanish information sovereignty, for its content is edited by UPI." José Luis Roldán, commented that he feared Nuestras Noticias would "distort the image of EFE" and warned of "the evident risk to the future independence of EFE exposed to the foreign monopolies.[12]

In spite of these xenophobic criticisms, the UPI-EFE radio news program continued. And in retrospect, the intimacy with UPI's operation, developed through the Nuestras Noticias program, contributed to inspiring Utrilla's EFE to aspire for partial ownership of the UPI in bankruptcy and engage in the 1985–1986 bidding war.

"Unconstitutional" EFE Statutes

Both Anson and Utrilla, like other EFE directors, reformed EFE statutes. These reforms became the targets of bitter feuds. The 1981 Anson statutes stipulated that both the president and director-general should have a minimum of 10 years' journalistic experience; and must not belong, or to have belonged to any political party in the 3 years before the EFE appointment.[13] Utrilla claimed that the latter conditions were "unconstitutional," and declared that it would be tantamount to "prohibiting from assuming the EFE positions to those who are not Catholics, whites, or even male."[14] Then Utrilla made his own changes to these qualifications and extended the restrictions to the members of the EFE administrative council, plus any other "directive" personnel. These EFE posts were "incompatible with" (1) the exercise of "parliamentary representation" and also (2) "any direct or indirect bond (*vinculación*) with other social communication media and enterprises producing radio and television programs or advertising" (*publicidad*).[15]

Condition 1 made it possible for political partisans to be appointed to high EFE posts, as long as they were not elected to the Cortes. Anson had excluded any party members from these positions. Condition 2 was a direct antithesis to the Ansonian requirements that the EFE president and director-general be professional journalists with a minimum 10-year experience. Under the Utrilla statute, not only the EFE president, director-general, and other high management personnel, but the administrative councilors as well would have to resign from mass communications positions in order to be able to serve in the top EFE management. Anson called the first Utrilla condition "unconstitutional" in an eye-for-eye payback to Utrilla's charge. Anson saw the second Utrillan stipulation as a sinister attempt to drive "competing and competent" journalists out of the EFE administrative council.

In the studied opinion of the present author, the statute controversy ended in a draw. On the "incompatibility" between the political partisanship and EFE management positions, Utrilla seems to have made a reasonable judgment. In a politically active, democratic post-Franco Spain, to exclude party militants up to 3 years previous to the EFE appointment —as Anson had attempted— was too restrictive a requirement, even undemocratic. Utrilla was also correct in excluding the current parliamentarians from top EFE posts; they would have too much political influence on EFE's basic structure.

Utrilla seems to have made a healthy decision to prohibit mass communications practitioners from simultaneously taking the post of EFE president and director-general. But it was unprofessional for him to try to apply that requirement to all EFE "directive" personnel, including the EFE councilors. The more journalistic participation in the EFE council, the better professionally qualified the council would be for the news agency. Anson and Carlos Mendo professed to have done their best to accord more press participation to EFE.[16] Utrilla's move to exclude other journalists from the

EFE council tended to show his desire to preclude journalistic competition at the top decision-making body of the news agency.

In his EFE council, Utrilla was the only journalist, surrounded by bureaucratic representatives of state entities, which owned 98% of EFE stocks. He, in fact, never promoted media participation in the EFE stockholders' general assembly (junta) either. Utrilla presided over an outright state news agency, all the while opposing vehemently —in a tremendous self-contradiction— parliamentary control of the EFE news agency, as envisaged in Article 20.3 of the 1978 Spanish constitution. Even the state-owned AFP —for which he worked for more than a dozen years— provides for strong media participation in its financial-administrative structure.

"J'Accuse" EFE Audits

Charges of Ansonian financial mismanagement were fought over a 1.5-year period, commencing in February 1983, immediately after Utrilla's takeover of EFE, and fizzling out in July 1984. Upon assuming the EFE post in January 1983, Utrilla requested a specific audit of Anson's EFE finances of 1982. The parliament under PSOE control also ordered comprehensive EFE audits of the years 1978–1982 by the Accounting Tribunal. Anson later claimed that he had been subjected to "no fewer than 12 audits in all."[17] Six audits by the Finance Ministry, and 5 by the Instituto Nacional de Industria (INI is 1/3 EFE owner) consumed 8 months of 1983. (These 11 audits will henceforth be referred to as "Finance Ministry" or "ministry" audits, since the INI interventors reported their audit results to the ministry.) A comprehensive audit by the Accounting Tribunal of the 1978–1982 EFE records occupied the entire 18-month period. (These inspections of the 1978–1982 accounting will be henceforward called the "Accounting Tribunal" or "tribunal" audit.)

After a 4-month check of Anson's 1982 books by the Finance Ministry, pro-Utrilla *El País* scooped preliminary audit figures on 24 June 1983, and publicized a 1982 EFE loss of P393.1 million (US$3.5 million at $1 = P112.4), and the 1978–1982 accumulated loss of P1.108 billion ($9.86 million). It blamed these losses on Anson's "important deviations in the salary and real estate investment policy."

Anson's *ABC* reported the story from an exactly opposite perspective. Its 24 June 1983 issue headlined, "The EFE Audit Without A Problem of Depth," implying that there may have been some minor flaws but no fundamental problems. The next day, Anson's paper had a longer story, headlined: "Not One Expense Without Justifying in the Audit of EFE." In it, Anson gave a detailed 10-point rebuttal to the story in *El País* of the previous day. *ABC*'s stories claimed that *El País* was running a "campaign of manipulation" against Anson and his paper.

The church paper, *Ya*, attempted to play middle ground, reporting on the polemics on both sides. The debate raged for the entire week, in which the *Diario 16* (Utrilla's old paper) even appeared to try to recruit the support of EFE's labor by bringing into the fray José Luis Roldán, president of the EFE union's committee before the business. He was reported to have "declared the EFE union committee in permanent session" to present the grievances, faced with the fantastic EFE losses being debated. Roldán would play an important role, but to the consternation of Utrilla, he would turn out to be a critical enemy.

The week-long dust storm on the 1982 audit was put down on 30 June 1983 by the sheer literary prowess of well-read Anson. His *ABC* published a signed article by Anson himself entitled, "I DENOUNCE," in which he eloquently expounded in the style of Emile Zola's *J'accuse* (I accuse) letter of 1898:[18]

> I denounce the audit of EFE as an offense against the liberty of expression. I denounce that audit as a political maneuver. I denounce it as an intellectual terrorism that attempts to silence the moderate criticism of *ABC* on the socialist policy. I denounce that a planned campaign is in march against the journalistic writers and professionals. I denounce that, in the press, radio, television and [news] agencies, my journalistic colleagues are threatened with the silence, the scandal or the unemployment.

He then closed his open letter with an expression of hope and optimism about the future of Spain. Said he:

> The liberty without fears or menaces so that we can exercise this profession in benefit of all will open new roads of hope, for all is not negative in Spain, but, to the contrary, there are reasons for the optimism and the clean horizons.

The "I DENOUNCE" open-letter article worked a miracle; it shut up the polemics about the EFE audit except for weak murmurs here and there. Anson had appealed powerfully to the national conscience. A month and a half later, on 17 September 1983, Anson's *ABC* published detailed accounts of the Finance audit being concluded and carried a short insert article. It reported an August statement of the secretary of state of budget that "the EFE 1982 audits [result] are completely normal and it is necessary to silence the 'organized noise.'" On 10 October 1983, the Finance audits of the EFE news agency were approved and accepted by the council of ministers. Anson had won the battle. Literary power of Anson's had saved the day.

During the 6-month period between 1983 and 1984, the EFE audits were no longer a big story. When the Accounting Tribunal came out with an audit report on 1 March 1984 on the 1978–1982 finances of Anson's EFE management, it did not provoke much public interest. Besides, the Tribunal report, in its introductory section, had a laudatory remark. It said: "In the years analyzed, [EFE] has had a strong growth, which situated it among the first world agencies."

Anson, now in the clear, could boldly face his enemies. Anson took offensive against the by then 2-year-old Utrilla management of EFE. In July 1984 Anson's paper attacked the Utrilla reform of the EFE statutes. Anson also criticized Utrilla's EFE, which had lost P724 million (US$4.8 million) in 1983. Utrilla had to defend himself now through the pages of his old paper, *Diario 16*. Utrilla attempted to blame his 1983 loss of P724 million on the accumulated P825 million losses he said "we inherited from Anson." Utrilla said his P724 million loss was actually "a P101 million savings from the bad inheritance." Since he had so viciously criticized Anson's 1982 loss of P393 million, the P724 million loss in 1983 was difficult to explain away; hence, Utrilla turned to the Ansonian accumulated P825 million losses.

Utrilla used another means of defense, citing a late 1983 study by the Central University of Venezuela on news agency penetration in Latin America. The Venezuelan study noted that EFE in 1983 was definitely the third-biggest news agency in Latin America, only after AP and UPI. It even placed AFP, ANSA, dpa, and Reuters after EFE, which it said had not even figured in the earlier (1962 and 1966) studies conducted by other researchers. Utrilla's contention was that, by 1983, EFE had become a giant agency. But that argument did not wash; if EFE had developed into a "giant" in the 20 years from 1962 to 1983, that growth was due to Utrilla's predecessors like Mendo and Anson.

Utrilla was now feeling the heat of Ansonian criticism of his P724 million loss of 1983, employee discontent, statutory contradictions, and other consequences of his EFE management. Lacking any factual means of defense, Utrilla employed rhetoric. He confided to interviewing reporters that Anson "appears to consider himself as a kind of EFE president in exile and I —Utrilla— would not be surprised, if Anson were to prepare a liberation army to recover a power that he thinks he has been given for life by God's grace." The table had now turned on Utrilla, and he was clearly on the defensive. He had better put up a lot of defense, for he had found a new formidable foe within his own agency.

EFE's Labor Union Attacks

Utrilla had created many malcontents among the EFE labor ranks because of his austerity cuts in personnel, salary, and perks. Employees remembered the exciting environment of Ansonian growth and expansion. It did not feel good to work in a shrinking outfit. EFE workers naturally compared Utrilla with the old boss, Anson, who had been so active and always kept in close contact with them. Utrilla, in comparison, seemed shy and aloof.[19] Taking advantage of this state of affairs was José Luis Roldán, president of the EFE labor union committee. Roldán saw, first, that the Utrilla–Anson battle was being engaged at the cost of the EFE labor, which turned out to be the final victim of the situation. Roldán also felt completely ignored. Named president of the EFE labor committee in 1980, Roldán regarded his function as maintaining an adversarial —although, not necessarily unfriendly— relationship with the EFE presidents. Under Utrilla, EFE labor suffered what Roldán considered tremendous deterioration because of austerity cuts.[20]

Roldán was a card-carrying member of the ruling PSOE and had been the "secretary" of the center-left UGT (Unión General de Trabajadores, or General Union of Workers) during 1978–1981. In EFE under Utrilla, Roldán was UGT's representative to the news agency. Roldán started complaining to the Utrilla management about the general downturn in labor interests. With each negotiation, their relationship deteriorated. Now, Roldán and Anson saw themselves as allies against Utrilla.

Anson was not above fanning the Utrilla–Roldán feud. Anson's *ABC* carried a story on the press conference Roldán held on 10 July 1985. In it, Roldán went all out against Utrilla. He said the EFE labor committee would ask for a permit for strikes, scheduled for 23 September. Roldán bitterly complained that there had been since July 1984 some 400 job changes, many of them "oppressive and penalizing" transfers. He himself, for example, had been demoted from subdirector of bureaus to the "morgue" (archives). He said 13 of 17 labor committee members suffered similar unreasonable job changes. Angry and frustrated at "the decadence EFE fell into under the Utrilla management," Roldán's EFE labor committee sent an "ample dossier" to all Spanish parliamentary groups about "the degradation that the [EFE] agency suffers." This dossier on the "sad-status-of-EFE" became a political bomb at the Spanish Cortes.

THE LEGAL STATUS OF EFE

Since 1939, the EFE agency had maintained an ambiguous and vexatious legal status. All concerned professed the belief that a news agency had to exercise journalistic independence. Yet, for its economic sustenance, EFE always had to depend on state support in the form of payments for claimed services as well as outright subsidies. In the Franco autocracy, that situation did not trouble people too much. Nobody pretended EFE was an independent news organization under the Franco regime. However, in Spain of the mid-1980s, in a parliamentary democratic monarchy, how should EFE status be defined?

All concerned acknowledged its dependence on official support. But did that support originate in an abstract but permanent Spanish "state," or in the shifting partisan "governments"? Was EFE a national or governmental news agency? Again, all concerned pretended that it performed a national role in the interest of Spanish information sovereignty nebulously defined. But they all knew the parties "on watch" changed the EFE management more for their own rather than the national interest. In the mid-1980s, the "national" agency was deeply embroiled in a partisan feud: What was the legal status of EFE?

The 1978 constitution stipulated in Article 20.3 that a law would be enacted that "will regulate the organization and the PARLIAMENTARY CONTROL of the media of social communication dependent on the State." Yet, in the 11 years since the promulgation of the constitution, no such law has been legislated. The Spanish opposition circles —political and journalistic— alleged that the PSOE in power manipulated the EFE agency to its political advantage and that EFE under socialist-appointed Utrilla performed poorly. The opposition also recalled that the PSOE had severely criticized the previous center-right government for its "inaction" in the constitutional provision for EFE's legal status. The PSOE now in power was, it seemed, as inactive, if not more so. In that environment, EFE labor chief José Luis Roldán supplied political dynamite in a "dossier on the sad state of EFE" in mid-July 1985.

On 25 September 1985 the PSOE administration was questioned on EFE's situation by Oscar Alzaga Villaamil, president of the right-wing splinter Popular Democratic Party (PDP, Partido Demócrata Popular). Responding to the Alzaga inquiry was Javier Moscoso, minister of the presidency of the government. ("President" of the government is the official title for the

Spanish premier, appointed by the king, who is the chief of state.) Animated, although moderate, debates ensued on EFE's legal status. Preceding this debate, however, were a series of exchanges on EFE in the Congress of Deputies (the lower house of the Cortes). On 18 July 1984, in the wake of the conclusion of the audit of 1978–1982 EFE finances under Anson, the PDP had threatened Utrilla's EFE with an audit of its 1983 books. Taking particular interest in the EFE affairs, the PDP presented a motion to legislate an EFE statute "to satisfy the precepts of ARTICLE 20.3" of the constitution that sets forth the "parliamentary control" of all state-run mass media. The PDP motion was soundly defeated by a 269-3 vote on 9 March 1985.

However, PDP president Alzaga insisted, again questioning the government on the state news agency on 13 March 1985. A week later (20 March), Alzaga presented another motion for EFE legislation. Two months later, EFE president Utrilla was called on the carpet before the congressional committee on public administration. Utrilla attempted to protect EFE from "partisan meddling fatal to the image overseas." In late September the PDP presented yet another challenge to EFE.[21] Alzaga doggedly pursued the EFE matter; he knew he had the PSOE on the defensive on EFE, given the constitutional mandate. There were also dissenting voices heard from within the EFE rank and file itself, such as that of José Luis Roldán, EFE labor committee chief. Alzaga realized too that the conservative press circles, particularly *ABC*'s Luis María Anson, entertained more than a passing interest in the alleged PSOE mismanagement of EFE.

"Byline Makes Journalists"

The issues being debated in 1985 on the state-run EFE agency were multifaceted and intertwined.

"Deviant" Agency EFE. PDP Deputy Alzaga charged that after 7 years under the constitutional democracy, the EFE agency still was functioning as an entity he characterized as "PARA-constitutional" ("para" signifying "deviant"). There was no ambiguity in the constitutional language, and there was no way the PSOE could cloud the issue, for the socialists —when they were in the opposition— had pounded on that line of argument themselves. But the political magicians found ways to avoid the issue. PSOE minister Moscoso first mused whether Article 20.3 applied to news agencies. Then Moscoso offered that Article 20.3 had been "imposed by the very important" (*importantísimo*) number of mass media in the public sector, existing at the moment when the constitution was written. Moscoso wondered about the wisdom of that constitutional proviso. He appeared to want to blame it on the excessive number of media units in the hands of the ruling Falange movement, which the PSOE government had inherited.

Moscoso also based his argument on "upside-down" logic. The EFE agency was a mercantile *sociedad anónima* (anonymous society, or an incorporated limited-responsibility company), equipped with its own statutes (charter), and with approximately one-third participation each of the state treasury, National Institute of Industry (INI), National Telephone Company of Spain, and minuscule private owners. "Modifying this situation would involve," he said, "the modification of the law on corporations." He was standing the juridical hierarchy on its head, saying that because a law was operating, the constitution could not be implemented against that law!

Anson's *ABC*, a newspaper not known for objectivity (especially in EFE's case) reported Moscoso as saying that "EFE is a private communication medium, for the [EFE] journalists do not sign [their stories]" or they do not get "bylines" for their articles. It was not clear whether it was muddled thinking on the part of Moscoso or of Anson's reporter.[22]

EFE president Utrilla did not present any more reasoned argument against the parliamentary control of his agency. He insisted that parliamentary control would deal a death blow to his agency's image abroad, for he contended —rightly— that "the believability and acceptance of international press agencies are 'inversely proportional' to the official character of the same." However, Utrilla could not demonstrate how parliamentary control would make the EFE agency any more "official" than the thoroughly known "fiction" of the "mercantile" nature of Agencia EFE, S.A. Utrilla preferred autocratic management of EFE to a democratic parliamentary thrashout. No one could blame his very human choice for a kingdom instead of a marketplace.

PSOE minister Moscoso, however, offered a compromise plan to the Cortes. He said that the PSOE administration would be well disposed to discuss the drafting of an EFE statute, if there were "sufficient parliamentary majority" in favor of that option. It was an obvious putdown for splinter groups like Alzaga's PDP. Moscoso made it known that only the ruling PSOE could decide on the status of EFE.

Privatizing EFE. Utrilla's EFE in 1984–1985 did not fare any better than Anson's in 1982, which Utrilla had attacked as "hyperatrophied." For the 1984 operations, the socialist government had to "endow" EFE with P2.992 billion (US$17.42 million). This was, PDP's Alzaga emphasized, 66.5% over the 1983 budget. Had not the PSOE, when it was in opposition in 1982, demanded that the EFE "endowment" be cut by 30%? In his congressional testimony on 21 May 1985, Utrilla tried to emphasize that "it cost the Spanish State less than P3 billion ($18.7 million) a year to maintain in the world 'a presence of first order' with projections, that are, really, unlimited."

Besides, Utrilla projected that he might be able to close the 1985 book for the first time in the history of EFE with a positive balance. This projection proved to have been disingenuous. The 1985 balance turned out to be again in the red by P216.9 million ($1.35 million).[23] Minister Moscoso did not even offer any defense of EFE finances, for none could be given.

So the socialist minister tried a privatization idea. Moscoso said the PSOE government might be willing to give up a part of the the state EFE stocks "in benefit of [future] Latin American stockholders." The EFE news agency could not have any non-Spanish stock owners. The thinking was that the Latin American media were the major beneficiaries of the Spanish government expenditures in the national news agency. But the "plan" to increase the private EFE capital with Latin American participation had not been thought through —it lacked both a politico-legal and economic basis. Anson's *ABC* particularly emphasized another economic point in the interpellation by the PDP president. Deputy Alzaga indicated that "the EFE news services sold to exterior [clients] constituted a percentage inferior to 5 percent of the total revenues of the EFE agency."[24] It indicated how little the Latin Americans would be interested in buying EFE stocks, Alzaga pointed out.

Again, it became manifest that both PSOE minister Moscoso and EFE president Utrilla were offering any seemingly plausible answers just to tide over the opposition interrogation. Given the political position of Anson —the former EFE president and current president of the National Press Federation— it ought have been clear to all concerned that plans for increased privatization of EFE capital by Latin American participation would never work. (Anson's draft press law had clearly spelled out in 1980 against non-Spaniard ownership of the mass media.

Buddyism in EFE Labor. The opposition interpellation directed particularly virulent criticism to the EFE management-employee relationship because it was assisted by the dossier from José Luis Roldán of the EFE labor committee. PDP deputy Alzaga said the EFE labor union had denounced "deterioration in labor climate, buddyism, and disorganization." Practically reading from Roldán's dossier on Utrilla, Alzaga complained there had been no fewer than 244 "unjustified" position transfers in less than a month during June–July 1985 and 400 job changes in a year. Most changes were "retaliatory and irrational": a lifetime sports writer is transferred to labor; a reporter who has worked for 10 years in international news has been forced to cover the Spanish courts; a person in charge of religious news has been sent to sports. "They were not job transfers but trampling," Alzaga intoned. Besides, EFE employees' purchasing power had dropped 45% in the past 3 years.

On the other hand, there were many examples of "buddy-buddyism and favoritism": the Central American (ACAN-EFE) bureau chief "gets a salary superior to the President of Government —plus house and a car on company expense." Another example of buddyism was the increase in per diem honorarium for attendance in the administrative council. It went up from P5,000 ($31) to P50,000 ($311). PDP deputy Alzaga recalled that Leopoldo Torres, now socialist acting president of the congress, had characterized, when in opposition, this kind of situation in EFE as that of "Oriental chieftain."

EFE in A "World Concert." A man of lifetime wire-service experience, Utrilla made an excellent case, flaunting catchy ideas and imaginative phrases, in his 21 May 1985 remarks to the committee on public administration of the congress. He avowed: "Thanks to EFE, Spain figures as the 'No. 4 country' of the world in international press agencies." Utrilla's new rhetorical twist to the situation was very inventive. Since AP and UPI both belonged to one country, Spain was only behind 3 Western nations —the United States, Great Britain, and France— in the matter of news agencies. That point appealed to Spaniards, for they heard from Utrilla's mouth that Spain was ahead of great political and industrial powers such as Germany, China, Japan, and Italy.

Utrilla cited some indisputable sources, so that his comments would not sound too self-serving. He said the prestigious International Press Institute (IPI) had picked out EFE "as [an] example of independence and professionalism" only a few months before. Utrilla then speculated that the annual report of the IPI, with its world headquarters in London, must have "favorably influenced the decision by the *Financial Times* of London to acquire our services." Utrilla concluded his plea against the "menace" to his agency with oratorical high pitch. Said he:

> The EFE agency is, definitely, something more than a mere information medium, Spain can offer to the countries that are her descendants in order to situate ourselves with dignity in the *World Concert* (emphasis added).

Five months later, on 25 September, government minister Moscoso picked up on some of the EFE president's eloquent rhetoric. The minister told the congress he wished that in the not far future, EFE would be an agency that configured itself as an instrument of communication of the state, not of the government, and that consolidated itself as the "first international agency" in the Castilian tongue. Oratorical symbolisms employed by Utrilla and Moscoso, however, did not change many people's minds. Opposition politicians were not the only ones who remained skeptical. Pilar Cernua, a reporter of the Barcelona newspaper *La Vanguardia*, made this cynical comment: "If [Moscoso] wants all that 'for the future,' [it] means that [he] thinks they are not the current conditions of the agency, no matter how much its president Utrilla may say to the contrary."[25]

"Peculiar UPI Connections."   At issue in the mid-1985 congressional debate on EFE as regards UPI were 2 factors: (1) Spaniards had deep-seated fears of UPI, "a monopolistic international giant," although financially moribund at the time; and (2) Spaniards also entertained mixed feelings on the century-old love-hate relationship with the United States.

PDP president Alzaga questioned PSOE Minister Moscoso on "this 'peculiar' contract [for 'Nuestras Noticias'] with the UPI agency a few months before its bankruptcy, which now extends to buy the said agency, over which there exists a major confusion among the professional media [circles]."[26] He was mystified. He saw something sinister in the UPI-EFE nexus at least. Alzaga showed off his intimate knowledge of "inside stories" of EFE, but swung confusingly between 1984 and 1985. His inside knowledge of EFE affairs was based on the equally spotty information supplied by José Luis Roldán of the EFE labor committe. All anti-Utrilla elements in the Spanish political and press circles were curious and deeply mistrustful of the Utrilla group and and the PSOE administration. The latter group had previously been as inquisitive and jealous of the old Anson team and its government backing. It was a "tit for tat."

Parkinsonian Committee on EFE

The Cortes exchanges of September 1985 produced one concrete result. A majority PSOE proposal was approved on 2 October to create a committee charged to study the EFE situation. Some 2 months later, on 11 December 1985, the EFE Committee was constituted. It was chaired naturally by a PSOE deputy. PDP's Alzaga —for his active intervention in the EFE affairs— was elected as vice chair of the committee. From the very first day the EFE committee began wrangling. Anson's *ABC* characterized the EFE committee as PSOE's "turns to the 'Parkinson's rule,' because when it is not desired to solve a problem [and] a committee is formed."[27]

When the year 1986 rolled around, the interests of the Spanish congress in EFE had been forgotten. The EFE committee never met, and the EFE statutes remained "in the same situation." José Mario Armero, the president of Europa Press and a prominent lawyer, wrote in August 1986: "On initiating a new legislature, and a new Government [Administration], it is possible that the issue might again be be presented. But, it does not appear to me that there is much interest for the issue."[28] Nothing has yet been done about the EFE statutes at this writing in April 1989.

THE POST-FRANCO PRESS

Anson's famous "I denounce" open-letter column of 30 June 1983 in which he defended his EFE management called *ABC* a "liberal" newspaper. At that time, and not so infrequently since then, Anson has publicly characterized *El País* and its director Juan Luis Cebrián as "Marxist." Another Spanish journalist, Waldo de Mier, has said: "I would never touch those two 'Communist newspapers' even with gloves on" —meaning *El País* and *ABC*. De Mier was EFE subdirector in 1957–1970, and has since been writing weekly book reviews for the ultra-right Madrid paper, *El Alcázar*.[29] How do these and other dailies line up in a left-right gamut in post-Franco Spanish journalism? It is a question vital to the undertanding of the role played by the Spanish press in general, and the EFE news agency in particular, in the democratizing process of Spain.

The Spanish press played a pivotal role in the post-Franco democratization, itself going through metamorphoses in 2 stages. In the 1976–1982 "transition" period, it courageously explored the possibilities. With the settling in of "democracy" in Spain upon the election of the PSOE government in 1982, the Spanish press started to behave like an arrogant and omniscient arbiter of society, at times stepping on its own toes. Nothing would better illustrate this development of the Spanish press than an 1985 episode whose main protagonist was *El País* (*The Country*), the very first daily to appear in the post-Franco era.

Inception of *El País*

The incubation period of *El País* started in 1972, some 3 years before Franco's death. Carlos Mendo, the former EFE director widely credited for having taken the Spanish agency to Latin America, sought a chance to put into practice his "Anglo-Saxon and [North] American mentality"[30] again in Spanish journalism. Franco —80 years old in 1972— showed some signs of mellowing. The dictator provided for a future premier to succeed him and allowed the signing of a trade agreement with the Soviet Union, the first open contact between the 2 countries since the Spanish civil war. Carlos Mendo, then job-hopping for some 3 years after leaving EFE in 1969, joined with 2 like-minded Spaniards to form a publishing company.[31] Carlos Mendo, José Ortega Spottorno (a son of philosopher Ortega y Gasset), and another journalist, Darío Valcarcel, scraped together P350,000 (US$5,400) to start a small, elite daily. The then MIT Alfredo Sánchez Bella required the company to boost its capital to an "impossible" P100 million ($1.54 million) in order to qualify for a publication permit. Sánchez, who had fired Mendo as the EFE director, wanted to stifle this potential voice of liberal opposition at any cost.

The Mendo group's publishing plan languished in abeyance for a while. When, in 1974, Franco fell ill, contributions poured in and *El País* finally hit the Madrid streets on 4 May 1976, only 6 months after Franco's death. By a lucky break, the Mendo group's publication became the first newspaper to come out in the post-Franco era, thus perceived as a symbol of democracy by Spaniards. Jumpy Mendo by then had assumed his second (and ephemeral) EFE command only 2 months before the apperance of *El País*. About 6 months later —in October 1976— a second new daily came out with the name *Diario 16* (*Daily 16*).

El País in Transition

Both new Spanish dailies at first had to tread dangerous waters. Their efforts to nurture democratic traditions after a 40-year dictatorship was a struggle. Loyal Franco followers still held onto their powerful positions in the bureaucracy, on the court benches, and especially in the army barracks. The old Falange movement press was in disgrace but still operated about 40 newspapers, until it was disbanded in April 1977. The center-right "transition" government established the "Medios de Comunicación Social del Estado" (MCSE, or State's Social Communication Media). Its functions were to administer and eventually dispose of the Falange and other Francoist press units. In addition to MSCE, the government operated 2 radio networks and 2 television systems. These "old forces" together put up resistance to changes.

Franco-era laws remained on the books even after the promulgation of the December 1978 constitution, and the judges applied old laws. In May 1980, some 18 months into the constitutional system, the Supreme Court handed a suspended prison sentence to *El País* editor Cebrián, for an editorial defending a magazine which had published photographs of nude women.

The highest court of constitutional Spain considered that editorial to be in "contempt of 'constituted' authority." Other outspoken journalists were continually summoned before civil and military tribunals. *Diario 16* editor Ramírez spent 5 days in January 1982 defending himself against civil charges. The International Press Institute (IPI) reported that, as of June 1980, more than 100 court cases were pending against some 700 journalists —"some in military tribunals"— which should not have jurisdiction over them.[32] These legal harassments and mental inhibitions even continued into the "democratic" Spain of the PSOE years since 1983. Cebrián told a U.S. PBS-television program in 1985,[33] that he had been hauled into civil and penal courts some 100 times in the 10 years since 1976. In May 1985, PSOE interior minister José Barrionuevo sued Cebrián and his paper for "having violated (the) personal honor," when the paper criticized the administration of the national police and the Civil Guard. The minister lost the case after a protracted trial, which cost the paper and Cebrián both money and time.[34]

Ignoring threats to their physical survival, the 2 new dailies called vehemently for defense of democracy, when the military officers and the Civil Guards attempted a coup, holding the Cortes at gunpoint on 23 February 1981. The incident naturally increased the Spanish military's hostility against the press. It quickly surfaced on 6 December 1981, when 100 army officers issued an ominous warning that the press must begin to show proper respect for the military. The failed coup entailed the most brazen violation of its rights to *Diario 16* in May 1981. About 50 police officers showed up late at night to halt the newspaper-delivery trucks, all loaded to distribute the issue with accounts of how the military had planned the coup. It was not released until 8:30 the next morning. Official explanation was that the newspaper had not fulfilled the legal-deposit requirement stipulated in the 1966 "Fraga" Press Law (LPI). That law had been repealed clearly by the 1978 constitution, if not yet with a specific reference, but certainly by a sweeping transition provision that "all dispositions shall remain revoked, which would oppose what is established in this Constitution."[35]

There were of course the reactionary press elements which supported the military coup, and consequently felt betrayed by the action of King Juan Carlos, who rallied the top military commands behind his stand against the rebellion. The extreme right-wing paper, *El Alcázar* (*The Fortress*), for example, openly criticized the king, on whose behalf the revolting military had supposedly acted.[36] The press was not exempt from violence rampant in post-Franco Spain —allegedly inflicted by the ETA separatists and their right-wing rivals of military or other extractions. Reporters at both new dailies and other publications were often threatened. Some, including the *El País* business editor, were beaten, and on 30 October 1978 a letter bomb killed an *El País* mailboy and blew his supervisor's hands off.[37] They never found the perpetrator(s).

In spite of all these difficulties, *El País* and others of the Spanish press forged on with determined contribution to the process of democratization. And the country readily embraced the pivotal role played by the press in dismantling the Franco-era institutions. Barely 2 months after its beginning, *El País* succeeded in bringing about the resignation, on 1 July 1976, of Premier Arias Navarro. The new daily had vocalized in its editorials the popular discontent against the slow pace of reforms under Arias, the Franco appointee. The newspaper, however, was not so rabidly antipast. It was willing to work with the new premier, Suárez González, another Franco-era holdover. Suárez carried out major political reforms during his tenure.

The press helped direct toward the center the reform measures started by the Suárez government. Spain established diplomatic relations with the Soviet Union in February 1977. Through 2 national referenda (of 1976 and 1978), Spain adopted a new constitution in December 1978. It legalized all political parties —including the Communist— except for the Falange, which was disbanded. The press was the mainstay in Spain's survival through the 1981 military coup attempt. It was instrumental in helping the minority government of the third "transition" premier, Calvo Sotelo, carry on until the 1982 elections, when the PSOE won a landslide victory. Spanish socialists who had been defeated in the civil war now came out as the victors in peace.

Through all this, the new Spanish press found itself in an unprecedented leadership position in Spain's transformation. *El País* especially "was a market success, and its influence surprised even those of us, who had prepared for the paper with so many hopes and illusions," editor Cebrián said.[38] By mid-1980 *El País* was quickly catching up in circulation with the old *La Vanguardia* of Barcelona (183,000 vs. 186,000) only to surpass the old leader by 1985 (191,800 vs. 348,000). The Sunday circulation figure of 600,000 of *El País* was a phenomenon never before seen in Spain. Cebrián attributes his paper's success to its mainstream position. He said his readers are on the "left," and its stockholders are on the "right," and between the 2 sides is the editorial position of the newspaper, which has stayed in the "center."[39]

Then, the paper's success went to Cebrián's head.

El País Steps on Its Own Toes

In its leading role in the democratizing process, *El País* had stepped on many people's toes. Then in January 1985, its tenth year of publication, *El*

País stepped on its own toes.

On 31 January 1985 *El País* ran a page in the "Society" section with 2 articles, accompanied by a big picture, on "The Crisis of the Spanish Press."[40] The edition also carried a lengthy editorial on the same subject. The crisis was that, the story alleged, almost all Spanish newspapers "owed to the State" debts totaling P5 billion (US$31 million). The editorial urged these press enterprises to pay up or they would lose lucrative government subsidies. The 1984 news-industry subsidy law would authorize the government to subtract all debt owed to the state from the 1985 subsidy, budgeted at P2.76 billion ($17.16 million). The newspapers could not ignore the accusation and implied threat. They jumped in unison at *El País* in their editorial rebuttals. *El País* rejected the countercharges. An ugly spat ensued on the newspaper pages.

Enterprising producers of the national Radio Televisión Española (RTVE) picked up the cue and aired a prime-time show entitled "Press— Anatomy of a Crisis" 2 weeks later. The television program stirred up the press wrangle which seemed to have simmered down, and also provoked a new squabble. The newspapers as a group —including *El País*— now turned on "state" television as the cause of the press crisis, because RTVE had "siphoned off more than half of the advertising revenues" from "private" press industry. Individual newspapers and the powerful Association of Editors of Spanish Dailies (AEDE) threatened the "national television entity" with a law suit.

Opposition newspapers also accused the PSOE government of using the debt issue as a political threat for their criticism of the administration. Opposition parties recalled the old charges by the PSOE when it was in the opposition that the RTVE was a "den of thieves" and PSOE's criminal suit of February 1981 filed against it for "using TV programs for political purposes in the upcoming elections in Catalonia."[41] It was a battle royal. And *El País* had started it all.

The other story in *El País* of 31 January 1985, headlined "The Multimedia in Spain," pointed out that some press businesses in debt owned and operated not only the press outfits but also radio and television. They still owed money to the state. A passage in the story boasted: "Practically, it can be said that EL PAIS is the only newspaper of national circulation that is up to date in its State accounts." "To help comprehend the magnitudes of the crisis the Spanish press suffers," it pointed to debts surpassing P1 billion ($6.2 million) owed to private financial institutions by some of these multimedia enterprises. How did the Spanish media businesses end up with such critical debts to the state totaling P5 billion ($31 million)?

The story did not attribute the information to any source, but simply said that "technicians of the Administration 'calculate' at some 5,000 million pesetas" the accumulated debts some press units owed to the state.

Table 8.1
Press Debts to the State, 1985

PAPER OWING (million P) to	Treasury	Social Security	Total
ABC	P 242	P 231	P 473
Diario 16	87	10	97
(Grupo 16)	97	222	319
La Vanguardia	292	n/a	292+
El Alcázar	137	480	617
Cinco Días	n/a	95	95+
El Noticiero Universal	597	642	1239
Avui	306	340	646
El Correo Catalán	158	264	422
El Periódico	122	74	196
DEBT TOTALS	P2,038	P2,358	P4,396+

The stories gave details of major Spanish papers' debts by name and amount without mincing words (see Table 8.1). The stories said the 91 press businesses that published 105 newspapers (hence "the 'multimedia' in Spain") owed only to Social Security more than P2 billion ($12.4 million), which, added to the debts to the treasury, amounted to P5 billion. This did not include "the debts of the press units to the governmenmtal banking institutions, principally to the Bank of Industrial Credit." It estimated those official bank credits "exceed the P5 billion owed to the Social Security and Treasury."

The 1984 newspaper and news-agency subsidies law provided for 3 categories of state assistance to news industry: (1) for diffusion (circulation), or to promote press circulations; (2) for use of Spanish-produced newsprint to promote national paper production against cheaper imported papers; and (3) for technological reconversion (renovation). These totaled P2,760.2 million ($17.16 million) in 1985.[42]

Though the *El País* story referred to the 1984 law on news-industry subsidies, the concepts were not limited to the post-Franco era. In Spain, government subsidies for the news industry dated centuries back. The Franco regime, however, kept the actual subsidy figures under tight cover. Until Franco's death, the EFE news agency, for example, never disclosed publicly how much money it received from the government. "Democratic" Spain continued on subsidies programs for the news industry, but with a slightly different perspective. The idea is that a democratic society needs to give the press positive aids and assistance, not just freedom. This idea is not limited to Spain. All Western capitalistic, so-called free societies give different degrees and magnitudes of special state subsidies to their media.[43]

The Spanish press as a whole, not counting a few like *El País*, owed the state some P5 billion ($31 million) as of 31 January 1985, while the government budgeted only P2.76 billion ($17.16 million) for press subsidies. If the government were to enforce the provisions of the subsidy law, and subtrcated all debts before any subsidy was given out, most media units would have to forego any state aid for almost 2 years at the current level of subsidy budget. That was the big crisis. Did that new "upstart" paper provoke this crisis in unfair competition against all its rivals?   Would Cebrián dare take on the whole Spanish press? The reaction was immediate and shrill.

The monarchist *ABC* hurled the most vitriolic invective on the very next day after the *El País* articles. Its editorial called Cebrián's paper "the governmental daily" that "lies in its figures and intent." *ABC*'s director, Luis María Anson —the 1976–1982 EFE president— called "the government daily's uncommon information" an "act of petulance of a new rich," which "betrayed its nervousness at the recent poll, relegating it to the second place after *ABC* in influence as well as in number of readers."[44] While disputing all the debt figures given by *El País*, *ABC* also explained how an 80-year-old paper could accumulate so much Social Security debt because of an overwhelming number of pensions, retirements, and excess of personnel —which "the eight-year-old government daily does not have." Besides, "the new newspaper received so much State subsidy and aids in technologcal investment."

The right-wing paper *El Alcázar* said that the government "owed [it] a lot of money," instead of the other way around. While it denounced "the lack of ethic" in Cebrián's "chiseling" action, it accused the PSOE government of "impeding official publicity from our pages" in violation of constitutional principle of equity. Besides, it said it was losing annually "P25 million ($155,444)" because the government "cancelled subscription for 2,000 copies of our paper to be placed on IBERIA," the national airline, which, in 10 years, had totaled P250 million ($1.55 million). *El Alcázar* pointed to another ugly open secret in government-press relationships, by alleging that "the REPTILE (bribe) FUND" (*fondo de reptiles*) "handed down to news outfits friendly to the governing parties in ample amounts impossible to figure out, and we never enjoyed."[45]

Ya, the Catholic church paper, which *El País* had not mentioned as owing money to the state, waited a single prudent day before joining the fray. It made sure to point out that it and all other church papers published by EDICA (Editorial Católica) did not have any state debts. *Ya* criticized *El País* for "having broken the traditional industry solidarity by revealing private information of its colleagues." Then it tried to take moral high ground above the disputes by analyzing the subsidy law, which it did not desist from criticizing for "favoring those dailies with a new plant."[46]

The controversy raged on between the newspapers as a group and the new daily, which obviously stepped on the toes of not only many of its colleagues but also its own.

El País twisted in agony.

The Spanish Press of 1985

This mudslinging fight among Spanish dailies lined them up in a sharp ideological gamut, as they branded one another as "Marxist, liberal, conservative, and ultra-right." In the studied opinion of the present author, Spain's major dailies line up in a left-to-right spectrum in the following order:

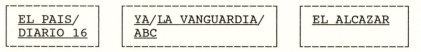

In the Spain of 1985, there was not a daily paper published by the Communist party or the ultra-left Comisiones Obreras (CC.OO. or Workers Committees). *El País* displays an editorial policy roughly akin to *The New York Times* and the *Washington Post*. *Diario 16* (Utrilla's paper and the distant third or fourth in circulation), although it pretends to follow a liberal line, is too "freakish" and haphazard to be taken seriously.[47] The 3 papers in the conservative middle in the above gamut would be comparable in their outlook to the *Washington Times*. These 3 conservative dailies —*La Vanguardia* (of Barcelona), *Ya*, and *ABC*— would place themselves in the above left-to-right order within the conservative grouping. One would be hard put to find an equivalant of the ultra-right *El Alcázar* in the U.S. mainstream press.

In the press-subsidy flak, Spanish television got into the act quickly. On the evening of 12 February 1985, the nationwide audience of Spanish national television (Radio Televisión Española, RTVE) was treated to a contentious program on the weekly series entitled "En Portada" (On [the] Cover). Similar to U.S. CBS's "60 Minutes" or ABC's "20/20" programs, "En Portada" is a very popular magazine presentation on current issues. On that evening the hour-long program dealt with only one story, "Prensa—Anatomía de Una Crisis" (Press—Anatomy of a Crisis). The press controversy, now in full public view on televison, became a tripartite dispute among television, press, and *El País*. The newspapers as a group were appalled that RTVE would present the print press in such a poor light to the public. Individual dailies and AEDE threatened to sue the national television entity, and they also renewed their attacks on Cebrián's paper. Cebrián found himself attacking RTVE on the one hand and, on the other hand, defending his paper against attacks from other newspapers.

The one-hour program, "En Portada," on the theme of "Press— Anatomy of a Crisis" broadcast on 14 February did not actually take up the whole 60-minute duration. It was only 43 minutes and 15 seconds long. The remainder of the time, or 16 minutes and 45 seconds, was allotted to commercials or advertisements. Spanish television is a state monopoly administered as a public entity, Radio Televisión Española (RTVE) —or "TVE" referring only to television. RTVE, a state monopoly, is engaged in lucrative advertising activities, unlike its U.S. counterpart PBS.[48] The "En Portada" program showed that commercial messages on RTVE take up roughly the same proportion —or 28% of air time— as on U.S. commercial television. The print media industry long claimed TVE, a governmental media operated with public funds, was putting up an unfair competition, siphoning off "more than half of the advertising revenues" from the private sector. The complaint came to a new boil with the "En Portada" program on the print media debt-subsidy relationship with the Spanish government.

Did TVE really siphon off more than half of the publicity?[49] *Ya*, the Catholic church paper, presented evidence that it did on 17 March 1985 with a long article, accompanied by pie-charts showing [50] TVE had indeed siphoned off 56.4% of the total 1984 advertising pesetas. Coming only a month after the 14 February 1985 "En Portada" show, the impact, if not the intent, of the story was paramount. *Ya* was disputing the data used by TVE on the distribution of advertising money, in a 1984 story in *Cinco Días* (*Five Days*). The TVE-plant story had indicated that television had drawn only 23.89% of adversing business, and it trailed the newspapers with 28.45%.[51] Such a large difference (56.4% vs. 23.89%) in TVE's advertising shares originated in the different data sources and the deceit-by-statistics tactic. *Ya* used Nielsen measurement service data. TVE turned to J. Walter Thompson (J.W.T.) as its sources. Tomás de la Cruz Serna, president of the Alas Group, a nationwide chain of advertising agencies and a neutral participant between television and print media, gave approximate data without consulting any "misleading" statistics: TVE (40%), radio (15%), dailies (30%), and magazines (15%). Broadcast media modestly outstripped the printed media (55% vs. 45%), but not as much as *Ya*'s claim (56.4% vs. 23.89%).[52]

The EFE news agency watched this subsidy-debt wrangle as a not so uninterested observer, carefully avoiding involvement. Utrilla's EFE discreetly declined to be interviewed for "En Portada" by RTVE. So, the "En Portada" program could only use photographs of the facade of the EFE building.

"AGENCY MAN" UTRILLA

Ricardo Utrilla assumed the EFE presidency on 25 January 1983. From the outset, he was besieged by many disputes. The first ones were of his own making and the later ones were payback he received for his original attacks on his predecessor. He completely avoided involvement in the *El País*—RTVE controversy. Utrilla needed no more disputes. Toward the end of 1985, the dust was settling on the controversy over his EFE management. By then the press–TVE flak had fizzled out also. The PSOE government that had appointed him to EFE also was firmly establishing itself. But even during the 3-year altercations, Utrilla amply displayed his management style, which was based on his long wire-service experience, mostly with AFP in the French capital, and Washington, D.C., the world's news capital.

Functional News Delivery

Utrilla made EFE's news delivery more functional. The Linkage Department (Departmento de Enlace), set up a few yards away from the national and international desks, linked national news to international circuits. Also called "Servicio de Lids" (Lead Service),[53] this department supplied the Latin American circuits with brief leading paragraphs of about 20 Spanish domestic news, culled for their potential importance for Hispanic American clients. Many Latin American nations have sizable clusters of Spaniards, who emigrated from particular Spanish regions and cities. Spanish local news are important for those emigrant communities in the Americas. The Linkage Department satisfied those needs, plus linking Spain spiritually to her former colonies.

Utrilla had learned from his AFP experience that the subscribing newspapers and other news media must be supplied with some kind of foreknowledge of what news items are to be expected. Generally called "budgets" in the English-language newsrooms, these lists —a collection of graph summaries of news stories being prepared for later dispatch— assist subscribers in planning for their "news cycle or news day" ahead. Utrilla called them "forecasts of the day" (previsiones del día).

Utrilla's News Scoops

Into the third year (1985) of his management, Utrilla had EFE under his control, even though partisan potshots continued. As a daily routine, president Utrilla inspected all the dispatches in the "EFE Básico" (Basic EFE), the basic wires on which 17 different circuits to Hispanic America are based. These 300 or so EFE wires were stapled together in 2- to 3-inch bunches and placed on his presidential desk by 3 "wire cutters" (*cortadores de cables*) in the central newsroom. Some wire stories were good, many were mediocre; most of them were acceptable but improvable. Shuffling through the stories filed by his correspondents all over the world, the wire-service man Utrilla yearned to cover news in far-away lands. Wanderlust would stir his mind. In early 1985 an the itinerant spirit got the better of him. A wander-bug bit him.[54] The president of world's fifth largest news agency went on a reporting junket himself.

Cuban President Fidel Castro gave an exclusive interview to Utrilla —and Marisol Marín, EFE's Havana bureau chief— on 13 February 1985. In a marathon 6-hour interview, —EFE claimed to be "the first Castro has granted to a news agency in more than 20 years"—the Cuban leader covered the current Spanish-Cuban and other world issues. On the afternoon of 18 February 1985 EFE-International dispatched 4 lengthy wires: (1) CASTRO-SPAIN = Fidel Laments Influence of U.S. in Relation with Spain (some 1,280 words); (2) CASTRO-LATIN AMERICA = Latin American Debt Menaces World Peace (1,370 words); (3) CASTRO-WORLD = Fidel Adjudges Cuban Relations with US, USSR, and Europe (1,300 words); and (4) CASTRO-SYNTHESIS = Exclusive Interview of Cuban Leader with EFE (1,050 words).

Spanish dailies gave at best mixed reactions to the big Castro interviews by Utrilla. The leading Madrid newspaper, *El País*, gave short shrift to the 5,000-word series —publishing a 250-word summary. *ABC* simply ignored them. Only Utrilla's old newspaper, *Diario 16*, gave the interview any decent coverage by placing a 250-word synopsis, with a Castro "mug shot," on the front page and full-page rewrites of the 4-dispatch series. Not a single original wire was carried.[55]

Utrilla continued with his self-imposed foreign reporting assignments. In late May 1985 the EFE president conducted an exclusive interview with Mexican President, Miguel de la Madrid Hurtado. The Mexican leader was preparing for a 19-day tour of Europe. De la Madrid's first leg of the European visits was in Spain during 5–6 June 1985. The junket was a countermeasure on the part of the Mexican president to pressures Mexico felt from the United States. Mexico was wracked with gigantic foreign debts —mostly owed to the U.S. banks— amounting to $100 billion. Though gradually waning, Mexico's economic support for Nicaragua and for regional groups, such as the Contadora Group and the Cartagena Agreement on Central America, also ran against the policies of the Reagan administration.

De la Madrid went to Europe with hopes of increasing European investments in and trade with his country, and also to gain support for his "anti-Reaganite" Central American policies. Given the importance of De la Madrid's visit to Madrid, many Spanish and Mexican media had conducted pretour interviews with the Mexican leader. Utrilla's position as the EFE president gave his encounter with President De la Madrid an above-average meaning. EFE's 1985 Memorial claimed, "This interview was amply used by the Spanish and Ibero American press."[56]

Then, a disaster hit Mexico. In the early morning of 19 September 1985 and the evening of the next day, earthquakes, measuring 8.1 and 7.5 on the Richter scale each, shook Mexico City and left more than 20,000 persons dead, at least 40,000 injured, and 31,000 homeless. These quakes left to rubble most of the central part of the Mexico City, which housed hotels, apartment buildings, government offices, and historic buildings. EFE's 1985 Memorial said that "the EFE Mexico bureau took 23 'interminable' minutes to respond to the 'nervous' messages that the copy-chief on duty was sending from the international desk in Madrid." EFE's correspondent in Los Angeles had barely informed the Madrid Central that the seismographs at the University of California had detected an earthquake of strong intensity with the epicenter possibly located in Mexico. For 23 minutes the EFE bureau in Mexico, as all other offices of the rest of international agencies, was isolated from the world.

At the end of those 23 tense minutes, Antonio Ortega of EFE's Mexico bureau sent out "the very first news from that country from within the ruins —the fear and the debris." EFE claimed that the communication of "all other news agencies remained interrupted for a week." As EFE-Mexico was off the center of the city —at Laffayette 69, in the Anzures suburb— it remained intact. From the EFE office, correspondents from the Spanish media, and "many colleagues of foreign news agencies —among them, those from AP, Reuters, and West German dpa— could transmit messages to their respective headquarters."[57] EFE had reaped its glory, though unwittingly, from disasters in a Third World (and a Latin American) country. It had assumed the exploitative character of the Western agencies against which the Third World had been complaining, for these news services thrive on "coups and earthquakes."[58]

Professional Newsroom "Game"

Around 5 P.M. —shift-changing time—, 29 March 1985, a sense of suspense reigned in the central news desk of the EFE agency. Top news directors were huddled around a VDT, anxiously awaiting a message from the Brussels bureau. EFE executive editor Manuel Velasco, associate editor Miguel Higueras, and others were trying different phrases on the central VDT.[59] They were preparing to dispatch a Priority 1, "Flash" wire on the final okay by the ministers of the European Common Market assembled in Brussels, a final agreement to let Spain join —along with Portugal— the European Communities (EC). She had aspired for EC membership for almost 2 decades in on-again-off-again negotiations with the 10 member nations.

The good word never came. At last around 11 P.M., Brussels sent a disappointing report that France again blocked Spain's entry in the Common Market at the last moment —as she had done so many times in the past. This time, the pretext was that Greece opposed the conditions of the entry of Spain; the 2 Mediterranean countries were direct competitors in the fishery industry. No FLASH wire was dispatched that night.

But was this really the way a FLASH wire is sent out by a news agency? A FLASH is supposed to be on surprise news of top importance; it had to deal with unexpected news. A FLASH must not be "concocted" this way. EFE's own style book says: "FLASH — goes out without dating and without EFE logo. [It] is so 'unusual' that [it] is used for very few occasions, for, otherwise, [it] would lose efficacy and become unnecessary."[60] Even if Spain had been admitted on that day in the Common Market, it was an "expected" news item. Indeed, the last-minute blockage should have merited a FLASH, for it was more "unexpected" than the "pending" admission. Editor Velasco defended his plan for a FLASH this way: (1) It would have been sent only to the subscribers in Spain; Latin Americans would not be that much interested. (2) It is not necessary that news be "unexpected" to qualify as a FLASH wire. Neil Armstrong's moon-landing on 20 July 1969 had not been "unexpected"; the whole world was "expecting" the news, even knowing the approximate time, but FLASH was used.

This FLASH business was an example of a "professional journalism game" played by the EFE managers. Utrilla —wire-service man— emphasized "professionalization" as opposed to the "reckless expansion" he blamed on his predecessor Anson. Thus "professionalized" EFE covered agilely other big news of 1985 such as: Ronald Reagan's 7–9 May visit to Spain, where he collided "with one of the most vociferous demonstrations of his entire European tour."[61] Events included Reagan's visit to a West German cemetery at Bitburg; the death of Spanish matador "Yiyo"; and the signing in Madrid in June of the long-awaited agreement by the European Common Market to admit Spain, this time, as of 1 January 1986.

English Language Service (ELS)

Utrilla was keenly aware of the journalistic importance of the U.S. capital. His increased dealings with the number 2 U.S. news service UPI, for "Nuestras Noticias UPI-EFE" program, led him to aspire to partial ownership of the failing UPI beginning in 1985. His second-in-command in the news side of EFE, editor "Manolo" Velasco, was also of the opinion that Washington definitely was the most important news source even for the "Hispanic news agency" EFE.[62] All these considerations led the EFE management to place increasing importance on the yet little-noticed English-language section of EFE.

EFE's English section was founded originally in 1969 by Carlos Mendo, another internationally minded EFE director. Its first chief was an Englishman named David Cemlyn-Jones, a friend of Mendo's. It was never given any importance by Mendo's immediate successor, Alejandro Armesto (1969–1975). Luis María Anson, great EFE expansionist (1975–1982), had a skewed view of the English service. He maintained that an English-language service of EFE should be located in London and should be chiefly a translation of the main EFE Spanish stories. The Utrilla–Velasco team started giving due importance to the EFE English department, upgrading it to the "English Language Service" (ELS). ELS was not to be a simple translation section but a semiautonomous news service with its own legitimate news function and its own clients. The head of the ELS was using the showy title of "editor-in-chief" (of ELS), which even Utrilla, let alone "Manolo" Velasco, did not employ.

The ELS editor-in-chief Dwight Porter was a world rover originally from San Francisco. Porter had worked for EFE during 1969–1971 for its start of the English section, and rejoined as ELS chief in 1982. He and his staff of 15 persons with U.S. and U.K. backgounds insisted that theirs was a news service in the English language, bristling at the suggestion that they were engaged in "translation" of EFE wires.[63] They in fact used the main EFE wires, but that did not make ELS a translation service. ELS sent out weekly 30 to 40 news stories of some 400 words each, dealing only with Spain and Latin America.

ELS's strong coverage of Hispanic America appealed to such world-girdling news media as the BBC and the *Financial Times*, plus the *Guardian* (Manchester), *Worldwatch*[64] magazine, and the weekly *Latin American Newsletter*, all British; and the DDP (Deutsch Dienst Presse), a small West German news agency. Porter said he attempted to sell the ELS news to *The New York Times*, the *Washington Post*, the *Boston Globe* and 3 U.S. television networks, plus the CBC (Canadian Broadcasting Corporation). He claimed his efforts had not succeeded because of "no support from the EFE" management.

"CAPITALIST" EFE

EFE under Utrilla management looked more "capitalist" than "socialist" in many respects. "Profitability" was among the 3 *leitmotifs* set forth when Utrilla took over EFE in 1983. The agency, he insisted, had to be an "enterprise." Utrilla's "capitalistic" policy might appear germane to several decisions taken by the PSOE government, which named him to the EFE post. The socialist (PSOE) government under Felipe González has betrayed its capitalist yearnings in several major decisions. Among them was its return to the private sector of the Rumasa Group, the largest privately owned holding concern, which it had nationalized in 1983. PSOE's persistent drive to gain entry to the European Communities was another. And then, the most meaningful was the PSOE reversal of its original anti-NATO position (now for Spain's continued membership in NATO). PSOE successfully campaigned in the national referendum of 12 March 1986. It was ironic that both PSOE and PSOE-appointee Utrilla tended to take more capitalistic actions than their respective opponents would have taken.

EFE's "Hotline" Products

In its search for profit in the news business operation, the Utrilla management marketed "news products" that were uncharacteristic of a news agency. The first of these "new products" was the EFE Databank (Banco de Datos), whose collection was started in May 1983. Some 100,000 documents were retrieved, classified, and filed for possible commercial use in the future.[65] Staff members of the Documentation Department were dispatched for training to Paris and Brussels, where they studied the databanks of the French government and the European Communities.

Red Teletype

In early 1984 Utrilla's EFE launched an elite-oriented news delivery system, trademarked "Red Teletype" (Teletipo Rojo). Only 100 teletypes, painted in bright red and emblazoned, with AGENCIA EFE \ RED LINE OF ALERT, were sold to exclusive high-society clients. The Spanish king received the very first Red Teletype. A threefold promotional brochure —naturally in red paper— had the following high-pitch sales message:

> The Red Telephone . . . joins Washington with Moscow, but it is a Red Teletype which became legendary, upon enabling an understanding between Kennedy and Kruschev in the Cuban Missle Crisis. An information service like this is offered by EFE to only 100 persons in Spain. Politics influences the finance. The social changes have much to do with the movement of the stock exchanges. A state visit opens markets and an industrial conversion changes strategies.

It is significant that EFE under the PSOE offered this service for the highly exclusive elite people of Spanish society, who are mainly interested in business and financial affairs. Utrilla was catering to only 100 movers and shakers in Spain's economic power structure.

EFE's Television Business

Unable to compete against RTVE, EFE-TV looked outside Madrid for commercial penetration. Along with establishing regional autonomy in the whole nation, several autonomous governments set up their own television services. By 1985 there were 3 autonomous regional television stations: Euskal Telebista of Basque Country, TV-3 of Catalunya, and Televisión de Galicia. The EFE-TV department has served these regional stations "through the offer of a daily 'menu' of projected news and the production of other topics directly commissioned" by these stations. For these activities, EFE-TV's 1985 revenues were double that of 1984, reaching P226 million (US$1.4 million). Financially EFE-TV showed the largest growth of all EFE departments in 1985.

EFE Computer Whiz

By 1985 EFE's news transmission had reached 1,200 bauds. Fifteeen years of experience had accorded the EFE communication department an opportunity to train itself to manufacture its own microcomputers, to be used in all EFE newsrooms and bureaus, domestic and foreign. In fact, the EFE-manufactured computer printers "were so good and versatile that such foreign news agencies as AP, the Merrill Lynch Financial News Network (FNN), and other businesses were considering to buy them" for their own use.[66]

Utrilla's News Bureaus

The Utrilla management made the most drastic cuts in its overseas bureau network. Expansionist Anson had listed the grand total of EFE's "news posts" at 91.

Table 8.2
EFE Network in the Pre-Anson, Anson, and Utrilla Eras

EFE NEWS OFFICES				
Regions/Categories	Pre-Anson	Anson	Utrilla	Change *
FOREIGN POSTS:				
South America	11	13	12	-1
Central America	6	7	7	0
The Caribbean	3	9	5	-4
Western Europe	9	16	12	-4
Eastern Europe	0	3	1	-2
North America	2	7	4	-3
Far East	1	7	5	-2
Middle East	1	6	6	0
Black Africa	0	6	2	-4
South Pacific	0	2	2	0
Foreign Total	33	76	56	-20
DOMESTIC POSTS:				
EFE Headquarters	1	1	1	0
Madrid Central	1	1	0	-1
Main Bureau	4	5	0	-5
Regional Bureau	1	1	16	+15
City Bureau	0	7	0	-7
Domestic Total	7	15	17	+2
GRAND TOTAL	40	91	73	-18

* Changes indicate +/- between the Anson and Utrilla eras.

One of these 91 posts —the "Madrid Central" office— was a bogus listing; there was no such post. The Central EFE National Desk took care of the capital-area news. The remaining 90 posts broke down to 60 real bureaus, 16 correspondents, and 14 stringers. But Anson always tended to call all of them "bureaus" in his expansionist expositions.

Foreign Bureaus. Of the 76 foreign EFE posts Anson had listed, only 46 were real bureaus; the remainder were 16 correspondents and 14 stringers. Utrilla effected 2 changes with regard to EFE's foreign posts: (1) he listed only 45 of the 56 total posts as bureaus and the remaining 11 as correspondents or stringers; and (2) he cut 20 foreign posts from Anson's 76, to wind up with only 56 EFE posts overseas. These changes were based on the basic "profitability" motif of the Utrilla management. All changes were made under down-to-earth considerations of cost-effectiveness of EFE posts abroad. Though a 20-post cut (from 76 to 56) was drastic, it was not reckless. Utrilla did not just cut and cut. New posts were even set up in the first year of his EFE management. In 1983 he reactivated correpondent offices in Ottawa and Belgrade and employed correspondents in Hong Kong, Singapore, and Bangkok. (Of these 5, only 2 had survived. By 1985 the, 3 at Belgrade, Hong Kong, and Bangkok, were eliminated, for they did not generate enough news of importance.)

The 20 foreign posts that received the Utrilla axe were: One South American —Brasilia; 4 Caribbean —Jamaica, Guadalupe, Tinidad-Tobago, and Martinique; 4 West European —Oslo, Berlin, Helsinki, and the Vatican; one East European —Belgrade; 3 North Amercan —Houston, Los Angeles, and the United Nations; 3 Far Eastern —Hong Kong, Jakarta, and New Delhi; and 4 Black African —Kampala, Uganda, Johannesburg, Dakar of Senegal, and Harare of Zimbabwe.[67] (See the Table 8.2.)

Domestic Bureaus. In 1984 Utrilla upgraded to regular bureaus the offices in Valladolid, Santander, Logrono, Zaragoza, and Murcia. This was in line with the progress in political regional autonomy being pushed by the PSOE administration. In early 1985, the Toledo bureau was established. Then, on 20 November 1985, EFE inaugurated its bureau in Mérida of Extremadura province, which completed EFE's domestic bureau network. The 16-bureau net, plus the Madrid Central, —for a total of 17 domestic posts— was in concurrence with the 17 autonomous regional governments. In the future, EFE intended to have 17 regional services, wire as well as television, to attend to the needs of these autonomous communities.

Utrilla's News Exchanges

Utrilla also gave a capitalistic tinge to the area of news exchange agreements with foreign agencies by emphasizing the "profitability" principle. This is declared unabashedly in the EFE memorials of the Utrilla years 1984 and 1985.[68] This was corroborated by the official charged with "external relations," Víctor Olmos, who said, in a formal "taped" interview that the commercial philosophy of EFE "begins in the direction of Utrilla."[69] Olmos said that there were 36 interchange agreements as of December 1985. Of this total, 4 had always been outright paid subscriptions by EFE for the "superior" services of the "Big-4" agencies, AP, UPI, Reuters, and AFP. Six "small" agencies paid for EFE news: Dutch ANP, Austrian APA, Belgian BELGA, Cuban Prensa Latina (PL), Hungarian MTI, and Angolan ANGOP.

With the remaining 70 to 80% of news "exchange" agreements, the Utrilla management started in 1984 a "campaign to obtain the 'profitability' from the deals." Since EFE had tremendously expanded its services "qualitatively as well as quantitatively," in the 2 decades of 1965 – 1985, the free interchange with many of these small agencies was no longer justified. But it was not easy to convince these foreign agencies to begin paying for their EFE subscriptions, as "they had many years of 'gratis' service exchanges." Seven of these —which Olmos did "not want to mention their names"— would or could not pay for EFE services. They would, however, "help EFE obtain clients in their respective countries," Olmos said. The approximately 20 remaining medium-range agencies were approached, beginning in 1984, "whenever the periodic contract renewal came around" for payment for service differences, which "are difficult to quantify" though they know EFE has had more extended and expensive information services. How successful has the Utrilla team been in getting these foreign agencies to pay for the service differential of EFE news? Olmos, to start with, was very much disinclined to provide any answers.[70]

The 1984 EFE Memorial listed 30 foreign news agencies with which EFE had different types of exchange agreements: (1) The "Big 4" (AP, UPI, Reuters, and AFP); (2) 8 Western European; (3) 8 Eastern European; (4) 5 Arab; (5) 3 Asian; (6) one Cuban; and (7) one Angolan agencies. The roster of the 26 foreign agencies did not vary significantly from what the Anson management had. This fact signifies that the Utrilla management —aside from its effort to commercialize more— did not alter much of what had been carried out by the Anson team in news exchanges. The same held true for EFE's participation in international association activities: IAPA (Inter American Press Association, or in Spanish SIP, Sociedad Interamericana de Prensa), AEAP (Alliance Europeenne des Agences de

Presse), Conference of the Euro-Arab Press Agencies (CAPEA), and EPA (European Photo Agency).[71]
  The only change from the Anson era was the visit EFE president Utrilla made to Moscow in July 1985 to sign the renewal of the exchange agreement with TASS. EFE had come a long way from the paranoid days of anticommunism under Franco.

THE BEST WOMAN FOR A MAN's JOB

Upon assuming power in January 1983, Utrilla hired as his chief of presidential staff, a first-class P.R. person, Charo de la Rica Gruber. An English sign in her office read: THE BEST MAN FOR THIS JOB IS A WOMAN. Under De la Rica's coordination, the EFE agency was engaged in glittering promotional activities during 1983–1985.

EFE Publications of 1983–1985

In 1983 EFE published a slick 28-page pamphlet entitled "Nuestro Mundo" ("Our World") in Spanish and English. These booklets were much superior in their appearance —though not in content— to Anson's "Agencia EFE, S.A., History and Organization," also in both languages. They were followed in 1984 by the fourth edition of the EFE manual of style, which carried —unlike its Ansonian predecessors— a catchy title: "Manual de Español Urgente" ("Manual of Urgent Spanish").[72] Then, between 1984 and 1985, EFE published a gigantic (1,552 pages, 4-inch thick) compendium, entitled: *Nuestro Mundo '85/'86, Banco de Información, OMNIDATA EFE*. This book contained encyclopedic descriptions of the Latin American nations, Spain, Portugal, Israel, and the United States, which EFE considers a vaguely defined "Hispanic world." Country sections were introduced by statements by the respective chiefs of state, plus individual essays written by representative national journalists. Some 300 journalists supposedly took part in the publication of the massive data book, replete with 4-color pictures, graphs, and maps.

Of Awards and Corporate Image

For the first time in its history, EFE set apart a section in its 1985 memorial to "public relations" activities. This was an indication of how image-conscious the EFE management had become. The Utrilla management —with the coordination of the Instituto de Cooperación Iberoamericana (ICI)— began giving out 5 annual journalism awards, ranging in cash amounts from P600,000 to P1 million ($3,715 to $6,192). In reality, Utrilla —socialist appointee— had altered monarchist Anson's old "Iberian Pulitzer" award to "King of Spain Prize" (*Premio Rey de España*), and had them bestowed by King Juan Carlos I and Queen Sofía at the Zarzuela Palace —unlike the ceremony at EFE headquarters officiated by the EFE president. Utrilla's EFE had become that good in P.R. —giving the old wine in a new bag.

EFE also received many prizes and recognition for excellence. It received the "Gold Mercury International Award" in 1985 for its "increasing contribution to knowledge and cooperation among the people of Latin origin" of the Special Conference for the Peace and the International Cooperation held at Brazzaville, organized by the International Organization for Cooperation (IOC). To put the "Gold Mercury" award in proper perspective, the EFE memorial pointed out a number of recipients of the award in previous years: French *Le Monde* (*The World*), the *London Times*, and Italy's *Corriere de la Sera* (*Evening Courier*). Spanish newspapers had also received the Gold Mercury: *El País* in 1978 and *La Vanguardia* of Barcelona in 1981.[73]

In 1985 the image-preoccupied EFE staged a *coup de theatre* in promotion of the news agency as a capitalistic corporation. EFE discarded its decades-old logo and had a new one designed. This was done to "mould its [EFE's] renovation" giving "a message of evolution that would identify the agency as [a] corporation of specific and unique form." Thus was set aside the EFE logo —the 3 letters *e-f-e* girdling the globe. This logo, used from the early days of EFE, was replaced with a modern emblem. EFE was prepared to spend a fortune in changing all its letterheads, business cards, and building signs across the world.

1985 Statistics and Finances

Statistical data under Utrilla are relegated to this P.R. section, for he considered all data purely as P.R. tools. Anson's reports —though exhibitionist— at least gave figures that explain themselves and are logically related. Utrilla's data have to be guessed at, or are simply unavailable. (Table 8.4 gives overall comparative pictures of the agency at different eras of its half-century.)

Information provided by the 1983-1985 EFE memorials is sketchy at best. The Utrilla memorials "insinuate" that EFE had "more than 1,000" national correspondents but this is not given as a hard piece of information. The memorials of the Utrilla years are "anecdotal," never "informational," and are contained in the picture-magazine type books. They never had such information as "EFE en Cifras" ("EFE in Figures"), as presented in Anson's books of 1980–1982. Utrilla's annual memorials never even tried to list the wordage(s) of the different sections or the total EFE services. One has to guess from the anecdotal reference in passing to have any idea of the news volume, which seemed to add up to 345,800 news items in a year. Anson's books were full of detailed wordages in millions by sections. Even though those figures may have been inflated, one can get some idea of the EFE news volume. The Utrilla books never listed how many domestic and foreign subscribers the agency had. So they are presented as "n/a" (not available) on the comparative Table 8.4.

Even in the financial statement, where the management had to render cold figures, the Utrilla team played the P.R. game. The Utrilla management juggled the financial figures as shown in Table 8.3.

It claimed total 1985 expenses of P4,689.1 million and a loss of P216.9 million in the cover letter for the financial statements of that year. These figures did not include P122.4 million in severance payments Utrilla had to make to the EFE employees he had fired. His excuse for this was that those payments should not be considered part of "his" 1985 accounts, because those employees had been hired during what Utrilla called "Anson's disorbited expansion binge." It was a ludicrous claim and represented a typical juggling of the books for the sake of image.

Table 8.3

Finances under Anson, Utrilla, and Palomares

EFE PRESIDENT	ANSON	UTRILLA	PALOMARES
Year.month	1982.12	1985.12	1986.12
EXPENSES	P3287.7m	P4689.1m	P4887.8m
(Severance pay)	—	P122.4m	—
Utrilla's REAL total expenses		P4811.5m	
REVENUES:			
From:			
Government Services	P1730.7m	P2629.4m	P2570.3m
Domestic Clients	P789.4m	P1440.0m	P1450.9m
Foreign Clients	P251.2m	P228.8m	P213.1m
Other revenues	P123.3m	P174.0m	P200.3m
TOTAL REVENUES	P2894.6m	P4472.2m	P4434.6m
BALANCE (loss)	(P393.1m)	(P216.9m)	(P453.2m)
Utrilla's REAL losses		(P339.3m)	
GOV'T CAPITAL SUBSIDY	P817.2m	P1322.9m	P1322.9m

P   amounts may not jibe with the figures in EFE financial statements because of rounding used here.
m   signifies million.

If one adds the P122.4 million figure to Utrilla's claimed expenditure of P4,689.1 million, then his truthful total 1985 expenses amounted to P4,811.5, and his real loss to P339.3 million. He had to list these real figures in the fine print of the 1985 financial statements, which had to be inspected by official bookkeepers.

On the revenue side, Utrilla listed a total of P4,472.2 million. But he never gave the breakdown of the global "interior (domestic) news service revenues" of P4,069.4 million. A researcher had to look all over the 1985 memorial and deduce from ambiguous statements to finally discover that 65% of that amount —or P2,629.4 million— had come from the government as payments for EFE's services. This was another Utrillan image-making game. Both his predecessor Anson and successor Palomares publicly listed their respective government revenues. Utrilla's "image-making" game went to such an extreme that it bordered on the disingenuous, if not outright false.[74]

It was fortunate for Utrilla —or maybe he had planned it that way all along— that he confronted only the government or semigovernment representatives as EFE stockholders; the entire EFE administrative council was made up of these officials. More than 98% of EFE stocks are owned by the government or semiofficial entities, and all 10 EFE councilors represented them, except for Utrilla himself, who, as the president of EFE, was just another official of the Spanish government. But Utrilla wanted to live the fiction that his EFE agency was not of the Spanish government and all his image-making gambits were directed toward that unreality. Despite all his image-conscious actions, his end came at the apogee of power of the PSOE government, whose political appointee he had been.

Utrilla Management Fizzles Out

As EFE entered 1986, the fourth year under Utrilla management, it became increasingly evident that Utrilla's ambitious bid for partial ownership of UPI was a futile effort. High-powered multiparty lawsuits were being filed in the United States capital in a complex fight over the legal and financial status of the U.S. news agency. It was no place for EFE. By mid-June 1986, a federal bankruptcy judge in Washington, D.C., had decided in favor of UPI's purchase by a Mexican-U.S. partnership.

At home, Spain was confronted with important diplomatic issues. Spain's official accession as of 1 January 1986 to the European Communities brought to Spain, along with an enormous spiritual uplift, a big economic challenge. Spain, the third-poorest nation in Europe, now had to compete with its much more industrialized neighbors without its former protectionist barriers. Barcelona's selection as the 1992 Olympics site also brought financial burdens along with a psychological boost. These and other national issues occupied Spain's national news agency during 1986.

Then came the oft-postponed referendum on NATO membership. In spite of national opinion polls suggesting negative results, the 12 March 1986 vote showed 52.5% in favor of continued Spanish membership in NATO: It was a personal victory for PSOE Premier Felipe González. Yet, it spelled —ironically— the ultimate downfall of EFE president Utrilla, a self-claimed González appointee.

Felipe González called an election for 22 June —4 months early— to capitalize on the NATO referendum victory. His PSOE won an absolute majority with 184 seats in Congress —18 seats fewer, however, than in the 1982 landslide. The election results were interpreted as an indication of the electorate's disillusionment with the PSOE's long rule. Though González reappointed most senior ministers in the July 1986 cabinet reshuffle, 4 new technical appointments were made, among them the labor portfolio that went to Manuel Chaves, a long-time colleague of González. Chaves' mandate was to resuscitate labor support, which González conceded in October 1985 that the PSOE had lost in its complacence. This upgrading of the labor portfolio, along with PSOE's general desire for a fresh beginning, foreshadowed doom for EFE president Utrilla.

José Luis Roldán, an EFE veteran and card-carrying PSOE member, had been "banished to meaningless positions" for his hostility toward Utrilla. Utrilla and his executive editor, Velasco, sensed a menace from Roldán, whom they perceived to aspire to the top EFE position. Roldán was elected president of EFE's labor committee. This allowed Roldán to challenge Utrilla's authority under the pretext of legitimate labor representation. He was a vice president of the PSOE labor commission and had been the secretary general of UGT (Unión General de Tabajadores = General Union of Workers), the power base for PSOE. During Utrilla's 1983–1984 feud in the Spanish congress with Anson, Roldán always raised completely new issues, as a third-party fisherman in troubled waters. With ascendancy to the labor ministry of Manuel Chaves, Roldán's labor colleague, there appeared writing on the walls of the presidential suite in the EFE building. Utrilla was a goner.

The 10 October 1986 issue of *El País* carried a story which speculated —without citing any sources— on the "possible" naming as EFE president of Alfonso Palomares, editor of the magazines *Posible* (*Possible*) and *Ciudadano* (*Citizen*). The "non-news" story recalled that, back in 1983, when Utrilla was appointed to the EFE post, Palomares had also been a candidate. The "news" item was a typical "plant story" commonplace in

Spanish journalism. Less than 2 weeks later, on 22 October 1986, Utrilla submitted his annual EFE report to the Congress. He did not even attempt to defend his position, but only rendered accounts of EFE's 1983–1986 activities and finances in a low-key, matter-of-fact delivery, pointing out that he had reduced the EFE labor force by 100.

A day later, on 23 October 1986, the PSOE government summarily dismissed PSOE appointee Utrilla as EFE president. Alfonso Sobrado Palomares was named in his place. [Sobrado] Palomares [75] immediately named José Luis Roldán as counselor, a post created to repay his "services" in causing the command change in EFE.

The new Palomares–Roldán team declared in the first paragraph of the opening statement of the 1986 EFE memorial:

> The news services of the Agency . . . maintained during the first three quarters of 1986 a decreasing activity [which was the] result of a rejected Personnel policy that sowed disenchantment [among EFE employees] upon 'computing' as maximum success the mere diminution of payroll. Besides, the increasing loss in salary lineup of the Agency with the communication businesses on the cutting edge in our country produced an exodus of some of the better prepared people of different writing sections of EFE.[76]

It was an open rebuke of Utrilla's management and a victory statement of the laborite Roldán. Utrilla had become another victim of the system that he had so ardently defended.

Utrilla was always vehemently opposed to the idea of parliamentary control of EFE, stipulated in Artcile 20.3 of the 1978 constitution. Utrilla preferred Administration control of EFE to parliamentary control, where EFE would be subject to multiparty give-and-take. He had replaced all nongovernmental EFE councilors —among them Palomares— with mid-level P.R. officials of the government or semigovernment corporations. Utrilla found them easy to order around and, indeed, they were, for they did not have any stake in EFE business. They, however, were also powerless to do anything when the PSOE government one-sidedly decided on Utrilla's removal.

If the EFE agency was under parliamentary control, there might be a wrangling in appointing an EFE president. But, dismissal would not be as easy or capricious, as Utrilla himself must have felt it to be in October 1986. He was simply discarded by the Spanish government, as had been all his predecessors.

EFE marked another era in its 50-year government service.

Table 8.4
EFE STATISTICS (1940s – 1980s)

Year	1940s	1950s	1962	1967/8	1969/75	1977.6	1982.12	1985.12	1986.12
EFE Director	Gállego	Gómez	Sentis	Mendo	Armesto	Anson	Anson	Utrilla	Palomares
EFE News									
Employees			200	500			735	635	640
Correspondents			710	1300			1640	1000+	
Bureaus			2	36	38	56	89	73	73
Domestic			2	4	5		13	17	17
Foreign			0	32	33		76	56	56
News Exchanges	2	5	5	7	19		31	33	33
Services									
Wordage		19m	21m	135m	136m	150m	265m	n/a	n/a
Photos							32850	59343	n/a
Subscribers				446		1500	1984	n/a	n/a
Domestic				163			840	n/a	n/a
Foreign			0	283	300		1144	n/a	n/a
Finances									
Capital	P10m			P20m	P50m	P200/400m	P800m	P1550m	P1300m
Expenses			P33.2m	P175.4m			P3287.7m	P4811.5m	P4887.8m
Revenues			P31.4m	P168.8m			P2894.6m	P4472.2m	P4434.6m
From:									
Government Services		- - - - - - - - - - - - - - - -(secret)- - - - - - - -					1730.7m	P2629.4m	P2570.3m
Domestic Clients		P23.0m		P86.3m			P789.4m	P1440.0m	P1450.9m
Foreign Clients		0		P71.4m			P251.2m	P228.8m	P213.1m
Other revenues							P123.3m	P174.0m	P200.3m
Balance				(P6.6m)		(P63m)	(P393.1m)	(P216.9m)	(P453.2m)
Government Subsidy		- - - - - - - - - - - - - - - - - - - -(secret)- - - - - - - -					P817.2m	P1322.9m	P1322.9m

m signifies million words or million pesetas (P).

P amounts may not jibe exactly with the figures in EFE financialstatements because of rounding.

Epilogue

Evaluation
(1986–1989)

The lengthy discussions and analyses thus far have traced the half-century history of Spain's EFE news agency. In that time span, EFE developed into the fifth-place Western news agency, only after the "Big-4" agencies AP, UPI, Reuters, and AFP. In 1985 —the 48th year of its formal operation— EFE even aspired to partial ownership of UPI. EFE has all the trappings of an international news agency in its organization, in its well-trained news personnel, and its material resources. Above all, EFE has "guaranteed" gigantic foreign markets in Latin America, where about 420 million Hispanics live in 20 former Spanish colonies, plus 130 million Portuguese-speaking "brothers" in Brazil.

EFE is operating as a "new conquistador" in the Americas. EFE has everything going for it. A U.S.-born editor of EFE's English Language Service observed in 1985 that EFE "has a potential of becoming a great agency. It has 'good individuals' working. Its system is crummy, which does not let the fine individuals work to their capacity,"[1] to convert it into a national as opposed governmental news enterprise.

EFE's STRUCTURAL DEFECTS

EFE has many structural defects that need to be corrected. But correction has not been possible, precisely because of that flawed structure. There have been meager efforts to break that vicious circle by 2 EFE managements —those of Carlos Mendo Baos (1965–1969) and Luis María Anson Oliart (1976–1982). However, their attempts scratched the surface. EFE's fallacious system would take much more than partial fixing. It would demand the reformist will of Spanish politicians and press practitioners to rectify EFE's multiple problems.

EFE's Capital Structure

EFE is legally a commercial corporation, denominated *Sociedad Anónima* (S.A., or anonymous society, equivalent to Anglo-American "limited responsibility" [Ltd.] or "incorporated" [Inc.] company). The current EFE statutes (commercial bylaws) of 17 July 1984 fix its "social" capital at P1,550 million, represented by 1.55 million shares of a nominal value of P1,000 pesetas each.[2] At the end of fiscal 1985, only 1.3 million shares had been paid in, thus pegging the actual value of the Agencia EFE, S.A., at P1.3 billion (or US$8.1 million).[3] The distribution of these 1.3 million shares is the cause of EFE's problems.

As shown in Table 9.1, practically all (98.9%) of the 1.3 million EFE shares are owned by the state of Spain or quasi-state entities, including some 425 public radio stations. Spain has only 17 commercial or independent stations.[4] These do not own EFE shares. The "Private Press," "Various of Press" (a curious expression), and "Private [Entities]" own a minuscule portion (1.099%), or 14,293 of the 1.3 million EFE shares. Of the 14,293 privately held shares, 10,000 are holdovers from the 10,000 original stocks imposed on bankers as voluntary contributions by the wartime interior minister Serrano Súñer and EFE founders. Most of the remaining 4,293 shares were sold out to the private press and press-related persons by EFE director Mendo in his dream to convert EFE into a press cooperative during his tenure.

With this capital status, EFE could not help but be controlled by the shifting Spanish administrations, which used, without exception, the prerogative to appoint their cronies to all state entities, including those owning the EFE stocks. Political appointments of course went to EFE presidents and directors. Every change in the Spanish government has produced without fail change in the EFE management. It mattered little whether the government changes involved only the director general of press (DGP), or the minister of information and tourism (MIT) during the Franco period, or the premiers or ministers in the post-Franco democracy. Government changes have *always* resulted in shifts in EFE management.

To camouflage this embarrassing state ownership of EFE, president Anson listed the number of stockholders as 375 and showed their names in a full-page listing in intentionally illegible typographical arrangements. He claimed to want to make EFE a Spanish press cooperative,[5] although he did very little to make it a reality. His successor since 1983, Utrilla, dropped all pretense at privatizing the EFE agency and started listing the number of EFE shares owned by different state entities as shown in Table 9.1.

Table 9.1
EFE Shareholders (December 1985)

STOCKHOLDER	# OF SHARES	% OF TOTAL
State of Spain	766,656	58.9 %
National Institute of Industry (INI)	266,660	20.5
[State] Savings Banks Federation	103,144	7.93
National Telephone Company of Spain	139,801	10.75
Social Communication Media of State (MCSE)	7,826	0.6
Radio Stations	1,620	0.12
STATE SUB-TOTAL - - -	1,285,707	98.9 %
Private Press	12,697	0.97
Various of Press	286	0.022
Private Entities	1,310	0.1
PRIVATE SUB-TOTAL - -	14,293	1.099%
GRAND-TOTAL - - - -	1,300,000	* 99.999%

* Total % is less than 100 because of rounding.

EFE's Revenue Structure

It is not only the capital structure that makes EFE a government agency. Most of EFE's operational revenues also come from the state. EFE's 1985 Memorial rendered that year's total operational revenue as P4,472.2 million. Of this income, P2,629.4 million, or a whopping 58.79%, was derived from government services (Table 9.2). The real picture is much more dismal. For among the domestic clients are hidden, at least, the public radio and television stations (RTVE) and the government-financed press association newspapers, like *Hojas del Lunes* (*Monday Sheets*). EFE could never operate without the money given by the government. And, no government will finance a news medium and let it operate as a free press.

Table 9.2
Sources of EFE 1985 Revenues (in P Millions)

SOURCE	AMOUNT	% of TOTAL
Government Services	P2629.4m	58.79 %
Domestic Clients	1440.0m	32.20
Foreign Clients	228.8m	5.12
Other revenues	174.0m	3.89
TOTAL REVENUES	P4472.2m	100.00 %

EFE Among Private Agencies

How did EFE escape the dismantling of the Franco institutions after1976? How do private Spanish news agencies reconcile the existence in their midst of a leftover from the Francoist propaganda institutions? They do not, according to an unsystematic survey conducted in late 1985 asking them if they regared EFE as a government or state agency.[6] Radial Press, one of the 5 private agencies [7]responding to the survey was most expressive: "In 1976–1985 [EFE has been the] mouthpiece of the GOVERNMENT, sustained with the money of all Spaniards, making illicit competition to the independent agencies." This was in sharp contrast with its understanding of EFE as a "mouthpiece of the STATE" up to the 1975 death of Franco. COLPISA (Colaboraciones Literarias para Prensa Independiente, S.A.) was not so vociferous. It said: "EFE has been 'Governmental' of late, but it can not be so much. It is not possible to rule over the 300–500 intellectual persons [at EFE]."

Europa Press (EP), the biggest of all private news agencies, founded in 1960, has been a feisty competitor of EFE. EP's president José Mario Armero Alcántara, prominent international lawyer, does not even make a distinction between a state or government news agency: "EFE is at the service of the Government, that represents the State," so it should serve the interests of the Spanish state in foreign affairs. But in domestic politics, an official agency cannot avoid serving the government in power, which is "unfair" to the rest of the news industry.

Armero cited an example to elaborate that the function of EFE is to be the organ of Spain. He asserted that EFE should have given only the Spanish version on the Spain-Morocco dispute over the Ceuta enclave in Morocco. He elaborated that EFE (in February–March 1984) should not have carried the statements by Moroccan King Hassan. Armero insisted that EFE should have given only the Spanish side of the dispute, because it is Spain's agency.[8]

Agencia SEIS (Servicio de Informaciones Especiales) concurred with other private agencies by observing that "politics returned to EFE" during 1976–1985. Agencia OTR (Off the Record) "lamented not being able to express our opinion on the functions and nature of EFE, for the respect that naturally is owed to the competition." It desired to stay "off the record" on EFE. The rest of the sources responding to the survey expressed in varying terms their general consensus that EFE is more "of the GOVERNMENT than the STATE." Marcelino Camacho Abad, leader of the ultra-left Comisiones Obreras (CC.OO. – Workers Committees) used the strongest terms: "No! EFE keeps being a Governmental Agency."

EFE Administrative Council

EFE, operated with funds from the state, owes its problems not entirely to state money. If operated with wisdom and fair play, it could still perform its national as opposed to the governmental role effectively, as in the case of AFP, the French state news agency.

As practically all (98%) EFE shares are held by the state or semistate entities, the annual stockholders' assembly has stamped the decisions presented from the EFE administrative council. Thus, EFE's direction has remained in the administrative council. EFE's current (1984) statutes fix the council membership at "a minimum of 9 and maximum of 12 residents in Spain and of Spanish nationality" to prevent the possibility of absentee or foreign control of the agency.[9] The administrative council elects its own president, and also the EFE director-general at the proposal of the president, who can exercise simultaneously the functions of director-general, if the council so approves. The last 2 presidents —Anson and Utrilla— have exercised that prerogative.

Nothing in this basic EFE structure presents problems, except the membership of the council. The council membership has made EFE a government "P.R." service rather than a "press" enterprise. EFE director Mendo (1965–1969), who made EFE a Latin American news agency, would emphasize that more than half (8 out of 15 once) of the EFE councilors were representatives of the Spanish press. To Mendo, it meant that EFE was a press-oriented news agency. Besides, Mendo at least tried to expand private parts in EFE proprietorship. EFE president Anson (1976–1982) also kept a few press representatives on the EFE council, besides his "camouflage attempt" to emphasize the number of EFE stockholders, though they owned only a tiny portion of EFE shares.

EFE president Utrilla (1983–1986), a political appointee of the PSOE government, not only did away with all the pretense of camouflaging the 98% state ownership of EFE stocks, but took several actions to make EFE completely governmental.

He dismissed all councilors representing the press. Ten of the 11 EFE councilors —except himself— were directly from 6 state entities that had nothing to do with the press. Utrilla's dislike of having other journalists on his EFE administrative council was not only shown de facto in the council membership, but made it de jure or statutory. Utrilla did not want any other journalists on his council or among EFE directive personnel. He wanted —and got— dictatorial powers in running the state-owned EFE.

Utrilla vehemently objected to "the parliamentary control of the media of social communication dependent on the state" including EFE, as stipulated in Article 20.3 of the 1978 constitution. He tried all administrative and parliamentary maneuvers to avoid the application of the fundamental law of the land to his agency. How did he reconcile his objection to parliamentary control when he himself conceded that "information control from the Parliament [is] more 'presentable' than from the Government"?[10] This was ludicrous in that everybody, including Utrilla himself and EFE clients, knew that the Spanish government controlled 98.9% of EFE's stock and it gave 84% of the total revenues.

How did he explain that his appointment to the EFE presidency was owed to the PSOE administration then in power? Utrilla did not want any control from the Spanish parliament with the clear constitutional mandate. Utrilla did not want any journalistic participation in his council. He did not want any control over his conduct of EFE business other than the political commission from the party in power. The EFE president under the first genuinely "democratic" government after 3 "transition" governments (1976–1982) did not want democracy in his state-run news agency!

AFP-EFE COMPARISON

Utrilla's reluctance to share power with anyone should not be construed as flaws inherent in every state-owned or -supported news agency. The Agence France-Presse (AFP) is a case in point. Of the capitalist "Big-4" (AFP, UPI, AP, and Reuters), the French news agency "is the only one to which its government has direct channel of influence in its policy-making."[11] Yet nobody has accused AFP of serving partisan interests.

AFP's Organization

AFP's political independence is assured by an autonomous board of directors (or administrative council), appointed by an intricate system of checks-and-balances. Its structure prevents its administrative council from being dominated by a single party. The multiparty French National Assembly practices a gentleman's agreement to reflect proportional partisan strength in AFP's administrative council. Political leaders of Spain should exercise statemanship in a state enterprise that is the EFE agency, and reflect a proportionate party representation in the composition of the EFE administrative council. Utrilla summarily brushed aside such a suggestion from the present author, as "little realistic"[12] without offering an explanation.

Utrilla even rejected a suggestion that EFE presidents be appointed for 5- or 7-year "fixed" terms as in the case of the U.S. Federal Reserve Board chairman with a proviso that the EFE position could only be vacated by a two-thirds vote in the Cortes. That way the EFE president would not become a "political football." His position was never to countenance any parliamentary control of EFE. It did not matter to him the Spanish constitution mandates it. Now that he was removed in 1986 by the PSOE without much ado, how does Utrilla feel about the suggestion for a stability for the top EFE post?

Journalists' Agency AFP

Eleven of the 15 administrative councilors of AFP are journalists. One-half of the 8-member AFP higher council also represents the media. As shown repeatedly, EFE president Utrilla allowed no competing journalists beside him on his administrative council. Utrilla's adamant refusal even to consider the example of AFP is inexplicable, when it is seen against his personal experience with AFP. He worked for AFP for 13 years (1960–1972) in Paris and in Washington, D.C. It was for that very reason that he claimed to have been named EFE president by PSOE Premier González, because (Utrilla asserted) "I am the best agency journalist of Spain."[13]

AFP's Finances

Spaniards may still put up EFE's dire economic situation as a pretext to keep the Spanish news service completely subservient to the government in power. Of EFE's total 1985 revenues, the receipts from the Spanish government were 84%, which broke down to 41.5% for service payments and 42% from direct subsidies. But AFP has not fared much better. The French news agency received state subsidies of more than 50% of its 1956 budget. In January 1957, when AFP got an autonomous administrative council, France's 150 daily newspapers had their AFP service charges boosted about 30% to compensate for the lost subsidies from the French government.[14] But 20 years later in 1976 AFP's budget still was overwhelmingly state-dependent. Of the $43 million of the 1976 operating revenues, AFP received 66% from the French state sector and 17% each from French and foreign private clients.[15] AFP continued to receive state subsidies, which in 1978 amounted to FR161 million (US$38.4).[16] This should persuade Spaniards that financial dependence is no excuse for political servitude.

SPANISH PROBLEMS

The faults with EFE should be borne by all sectors of society involved in the business of the national news service, which definitely is a national enterprise, not a profit-seeking business nor political-spoils system.

Political Will

The political influence of Spain is undoubtedly enhanced by EFE's worldwide news-gathering operations and its penetration in Hispanic America. Thanks to Spain's historical heritage, EFE has become the number 5 Western news agency in operational scope, leaving behind dpa and ANSA —of West Germany and Italy— whose industrial potentials are much higher. Political will and statesmanlike leadership are required on the part of all concerned. A healthy plan must be developed to implement the parliamentary control provisions stipulated by Article 20.3 of the Spanish constitution. Partisan competition should be elevated to higher levels for the national good. The PSOE —when it was in opposition in the 1976 – 1982 transition period— accused the Centrist Union (UCD) of not implementing Article 20.3. The PSOE is now being condemned for its reluctance to take action on the long-pending (10 years) constitutional requirement.

At the persistent demand for action from a splinter party, the PSOE agreed to form a parliamentary committee on EFE concerning Article 20.3 in late December 1985, as described in chapter 8 of this book. The EFE committee was to have its first meeting in February 1986. No such meeting had yet taken place at this writing. And there "does not seem to be much interest on the subject" of EFE's compliance with the constitution.[17] The control of the national news agency naturally is a political advantage for the party in power. It is for this reason that the shifting Spanish governments have been reluctant to implement Article 20.3 of the constitution, because of mutual mistrust among the competing political groups. A long-time EFE employee and EFE executive editor during 1986 suggested a solution to this political problem. Miguel Higueras Cleries said:

> EFE cannot avoid governmental meddling, given its financial structure. A solution would be to make it belong to the Crown (King). All media in the U.S.A., U.K., France, etc.; all suffer government

influence. The important thing is to see how to reduce that influence. Perhaps, through the Crown [in Spain]. Let's make a good use of the Crown.[18]

The idea sounded plausible, given the king's role in suffocating a military coup attempt in February 1981, which saved the fragile democracy of Spain.

Role of the Spanish Press

The EFE news agency is too important a national enterprise to be left to the politicians. The Spanish press, a direct beneficiary of the EFE services, should take the leadership in voicing a collective advocacy for participation in the affairs of the Spanish national news agency. It should claim its rightful representation in the administrative council of the EFE agency. The EFE news services can be markedly improved in its quality and quantity. The Spanish press as a whole should contribute to further progress in EFE's news services. Self-deprecating disregard for national news service, and toady preference for foreign news —especially from the "Big 4"— represent defeatism unbecoming of a once globe-girdling nation. The Spanish press must and can demand better service from EFE and help accomplish it.

Carlos Mendo once expressed "great surprise that the [Spanish] press did not show very much interest in active participation in the EFE agency." He said: "In the end, they were not disposed for such active participation, for cheap EFE services resulted in an indirect subsidy for them, thanks to the state subsidies for EFE. They didn't want more expensive EFE service."[19] Such an attitude may have been justified during the Franco dictatorship, for EFE then did not really give them news services, but acted as a tool for state control of the press. Now in democratic Spain, all should share the cost of improved services of the national news agency. The French papers accepted a 50% rate hike in 1957. Spanish colleagues should also bear the burden for the national good.

Subscription rates for EFE services are not "cheap" in Mendo's term, given the Spanish and Latin American economies.[20] The monthly rates for 1985–1986 were P57,743 (US$360) for EFE's national, international, and sports news for *La Tribuna*, published in the small Mediterranean town Marbella (pop. 10,000). Bolivia's daily *Opinión*, published in Cochabamba (pop. 190,000), paid a relatively low monthly rate of $200 in 1984–1985 for EFE-International.

Table 9.3
EFE Subscription Rates for Radio   Stations

TYPE OF SERVICES	MONTHLY RATES	(in P & $)
EFE national	P 113,605	$ 661.61
EFE international	119,444	695.61
EFE sports	112,671	656.17
EFE Hispanoamerica	35,850	208.78
EFE press summaries	200,000	1,164.75

RECOMMENDATIONS FOR IMPROVEMENT

Four specific recommendations are presented here in order that the undisputed potential of the EFE news agency as a national enterprise be fully developed without being exploited by Spain's domestic politics. The following measures should be taken to rid EFE of interference from shifting governments:

1. The EFE administrative council —kept to no more than 15 members— should be appointed by political parties in the Congress of Deputies of the Cortes, in proportion with their political representations. Councilors should all be directors of dailies, two-fifths from Madrid and the other three-fifths from the provinces. No government official should sit on the council.

2. EFE's president/director-general should be selected from among EFE councilors by the Congress and be appointed by the Crown, to free him/her of political influence from the party in power.

3. The term of office in the council, including that of the president/director-general, should be "fixed" at 5 or 7 years, so that it will not coincide with the political electoral process in order to give the council stability and independence.

4. The composition of the EFE personnel should be 70 to 30% between journalists and nonjournalists, respectively, to keep the administrative bureaucracy to a minimum. All journalists should be graduates of the recognized Colleges of Information Sciences, division of journalism.

EFE's CLIENTS ABROAD

In spite of structural defects and other problems, EFE has been a success story in Latin America, the area where, up until the mid-1970s, the "Big-4" agencies enjoyed predominance and EFE had been virtually ignored. Now who are the users of the EFE news? And, how do they utilize the EFE news as opposed to that provided by competing international agencies?

Recent EFE managements have generally claimed a clientele of some 2,200 subscribers, about 600 in Spain and 1,600 abroad. EFE enjoyed de facto and legal monopoly on foreign news in Spain for 40 years until 1978. And EFE passed the state subsidies on to its customers in the form of relatively inexpensive news-service quotas. Because of these factors all the Spanish media units had been clients of EFE in the Franco epoch, and the practice continued into the present decade, making all 600 or so Spanish media outfits customers of EFE. However, the figure of 1,600 subscribers overseas is highly debatable.[21] Foreign —mostly Latin American— media outlets do not feel compelled to subscribe to EFE's news services, unless EFE offers them news and features at least comparable to, if not more palatable than, the other international press associations. For these reasons, successive EFE managements have paid keen attention to the relative position EFE has occupied among the Latin American media.

Venezuelan University Study

Ricardo Utrilla assumed the EFE administration from Luis María Anson in January 1983 and that year there emerged among the left-leaning Latin American scholars a project to organize an alternate news agency known as ALASEI. Its long title was "Agencia Latino-Americana de Servicios Especiales de Información" (Latin American Agency for Special Information Services). ALASEI charged one of its founders from Venezuela to conduct a feasibility study. A research team headed by Eleazar Díaz Rángel, journalism researcher of the Central University of Venezuela, studied dailies of 11 Latin American countries during 19–25 September 1983.[22]

This study, called henceforward "ALASEI-1983," concluded that EFE was the "third in the Continent after the 2 North American giants [AP and UPI] since 1983, in the penetration of the news agencies" in Hispanic America. ALASEI-1983 found that the EFE news placed third in the frequency of use by the 11 newspapers with 16.95%, only behind AP and UPI which took the first and second positions, respectively, with 36.96% and 19.98% (see Table 9.4). EFE's penetration was far ahead (almost double) of the giant AFP's share (8.87%) —an amazing feat, when seen against the traditional Latin American strength of the French agency. EFE also soundly beat the Italian ANSA (7.28%). By then, the British Reuters had practically withdrawn from Latin America, scoring only 0.73%.

The Díaz Rángel report was a windfall for the extremely image-conscious
EFE agency. EFE president Utrilla hungrily grabbed this bonanza and had
its "summary" publicized in an "academic-looking" paper.

Table 9.4
EFE's "Ascendancy"

Sources of News	1962 CIESPAL	1966 DIAZ RANGEL	1976 REYES MATTA	1983 ALASEI	1985 EFE CONTROL
AP	27.93 %	40.80 %	21.00 %	36.96 %	20.04 %
UPI	46.39	31.30	39.00	19.98	19.13
EFE	0	0	8.00	16.95	30.69
AFP	12.56	18.60	10.00	8.87	15.26
ANSA	1.50	1.20	7.00	7.28	4.37
Reuters	0	1.60	9.00	0.73	3.50
LATIN	-	-	4.00	-	-
Corresp	9.37	-	-	3.32	-
DPA	-	-	-	-	4.82
Others	2.25	6.20	1.50	5.92	2.18
TOTAL *	100.00	99.70	99.50	100.01	99.99

LATIN is a 'subsidiary' agency of British Reuters.[23]
* Some totals do not add up to exact 100% because of rounding.
- means it was not counted, whereas 0 signifies there was no news from that source.
% figures were adjusted to total near 100%. Each study had extraneous sources, excluded
   from this table.
% represents media usage of different news sources.

ALASEI-1983 compared its results with 3 earlier studies on the
comparative penetrations among the news agencies operating in Latin
America. These previous studies were: (1) a 1962 study by CIESPAL
(Centro Internacional de Estudios Superirores Para América Latina)[24] in
Quito, Ecuardor; (2) a study done in 1966 also by Díaz Rángel;[25] and (3) a
1976 comparative analysis carried out by Chilean Fernando Reyes Matta, a
leading Third World communications scholar and activist.[26] EFE had not
figured at all in the 1962 and 1966 studies. And in the 1976 research, EFE
had "scored" an 8% share among the 7 news agencies compared. Table 9.4
presents these 4 studies by the communications scholars unrelated to EFE,
and a fifth study, of the 1985 periodic "controls" conducted by EFE's
"editing department" (a misnomer).

EFE's "Self-Study"

The editing department (a misnomer for "editorial control" department) of EFE compiles periodical (most of them monthly) statistical summaries of the usage of EFE news items by its Latin American subscribers, as compared to their usage of dispatches from other international news agencies.

In November 1985 EFE Editing compiled a statistical summary of a 7-month period (May–November) and circulated the results in an internal EFE report. The report placed EFE far ahead of all other competing agencies. It gave the EFE news agency a large (30.69%) share in news usage by Latin American papers, as opposed to the poorer showings obtained by AP (20.04%), UPI (19.13%), and AFP (15.26%). EFE was also far ahead of the smaller dpa (4.82%) and ANSA (4.37%). Reuters again trailed with only 3.50% showing. (See Table 9.4) How was this possible?

These periodical EFE statistical reports are compiled from the "Publications Control" (Control de Publicaciones). Every EFE Latin American bureau files a daily summary of comparative foreign-news use by EFE client papers. Madrid's editing department processes these bureau publications controls and issues monthly (and semiannual) analyses and studies reports. In addition to the lack of coverage of broadcast clients, this control system suffers from 3 inherent defects.

First, the bureaus are not punctual with these daily controls. EFE editing admittedly could not enforce the daily publications controls because of the busyness of the EFE wire traffic. The second problem is the subjectivity of the reporting bureaus. Besides, publications control is generally looked upon as a bureaucratic "busy work" at best, and tends to be attended to cursorily during the busy work schedule of the bureaus' personnel.

The third and most glaring defect is that this publications control surveys only those dailies subscribing to EFE. Some important Latin American papers do not receive the EFE news service and subscribe only to EFE's competitors.

What does all this mean for the EFE audience? The 4 scholarly teams cited above took supposedly scientific measurements of agency penetration during 1962–1983. But their objectives were not that of taking a hard look at comparative performances of agencies. Rather, they had been prompted by disparate ideological motives far removed from taking a measure of

EFE's health. EFE under Utrilla picked out whatever looked good for its P.R. gambit. The claimed "studies and analyses" by EFE "editing," for their inherent flaws, would always turn out to be a narscisstic exercise. Besides, no one —even those in EFE— took them seriously.

If EFE wants to know the real picture of its relative position in Latin American media, it should commission a specific and unbiased survey of its clients and nonsubscribers by an informed and neutral researcher. But it is not to be. The EFE administration has always opted to take Pollyannish pleasure from figures and data that it knows are fallacious. It has lived in a self-serving and self-deceiving dream world.

Has EFE not gained any international recognition at all, then? It certainly has. Yet a measure of that recognition cannot derive from any of these "scientific sorcerers" and EFE's misuse of these sources, but rather from its peers. The giant Associated Press has, of late, started using EFE as a legitimate news source. A short AP wire in early February 1987, for example, cited EFE's report on a speculated 21 April visit to Spain by Prince Charles and his wife, Diana.[27] AP did not turn to the British Reuters nor to Buckingham Palace in London to confirm the rumor but to the Spanish EFE and El Pardo Palace in Madrid. This is legitimate —although small— proof of international recognition of the EFE news agency.

Notes

All end-note references are grouped by chapters, and presented collectively. The end-note numbers are preceded by chapter numbers, e.g.: P-5 (Note 5 of Prologue); 5-13 (Note 13 of Chapter 5); and E-1 (Note 1 of Epilogue). Reference to the sources is facilitated by this numbering system plus the page titles of this section, and the alphabetically arranged bibliography in the next section. Full reference data will be given when a source appears first time; the subsequent appearances will be abbreviated to the bare bones.

NOTES TO PROLOGUE

P-1.   An EFE English Language Service (ELS) wire datelined "MADRID, MAY 11" [1985], headlined "EFE-UPI: Spanish News Agency Bids for Share of Ailing U.S. Wire Service" [UPI].

P-2.   *Editor & Publisher*, 21 September 1985, p. 14, listed among the "individuals [sic] interested in buying UPI" British Reuters, Tele-Communications Inc. of Denver, Gulf & Western Industries, the Spanish news agency EFE, Comtes Scientific Corp., Turner Broadcasting System (owner of superstation WTBS of Atlanta and CNN), Citibank of New York, and the Wire Service Guild on behalf of its UPI members. The "individuals" listed by the newspaper industry journal included Beurt SerVaas, president of Curtis Publishing Co.; Max Hugel, former CIA assistant director; Pedro López, president of a Miami savings bank; Richard Cunningham, former owner of the *Daily American* in Rome and former CIA employee; Mario Vázquez Raña, owner of a Mexican chain of about 70 newspapers; and Joseph E. Russo, Houston-based developer. As it turned out by mid-1986, the last 2, Vázquez and Russo, became the new owners of UPI.

P-3.   Manuel "Manolo" Velasco López, executive or managing editor (*director de información* = news director), on 17 December 1985, in a daily conversation with the author, who was "installed" in an office in the EFE building for research and observation for this book during the year of 1985. EFE editor (1983–1985) Velasco had served as EFE correspondent stationed in New York City (at the UN complex) and Washington, D.C., from 1969 through 1973. Among the group of EFE news staff members that this author dealt with in 1985, Velasco proved to be best informed of the history of the U.S. journalism and his command of English demonstrated his intimacy with the folklores of the United States.

P-4.   Juan Luis Cebrián to John Darnton, former *New York Times* correspondent in Madrid, in a PBS program, "Spain Ten Years After," as aired by WETA-Channel of Washington, D.C., at various times in March–April 1986.

P-5.   The "First Republic" had ruled Spain for only 22 months (Feb. 1873–Dec. 1874).

P-6.   Alfonso Nieto Tamargo, *La Empresa Periodística en España*, Pamplona, Spain: Ediciones Universidad de Navarra,
S.A., 1973, p. 93.

P-7.   PBS program, "Spain Ten Years After."

P-8.   Carlos Mendo Baos, interview, 5 December 1985, when he was a London correspondent for *El País*. He gave this interview at the EFE headquarters on a home visit.

P-9.   Ibid.

P-10.   Ricardo Utrilla, interview, Madrid, 20 December 1985.

P-11.   Mendo interview.

NOTES TO CHAPTER 1

1-1.   In a 14 November 1985 interview, José Luis García Gallego (of the *Casino de Burgos tertulia* group, who worked for EFE from its foundation until his Dec. 1981 retirement) said that Vicente Gállego Castro "had belonged to the Associated Press previously." But he was not sure what kind of AP relationship Gállego Castro had had.

1-2.   A typed biography of Vicente Gállego Castro in the files at the Madrid EFE headquarters.

1-3.   Nobody seems to know exactly when EFE was started (months before its formal constitution as a limited stock company either on 3 December 1938 or 3 January 1939—there even exist 2 notarized documents on company formation, hence these 2 dates). "The 1 October 1938 was the date of the founding of 'La Agencia EFE,'" was a passing note in a 2-page typed note on "Biographical Data of Pedro Gómez Aparicio" (the EFE founding subdirector and its director [1944–1958], in "EFE Documentation" file at File and Documentary Service of EFE Madrid headquarters.

1-4.   Ramón Serrano Súñer, interview on 27 November 1985.

1-5.   James W. Cortada, ed., *Historical Dictionary of the Spanish Civil War, 1936–1939* (Westport, Conn.: Greenwood, 1982), p. 365.

1-6.   Serrano Súñer interview.

1-7.   Juan Montero-Ríos y Rodríguez, *De Fabra A EFE*, unpublished graduation thesis of, Escuela Oficial de Periodismo (Official School of Journalism), 1956, kept for restricted access to persons with the author's written permit at the Ministy of Culture Central Archive, Madrid. Most of the information on the Fabra news agency in this book is based on this rare scholarly work.

1-8.   The trademark *Hell* in German means "clear, as in sound or voice."

1-9.   *Ya*, 11 December 1982.

1-10.   On the historical data surrounding the Fabra news agency, the EFE "Foundational Memorial" is most sketchy when compared to the more disciplined thesis by Montero-Ríos.

1-11.   The Spaniards in general are sensitive about, and even resent, the term *Latin America*. They say it should be called "Hispanic America." Luis Bergareche Maruri, president of COLPISA news agency of Madrid, heatedly told the author in November 1985: "There is nothing 'Latin' or even 'Mediterranean' about the Spanish America; it was discovered, conquered, and developed by Spain. It should be called 'Hispanic America,' not Latin America."

1-12.   The major Argentine newspapers were: *Crítica* (*Critique*); *Noticias Gráficas* (*Graphic News*); *Pregón* (*Proclamation*); *L'Italia del Popolo* (*The Italy of the People*); *Argentinisches Tageblatt* (*Argentine Daily*); *El Diario* (*The Daily*); *Ultima Hora* (*Last Hour*); *La Vanguardia* (*The Vanguard*); *El Mundo* (*The World*); *España Republicana* (*Republican Spain*); *La España Nueva* (*The New Spain*); *Correo de Asturias* (*Mail from Asturias*); *El Boletín de la CGT* (*The Bulletin of the CGT* [Comisión General de Trabajadores = General Workers Commission]); and *Noticiero Español* (*Spanish News Bulletin*).

1-13.   Real Academia Española, *Diccionario de la Lengua Española* (Madrid: Real Academia Española, 1970), p. 937; Maria Moliner, *Diccionario de Uso del Español*, 2 vols., Madrid: Editorial Gredos, 1971, 2:553.

1-14.   Cortada, *Historical Dictionary*, pp. 90–91, characterized as "crucial" Bolin's contribution to the Franco uprising. Details of the Bolin missions in this book are drawn from both this Cortada dictionary and Luis Bolin's own book, *Spain: The Vital Years* (London: Cassell, 1967), pp. 9–49.

1-15.   Unbeknownst to the outside world, another Spaniard, Isaac Peral (1851-1895), physics and chemistry professor at the Academy of Amplification of Navy in Madrid, invented a type of submarine first tested in 1888. A street named after him cuts through an uptown section of Madrid.

1-16.   Cortada, *Historical Dictionary*, p. 234.

1-17.   Their memoirs are: Bolin, *Spain*; Ramón Serrano Súñer, *Entre Hendaya y Gibraltar* (Madrid: Ediciones/Publicaciones Españolas), 1947, and *Entre el Silencio y la Propaganda: Memorias* (Barcelona: Planeta), 1977.

NOTES TO CHAPTER 2

2-1.   Manuel Aznar Zubigaray, *Historia Militar de la Guerra de España*, Madrid: Ediciones Idea, S.A., 1940, pp. 872–3.

2-2.   Information on the DUX agency comes mostly from Montero-Ríos's thesis, pp. 50–53.

2-3.   Fernando Cendan Pazos, *Historia del Derecho Español de Prensa e Imprenta (1502–1966)*, Madrid: Editora Nacional, 1974, p. 182.

2-4.   Ibid., p. 184.

2-5.   Antonio Castro Bobillo, *Elementos Básicos para el Análisis de la Censura Cinematográfica Estatal en España desde 1936 hasta Nuestros Días,* unpublished thesis, Facultad de de Ciencias de la Información, Universidad Complutense de Madrid, September 1980, p. 91.

2-6.   All these citations and references to the 1938 Press Law are based on: César Molinero, *La Intervención del Estado en la Prensa*, Madrid: DOPESA, 1971, pp. 91–99.

2-7.   Nieto Tamargo, *La Empresa Periodística*, p. 90.

2-8.   Serrano Súñer, *Entre Hondaya y Gibraltar*, p. 57.

2-9.   Alberto Poveda Longo, interview, 6 November 1985, and subsequent conversations. In Spanish usage, the word *información* carries a slightly different connotation from the English word *information*. The Spanish *información*—which, unlike English *information*, can be singular and plural—is more equivalent to the English term *news*. The Spanish words *actual* and *actualidad* are not direct equivalents of English *actual* and *actuality*. The English words carry connotations similar to English *real* and *reality*. In Spanish, *actual* and *actualidad* do not carry that meaning at all but refer to "present" and "present time." This tricky differentiation between Spanish *actual* and English *actual* has been a stumbling block to the beginning learner of both languages. At times it has caused social mishaps and sometimes contractual disasters.

2-10.   Antonio Herreo Losada, director of Europa Press, in a letter cited in *Diario 16,* 26 December 1982, p. 8.

2-11.   Vicente Gállego Castro, interview with an unidentified reporter of *Dígame (Tell Me)*, for an article on 10 September 1940.

2-12.   Ramón Garriga, *La España de Franco*. Vol. 1; *Las Relaciones con Hitler*, Madrid: Toro, 1976, pp. 99–100.

2-13.   Oliver Boyd-Barrett, *The International News Agencies,* (Beverly Hills, Calif.: SAGE, 1980, p. 158n.

2-14.   Group interview. On 14 November 1985 the author held lengthy taped interviews with "La Vieja Guardia" (the Old Guard) now in retirement: José Luis García Gallego (of the *Casino de Burgos tertulia*), Jesús Martínez Tessier, and Francisco del Valle Arroyo.

2-15.   Serrano Súñer, *Entre el Silencio*, pp. 408–10.

2-16.   Max Gallo, *Spain Under Franco: A History* (New York: E. P. Dutton, Inc., 1974), p. 17.

2-17.   George Hills, *Franco: The Man and His Nation* (New York: Macmillan, 1967), p. 342.

2-18.   Garriga, *Las Relaciones*, p. 113.

2-19.   Felipe Maraña Marcos, *La Información Internacional en España*, unpublished doctoral thesis, Faculty of Information Sciences of the Complutense University, Madrid, 1984, pp. 389–90, vol. 1, citing news reports in the Madrid dailies: *ABC* of 22–29 [sic] August 1939 and *El Alcázar* of 22 [sic] August 1939. (Since the Soviet-German pact was signed in Moscow overnight 23–24 August, the news could not have been reported by the Spanish papers until 25 August.)

2-20.   Brian Crozier, *Franco* (Boston: Little, Brown, 1967), p. 299.

2-21.   Maraña, *La Información Internacional*, p. 391, citing the Madrid Catholic daily *Ya* of 5 September 1939.

2-22.   Samuel Hoare, *Ambassador on Special Mission* (London: Collins, 1946), pp. 7–77.

2-23.   Poveda interview.

2-24.   Gállego Castro interview with *Dígame*. (See n. 2-11 above.)

2-25.   Hugh Thomas, *The Spanish Civil War* (New York: Harper and Row, 1977), pp. 921–22.

2-26.   EFE, "La Agencia EFE, S.A.: History and Organization," Madrid, 1980, p. 4. (This 44-page promotional booklet was published both in English and Spanish in 1980, 1981, and 1982.)

2-27.   *SP* * magazine, "EFE, agencia hispanoamericana de prensa," 10 July 1966, pp. 48-50.

          * There is a curious story on the *SP* title of this weekly news magazine patterned after the U.S. *Time* magazine. General Spanish public —including even some former editorial employees of this once-defunct magazine— believed that "SP" was a short for "Servicio Público" (Public Service), as it was published by the company, "Servicio de Publicaciones, S.A." Not so, said Vicente Royo Masía in a 26 November 1985 interview. Royo was the "director" (editor) of the *SP* weekly from 1968 to 1972, when it "was strangled economically by the Franco censors for its 'TIME–style' objectivity." Royo said that an *SP* cofounder–editor had seen a commercial neon sign once at the San Francisco Golden Gate that blinked "SP — South Pacific," which caught his fancy and named the magazine *SP* without ever explaining its origin in its masthead or anywhere else. *SP* was resuscitated in the post-Franco era.

          Lawyer Royo has been EFE's "asesor jurídico" (legal advisor) since 1972. Royo could also be a busybody censor. He suggested in November 1985 that this book on EFE history be "approved" by EFE, the idea rejected out of hand. The present author is not sure if Royo withdrew his fangs because of the quiet yet intense rejection by the author, or Royo was reminded of the demise of his own *SP* at the hand of Francoist censors.

2-28.   José Sotomayor y Ojeda, *La Información Nacional de la Agencia EFE*, unpublished graduation thesis, Escuela Oficial de Periodismo (Official School of Journalism), Madrid: Ministry of Culture Central Archive, 1963, pp. 12, 18. (Sotomayor was a chief of the EFE national desk in 1985.)

2-29.   Group interview.

2-30.   Hills, *Franco*, p. 344.

2-31.   Garriga, *Las Relaciones*, 1: 288–292.

2-32.   From the Madrid daily, *Arriba* (*Hurrah*), 24 October 1940, vol. 2, no. 189, p. 1.

2-33.   Gallo, *Spain Under Franco*, pp. 100–101; Hills, *Franco*, p. 345–46; and Lloyd, *Franco*, pp. 180–81.

2-34.   Serrano Súñer, *Entre el Silencio*, pp. 290–91.

2-35.   Group interview.

2-36.   Manuel Prados y López, *Etica y Estética del Periodismo Español* (Madrid: Espasa-Calpe, 1943), pp. 159–60.

2-37.   Gonzalo Dueñas, *La Ley de Prensa de Manuel Fraga Iribarne*, (Paris: Editorial Ruedo Ibérico, 1969), p. 15.

2-38.   Gabriel Arias-Salgado, *Textos de Doctrina y Política de la Información*, 3 vols., (Madrid: Mnisterio de Información y Turismo, 1960), 1:22.

2-39.   Manuel Fernández Areal, *Libertad de Prensa en España (1938-1971)* (Madrid: Cuadernos para el Diálogo, S.A., 1968), p. 73. (The author insisted on leaving the 1968 publication date intact, as a silent protest against the censorship that held up the book's publication for 3 years until 1971, when he added a 56-page chapter to the original 178-page book.)

2-40.   Ibid., pp. 25–26.

2-41.   Miguel Delibes, *La Censura de Prensa en los Años 40* (Madrid: Ambito Ediciones, S.A., 1985), pp. 26–27.

2-42.   Castro Bobillo, *Elementos Básicos*, p. 95.

2-43.   Cortada, *Historical Dictionary*, p. 350.

2-44.   Cendan, *Historia*, pp. 93–94.

2-45.   Cortada, *Historical Dictionary*, p. 266.

2-46.   Fernández Areal, *Libertad de Prensa*, pp. 38–39.

2-47.   Delibes, *La Censura de Prensa*, pp. 8-11.

2-48.   Fernández Areal, *Libertad de Prensa*, pp. 62–63.

2-49.   Ibid., p. 45.

2-50.   Poveda interview.

2-51.   Group interview.

2-52.   Henry F. Schulte, *The Spanish Press, 1470–1966* (Urbana: University of Illinois Press, 1968), pp. 76–78.

2-53.   Ramón Garriga, *La España de Franco*, vol. 2 (Madrid: G. del Toro, Editor, 1976), pp. 98–99, 286–87.

2-54.   *Hojas del Lunes (Monday Sheets)* are a unique Spanish press institution. Originally instituted by the Royal Order of 1 January 1926 as beneficient publications, these Monday Sheets had monopoly right to publish Monday mornings —when all other "dailies" were not allowed to come out— by each and every one of the Spanish press associations. Revenues from their circulation and advertising were used for different social benefits for association members, including medical services, emergency loans, scholarships for the children of newsmen, and other professional activities for retired or incapacitated members. In 1979 there were 30 Monday Sheets in Spain with a combined national circulation of 700,000, receiving a government subsidy of some $650,000. These figures derive from Henry F. Schulte, "Spain," in *World Press Encyclopedia*, 2 vols. (New York: Facts on File, 1982), pp. 807, 815, and 818, vol. 2.

2-55.   EFE, "Nota Informativa a la Dirección General de Prensa," 1 February 1946, p. 2.

2-56.   EFE, "Ejercicio de 1950, Informe," April 1951, p. 2.

2-57.   Víctor Olmos, interview, 17 December 1985. (Olmos's job as the "exterior relations" man was not easy to pin down. Olmos had a business card that did not give a clear-cut title, but these two cryptic lines: "Adjunct to the Presidency/Exterior Relations." Olmos worked for EFE intermittently (1961, 1976–1977, 1985–present) and in Washington, D.C., from June 1986 to March 1987 as its "general manager for the United States and Canada." He says he worked at the Madrid bureau of Reuters in 1961, and later as editor-in-chief of the Spanish edition of the *Reader's Digest* (1964–1976 and 1977–1984).

2-58.   EFE, "Nota para la Subsecretaría de Educación Popular," 6 November 1946, p. 4.

2-59.   The International Organization of Journalists (IOJ), *Handbook of News Agencies in the World*, Prague: IOJ Books Dept., 1986, pp. 44, 127, 106, 153.

NOTES TO CHAPTER 3

3-1.   Molinero, *La Intervención*, pp. 99-100.

3-2.   Cendan, *Historia*, p. 191.

3-3.   EFE news carried by *ABC*, 9–14 December 1946.

3-4.   Alberto Martín Artajo to H.E. Knoblaugh of International News Service (INS), according to a FET-JONS note of 3 May 1950, by Bartolomé Mostaza, p. 2.

3-5.   Juan Antonio Gíner Junquera, "Journalists, Mass Media, and Public Opinion in Spain, 1938–1982," in Kenneth Maxwell, ed., *The Press and the Rebirth of Iberian Democracy* (Westport, Conn.: Greenwood, 1983), p. 34. This date, 13 "June" 1940, is refuted by other Spanish scholars. The law to create the Falange Movimiento press was decreed on 13 "July" —not "June"— 1940, according to Nieto Tamargo, *La Empresa Periodística*, p. 91 – 92; and Enrique Bustamante Ramírez, *Los Amos de la Información en España* (Madrid: AKAL Editor, 1982), p. 197.

3-6. There is no consensus or documental proof of the exact meaning of this acronym. Poveda said in a November 1985 interview that it stood for "Prensa y Radio Españolas, Sociedad Anónima." He, after checking with several persons in the EFE agency, changed it to "Periódicos y Revistas Españoles, Servicio de Agencia." Since the Spanish radio was under the control of "Radio Nacional Española" and now under RTVE ("Radio-Televisión Española"), the former definition is less credible.

A source in the United States —not necessarily more accurate than the Spanish ones— agrees with the former denomination that included "Radio." See John C. Merrill, Carter R. Bryan, and Marvin Aliksy, *The Foreign Press*, Baton Rouge: Louisiana State University Press, 1970, pp. 122-3.

There is yet a third Spanish source, which indicates that the letter *R* represents "radio" not "revistas"; see Ministerio de Información y Turismo, *Gobierno Informa* (Madrid: Editora Nacional, 1964), p. 448. (Since PYRESA was formed in the 1940s and this MIT publication on the occasion of the "25th Anniversary of the Spanish Peace" was done in the hyperbole of 1964, it is not very dependable.)

3-7. Carlton J. H. Hayes, *Wartime Mission in Spain* (New York: Macmillan, 1945).

3-8. Ataulfo G. Asenjo, "Con los Compañeros de la Prensa de Cuba," *Informaciones*, 28 November 1946, p. 5.

3-9. Edwin Emery and Michael Emery, *The Press and America* (Englewood Cliffs, N.J.: Prentice-Hall, 1984), p. 342.

3-10. Oliver Gramling, *AP —The Story of News* (Port Washington, N.Y.: Kennikat, 1969), pp. 442, 450.

3-11. Mostaza, nn. 3 – 4 above.

3-12. Nieto Tamargo, *La Empresa Periodística*, p. 92.

3-13. These figures, from page 2 of EFE White Paper No. 7 of 1949, are sketchy at best as are most EFE factual data throughout this book. They do not give comparable numbers of EFE correspondents, of total EFE employees, of EFE daily wordage in 1938 – 1939, or other information.

NOTES TO CHAPTER 4

4-1. Schulte said that Gállego Castro resigned in 1944, for "he could not stop the government encroachment." Gómez Aparicio took over. "From then on," Schulte also alleged, "the EFE agency received subsidies of varying amounts and in various forms from the government" (Schulte, *Spanish Press*, p. 27). Schulte's first point misses the focus; it was more of the Nazi pressure than the "government encroachment" that forced Gállego Castro out of EFE. The second allegation makes too hasty a sweep of the history and does no justice to the honest —though frustrated— efforts by EFE executives to maintain EFE's independence by means of "government payments for contracted services." The EFE White Papers amply demostrated how EFE executives aspired to live honestly "with government assistance without suffering in independence."

4-2. Ibid., 1968, p. 31 n. 80.

4-3. Juan Beneyto authored in 1957 a 296-page book, which was the Spanish pioneer in the novel social science of mass communications. He gave it an English title, *Mass Communications*, issued by the Instituto de Estudios Políticos.

4-4. Beneyto in answer to a written survey questionnaire that the author conducted among Spanish journalism scholars and professionals in November 1985.

4-5. Crozier, *Franco*, pp. 466 – 67.

4-6. Fernández Areal, *Libertad de Prensa*, pp. 69 – 70, says Fraga made this declaration to a French reporter from the Paris daily *Combat*.

4-7.   "Semblanza Biográfica de Carlos Mendo," 12 February 1976, a typed Mendo profile preserved in the EFE archive.

4-8.   These figures are pieced together principally from 2 major sources. One is the 1962 Annual Memorial to the General Assembly of EFE stockholders, held on 29-30 April 1963. The other is Sotomayor's graduation thesis, pp. 14-38.

4-9.   Montero-Rios, *De Fabra A EFE*, p. 60.

4-10.   The Press Club was named after Jaime Luciano Balmes, the prominent and short-lived thinker and writer (1810-1848), who, among many intellectual activities, published the weekly *El Pensamiento de la Nación* (*Thought of the Nation*).

4-11.   An anonymous article, "Las Agencias periodísticas" published in *Revista Política y Parlamentaria*, Madrid, 15 September 1900, as quoted by José Altabella in his "Notas para la prehistoria de las agencias de prensa en España," *Estudios de Información*, January-June 1972 (Nos. 21-22), Madrid: Instituto de la Opinión Pública, pp. 11-39. (Most information in this section derives from this article, unless otherwise indicated.)

4-12.   In disccussing Spanish news agencies, most writers tend to include the press endeavors by Manuel María Santa Ana from 1848 to 1924. But that is a misconception. His were "newspapers" rather than a news agency. The writers are: Montero-Ríos (thesis, pp. 9-14); Schulte (1968, p. 182); Altabella (1972, pp. 11-12); and Pedro Gómez Aparicio, *Historia del Periodismo Español*, 4 vols. (Madrid: Editora Nacional, 1971), 2: 256.

4-13.   The paternal surname *Peris* was soon dropped for a better Spanish sound, *La Agencia Mencheta*.

4-14.   Mendo interview.

4-15.   Francisco Casares, "Artesanía Periodística," *Ya*, 13 April 1948.

4-16.   Alejandro Fernández Pombo, "La Agencia Prensa Asociada Fue Fundada en 1909," *Gaceta de la Prensa Española*, 15 November 1964, p. 60, as cited by Schulte, *Spanish Press*, p. 218.

4-17.   The 1916 founding date of *El Sol* (as alleged by Schulte, *Spanish Press*, p. 224) is disputed by Spanish journalist Montero-Ríos, who dates it 1 December 1917 (p. 38).

4-18.   Antonio Espina, *El Cuarto Poder* (Madrid: Aguilar, 1960), p. 283, as cited by ibid., p. 224.

4-19.   Montero-Ríos thesis.

4-20.   Ibid., p. 42.

4-21. Since the current Spanish-Portuguese news agreement of 1978 is between EFE and ANOP (Agencia Noticiosa Portuguesa), no documentation exists on the EFE-ANI contract. ANOP was formed after the 1974 Portuguese "second republic."

4-22. Serrano Súñer interview.

4-23. Serrano Súñer, at age 84, still had a quick enough mind to slap the wrist of the author for asking why he thought the Ibero-American news agency did not materialize. He called the author "a man of *oficio* who has a bad intention, a little perfidious intention of the journalist." Inquired of his age, Serrano came back with: "I do not have age, I am timeless (*intemporal*)."

4-24. Gállego Castro biography.

4-25. De Mier interview.

4-26. Pedro Gómez Aparicio, *Historia del Periodismo Español*, 4 vols., vol. 4, *De la Dictadura a la Guerra Civil* (Madrid: Editora Nacional, 1981), pp. 193-95.

4-27. The EOP applicant had to be a *bachiller* (bachelor), a *maestro* (teacher), or equivalent. In the Hispanic educational system —both of Spain and the Americas— a "bachelor" degree is conferred to the graduate of *colegios*, equivalent to U.S. high school plus one year, probably. Normal schools which specialize in teacher training (*profesorado*) at a level slightly higher than *colegios* confer a *maestro* or *profesor* degree depending on the country. The Spanish terms *bachiller*, *colegio*, and *profesor* cause at times endless confusion.

4-28. Gallo, *Spain under Franco*, p. 321.

4-29.   Gíner, "Journalists, Mass Media, and Public Opinion," p. 37; Schulte, *Spanish Press*, p. 38.

4-30.   Serrano Súñer, *Entre el Silencio*, p. 14.

4-31.   José Luis Rubio, "Agencia Norteamericana Nos Separa de Hispanoamérica,"

Juventud, 11 December 1953.

4-32. An EFE Paris dispatch carried by the Madrid Falange daily *Arriba* of 8 May 1964 did not detect Dali's "surrealist" pique at the Spanish press control.

4-33. Mendo interview.

4-34. *Arriba,* 27 October 1965.

4-35. MIT, *Textos Legales,* 1969, pp.ix–xxix.

4-36. Merrill et al., *Foreign Press,* p. 120.

4-37. Cendan, *Historia,* p. 199.

4-38. De Mier interview.

4-39. On this day (31 March 1966), 13 other decrees were also issued to implement numerous provisions of the new Press and Print Law, according to Cendan, *Historia,* pp. 221–22.

4-40. Mendo interview.

4-41. A news account in *Arriba* (9 March 1965) said the following private owners "offered" their EFE stocks for sale, but they were, in reality, ordered to surrender to the state their shares: *La Geceta del Norte* of Bilbao (100 shares), Banco Hispano Americano (1,250), Banco de Vizcaya (1,046), Banco Español de Crédito (804), Banco Urquijo (629), Banco de Bilbao (560), Banco de Santander (7), and unnamed others (270). All shares were paid the 1939 face value of P1,000. The 1939 interior minister, Ramón Serrano Súñer, had solicited ("extorted") the capital from those bankers, whom the original EFE group (*Casino de Burgos*) called "the pyramids" for their old ages, as described in chapter 1.

NOTES TO CHAPTER 5

5-1. Gallo, *Spain under Franco,* p. 325.

5-2. *ABC,* 1 January 1969.

5-3. As cited by Miguel Higueras Cleries (EFE executive editor in 1986), *La Agencia EFE y la Información de España al Exterior,* unpublished graduation thesis, Escuela Oficial de Periodismo (preserved in the Ministry of Culture Central Archive), Madrid, May 1967, pp. 101–102.

5-4. José Antonio Rodríguez Couceiro (EFE Mexico City bureau chief circa 1985), *Proyección en América de la Agencia EFE,* an unpublished graduation thesis, Escuela Oficial de Periodismo (preserved in the Ministry of Culture Central Archive), Madrid, September 1967, pp. 7–9.

5-5. These statistical data again are "pieced together" —with sound educated estimate— from different sources of varying degrees of objectivity, such as EFE's 1966 and 1971 Annual Memorials; a 1967 report; 2 theses in 1967 by future EFE reporters (Higueras Cleries and Rodríguez Couceiro); 2 EFE promotional pamphlets of 1969; and numerous interview-accounts by Spanish and foreign publications of the years 1966–1969.

5-6. Higueras, *La Agencia EFE,* p. 87. While Higueras did not cite any source(s) for his statistics on these world agencies, his figures can at least be considered an indication of how he and other EFE journalists looked at EFE and other agencies. (From 1966, still in the Official Journalism School, Higueras had started working as an apprentice reporter for EFE, which he joined upon his graduation in 1968. In his continuous service for EFE, he served as a New York City and Washington, D.C., correspondent, 1968–1973; at the Mexico bureau, 1973–76; as the chief of various Madrid central desks, 1976–1979; as a Lisbon correspondent, 1980–1983; and as an assistant executive editor at the Madrid EFE headquarters, to become, in 1986, the executive editor, the highest news position at the EFE agency, and finally to be Lisbon correspondent again in 1987.

5-7. Ibid., p. 167.

5-8. *ABC,* 16 January 1966.

5-9. Mendo's statement cited in Higueras, *La Agencia EFE,* pp. 147–48; and Mendo's "report" to EFE's administrative council, 27 June 1967, p. 1.

5-10. Mendo to *Pueblo,* 13 March 1968, and *El Alcázar,* 14 January 1969.

5-11.   Poveda interview.

5-12.   Fernánez Areal, *Libertad de Prensa*, p. 186.

5-13.   Mendo interview.

5-14.   Gallo, *Spain under Franco*, p. 342.

5-15.   Ibid., p. 343.

5-16.   The wartime U.K. ambassador to Spain, Sir Samuel Hoare, once said, "the Spanish newspapers were not only unreadable but unread" (Hoare, *Ambassador*, p. 55).

5-17.   A brief historical sketch below will explain how successive Spanish governments have used the Rock issue as a xenophobic propaganda punching-bag to divert attention of Spaniards whenever there have been domestic crises. The EFE news agency under Franco did its share of anti-British drum-beating about the "Rock."

    The Rock of Gibraltar commands the highly strategic, 8-mile-wide western entrance to the Mediterranean Sea, connected to the Iberian peninsula by a one-mile low-lying sandy isthmus. The 2.25-square-mile (5.8 sq. km.) rock was captured by an Anglo-Dutch force in 1704 during the war of Spanish succession and passed to Great Britain by the 1713 Utrecht Treaty. Ever since the rock has been the source of Spanish-British disagreements. In 1779 Spain joined France in aiding the fledgling United States, declaring war on England. Then, a 2-year Gibraltar siege failed. Spain's effort to recover Gibraltar culminated in a referendum in 1967, when 99% of the residents (31,000 in 1985 mostly of Spanish, Italian, and Maltese descent) voted to retain the link with Great Britain. Spain rejected the referendum as a violation of her sovereignty and of the Utrech Treaty, sealed Gibraltar's land border in 1969, and did not reopen communication until April 1980, when Spain and Great Britain agreed —by the Lisbon Declaration— to solve their dispute in keeping with a UN resolution, calling for eventual restoration of the rock to Spain. The Brussels Agreement of November 1984 led to lifting of the 16-year Spanish blockade in February 1985 in exchange for British support for Spanish accession to the European Communities in 1986. The status of the rock has remained deadlocked past 2 years between the Spanish claim of her sovereignty and the British commitment not to transfer it against the expressed wishes of the Gibraltarians.

5-18.   Fernández Areal, *Libertad de Prensa*, pp. 155–156.

5-19.   The figure P10 billion ($143 million) derives from the *1970 Book of the Year of the Encyclopaedia Britannica*, p. 697; while Gíner, "Journalists, Mass Media, and Public Opinion," p. 40, raises it to P14 billion ($200 million).

5-20.   Mendo interview.

5-21.   De Mier interview.

NOTES TO CHAPTER 6

6-1.   Franco was born on 3 December 1892, making his age at his 20 November 1975 death "practically 83" —minus 13 days.

6-2.   Kenneth Maxwell, "Introduction: The Transition to Democracy in Spain and Portugal," in Maxwell, *Press and the Rebirth of Iberian Democracy*, p. 5.

6-3.   Gíner, "Journalists, Mass Media, and Public Opinion," p. 41.

6-4.   Castro Bobillo, *Elementos Básicos*, p. 120.

6-5.   EFE, *1969: Un Año de Desarrollo Constitucional* (Madrid: Agencia EFE, S.A., 1970).

6-6.   Fernández Areal, *Libertad de Prensa*, pp. 225-26.

6-7.   Mendo interview.

6-8.   "MEC" was an unexplained abbreviation for "España-Mercado Común," or Spain-Common Market, instead of "EMC."

6-9.   Historical Central America does not include Panamá, even though the geographical Central America refers to the Isthmian area down to Panama. Guatemala, El Salvador, Honduras, Nicaragua, and Costa Rica were the Spanish colonial provinces administered as the Capitancy General of Central America by "La Audiencia" at the Guatemalan capital from the 1523–1524 conquest by Pedro de Alvarado until the 1821 independence from Spain. After a brief (1822–1823) annexation to the Mexican Iturbide Empire, the 5 former Spanish colonies constituted the Federation of United Provinces of the Center of America from 1824 to 1839, when it broke up into 5 separate states. Panamá is of a completely different origin. It was a northern province of the South American state of Colombia. Theodore Roosevelt separated Panamá by force and intrigue in 1903–1904 to build the Panama Canal. In the 1960s, these 5 nations formed the Central American Common Market (MCCA) to reunite the common economic and cultural heritage, to which Panamá was admitted as an "associate member." MCCA has faced disintegration since the late 1970s because of the political turmoils afflicting these nations. Central America should be also distinguished from Meso America, which includes Mexico in the north, Central America and Panama in the middle, and the northern parts of the South American continent. Meso America includes Belize, the former British colony on which Guatemala claims sovereignty. Belize forms part of ACAN-EFE.

6-10.　Interview on 16 September 1985 in Panama City with Manuel R. Mora, director-manager of ACAN, who had worked for EFE from 1966 at different posts, including that of director of the EFE national desk.

6-11.　Ricardo Utrilla Carlón, "ACAN: Una Pequeña Gran Agencia para Centro América," speech given by the EFE president/director-general on 19 July 1984, to a seminar at the Universidad Internacional Menéndez Pelayo of Santander, Spain, on "Ibero America and the New Information Order." Most of the information on ACAN-EFE, other than the data on its legal and financial constitution, derives from this speech text of 23 pages.

6-12.　Panamá does not have its own money and uses the U.S. dollar as legal tender. The ACAN constitution specifically used "United States dollar" as the legal instrument of share accounting. The Republic of Panama's monetary unit, the "Balboa," is in name only, as Panamá does not print Balboa bills, and only makes 0.5 and 1-balboa silver coins. This practice is considered another symbol of the U.S. colonialism, to which Panamá owes its birth.

6-13.　"ACAN" is the official name of the news agency, but all in the agency seem to prefer to attach "EFE" to it. Their formal business cards, the company letterhead, and other papers carry the logotype "ACAN-EFE."

6-14.　This is obvious hyperbole on an imagined anecdote, if a one-page biographical note on the EFE president/director-general in the EFE archive is to be believed. The note said that Utrilla was called back to the AFP Paris headquarters in December 1972. ACAN-EFE was legally constituted on 30 November 1972, its papers were registered on 5 December 1972, and the ACAN-EFE operations did not begin until early 1973, according to his own ACAN 1984 speech cited in n. 11 above. The 22–23 December 1972 earthquake that devastated the Nicaraguan capital of Managua was covered by EFE's Costa Rican bureau chief, not by ACAN. EFE's (not ACAN's) coverage of the Managua disaster was praised by *Le Soir* of Brussels and Spanish newspapers, which was carried as a 2-bell "urgent!" dispatch by CIFRA wire on 11 Janauury 1973. This "news" item does not give any inkling of the pending ACAN operations.

6-15.　"Malestar Entre los Trabajadores de EFE," *Nuevo Diario*, 30 September 1973.

6-16.　"El Plan de Desarrollo a Favor de Una Agencia en Prensa," *Actualiad Española*, 23 November 1967.

6-17.　Clipping from an unidentified newspaper, 3 August 1972.

6-18.　Walter Pincus, "CIA Funding Journalistic Network Abroad," *Washington Post*, 16 January 1976, p. A15.

6-19.　Poveda interview.

6-20.　"EFE Desmiente que Haya Recibido Nunca Subsidios de la CIA" ("EFE Contradicts that It Has Never Received Subsidies from the CIA" —emphatic Spanish double negative), *Ya*, 17 January 1976. *Ya*, the leading Catholic Church daily published by the EDICA (Editorial Católica, surprisingly was not knowledgeable about the Inter American Press Association [IAPA]). It transliterated the IAPA into Spanish, "La Asociación Interamericana de Prensa," ignorant of the IAPA's official Spanish (and Portuguese) title, which is "La Sociedad Interamericana de Prensa" (SIP).

6-21. *Washington Post*, 19 February 1976, p. A18.

6-22. Agustín Edwards traveled to the United States frequently and was widely recognized as a conservative publisher and an important member of IAPA. He was among the 6 "honor medalists" given the 1969 "Missouri Honor Awards for Distinguished Service in Journalism" by the University of Missouri School of Journalism in May 1969 during "Journalism Week" at Columbia, Missouri. The author —then a graduate student— witnessed the conferral of awards and heard Edwards' speech.

NOTES TO CHAPTER 7

7-1. Spain's membership in the European Communities (EC), including the European Common Market, became legally effective on 1 January 1986, but her full-fledged accession had been obtained in 1985. In the case of NATO, Spain ratified the North Atlantic Treaty on 30 May 1982, thus formally becoming its16th member. The socialist government coming to power in December 1982 held Spain's NATO status in abeyance for 3 years. It, however, reversed its position and supported NATO membership in a national referendum, which it won by what was termed a "landslide" vote —52.5% for and 39.8% against— on 12 March 1986. Groundwork for this "victory" had been laid again in 1985.

7-2. Information on Anson derives from a one-page "Nota Biográfica de Luis María Anson," in "Boletín Mensual de Información, Madrid: Editorial Dawson and Fry, March 1981, preserved in the EFE archives.

7-3. Mendo interview; and also see the section "Command Changes II" in the preceding chapter.

7-4. News account in *ABC*, 20 October 1976.

7-5. For example, *El Alcázar*, 6 January 1978, p. 17.

7-6. "EFE Renuncia a la Exclusiva de Distribución de Noticas del Extranjero en España," *Ya*, 12 May 1978, p. 41.

7-7. Luis María Anson, "Palabras Preliminares" to Agencia EFE, "Manual de Estilo," 3d ed., 1981, p. 10.

7-8. The Panamanian reporter was Rafael Candanedo Acosta, who had worked for ACAN-EFE for 5 years before he came to Madrid in 1985 for a 2-year scholarship sojourn. The present author was lodged at the same university housing with Candanedo during his field research work in Spain on the present book.

7-9. Of the 38.99 million Spaniards, 28.38 million (72.8%) speak Castilian Spanish —the official language, 6.40 million (16.4%) Catalán, 3.19 million (8.2%) Galician, 0.89 million (2.3%) Basque, and 130,000 (0.3%) speak other tongues. See "World Data," *1989 Britannica Book of the Year* (Chicago: Encyclopaedia Britannica, 1989), p. 701 and p. 761.

7-10. Anson interview.

7-11. The 6 other Hispanic "Great Writers" were: Julio Cortazar, Eduardo Carranza, José Donoso, Miguel Delibes, Juan Carlos Onetti, and Salvador de Madariaga.

7-12. The Hispanics who were added to the "Great Writers" club were: Carlos Barral, Camilo José Cola, José María Gironella, Nicolás Guillén, Claudio Sánchez Albornoz, Fernando Lázaro Carreter, Francisco Miró Quesada, Ramón Sender, Gilberto Freyre, Juan Rulfo, Ernesto Sabato, Fernando Díaz-Plaja, and Carlos Franqui.

7-13. EFE 1981 Memorial, p. 13.

7-14. These EFE and COMTELSA figures are from Bustamante, *Los Amos*, pp. 224, 234.

7-15. EFE's 11 "traditional" Latin American bureaus were located in Buenos Aires, Montevideo, Rio de Janeiro, Asuncion, Santiago (Chile), Lima, Quito, Caracas, La Paz, Bogotá, and Mexico City.

7-16. IOJ Handbook. [These self-claimed figures of the reporting agencies should be taken with a grain of salt.]

7-17. The population figures —rounded off to millions— are from the "1986 World Population Data Sheet," Washington, D.C.; Population Reference Bureau.

7-18.   The 1978 Spanish constitution vested legislative power in the Cortes Generales, adopting the centuries-old title comprising 2 houses—the Congress of Deputies and the Senate.

7-19.   These EFE real-estate "inventories" derive from EFE's own publications, "Historia y Organización", 1980, 1981, and 1982 editions, the EFE Annual Memorials for the years 1981 and 1982; and other assorted accounts appearing in Spanish papers. In the 1984–1985 field-work research for this book, the author visited many EFE foreign bureaus in North and Latin America and Western and Eastern Europe. In most foreign posts, EFE bureau chiefs lived on the premises of the EFE buildings, which facilitated instantaneous and constant access to communication.

7-20.   A Russian-language expert at the National Security Agency translated "Sadovo-Samotiochnaya" into "natural garden." *Sadovo* is a "garden"; *Samotiochnaya* is a Russian word hard to translate into English. She explained that it can mean "self-watering" or "self-seated." The best plausible English rendition of the name of the Moscow street in question is, thus, "natural garden."

7-21.   The account of the Kremlin expulsion threat to the EFE correspondent comes from "Amenaza de Expulsión del Corresponsal de 'Efe' y TVE en Moscú," *El País*, 31 May 1979, p. 8.

7-22.   IOJ Handbook. [These self-claimed figures of the reporting agencies should be taken with a grain of salt.]

7-23.   Bustamante, *Los Amos*, p. 231.

7-24.   "El Convenio Colectivo de Este Año, al Laudo," *Entre Nosotros* (*Among Ourselves*), April 1979, preserved in the EFE central archive.

7-25.   Spanish Government, "Boletín Oficial del Estado," 10 May 1982, pp. 12026–29 (Dirección General de Trabajo, Ministerio de Trabajo y Seguridad Social).

7-26.   The sources for these international agencies are: various EFE documents, such as Annual Memorials; "AP Fact Sheet #2," AP Corporate Communications, 7 December 1983; "Reuters Holdings PLC, Offer for Sale by Tender," early unspecified 1984 date; and "Agenzia ANSA," Relazioni e Bilancio al 31 Dicembre 1984, Ordinary Assembly of 30 April 1985.

7-27.   Schulte, "Spain," p. 812.

7-28.   Nieto, *La Empresa Periodística*, p. 93.

7-29.   Schulte, "Spain," 1982, pp. 808–9.

7-30.   Spanish Government, "Boletín Oficial del Estado," 14 May 1982, pp. 12546–48 (Jefatura del Estado).

7-31.   Maraña, *La Información International*, p. 1183.

7-32.   Juan Luis Cebrián Echarri, interview, 10 December 1985. The director of *El País* also completed an opinion survey form for the author.

7-33.   The 1980 figure derived from Schulte, "Spain," p. 817; and the 1981 and 1982 figures from respective EFE memorials.

7-34.   *Cambio 16*, 17 October 1976, no. 255, as cited by a PYRESA agency's wire of 23 October 1976.

7-35.   Bustamante, *Los Amos*, p. 228.

7-36.   *Diario 16*, 20 October 1981.

7-37.   For example, *El País* carried a lengthy article on 24 November 1981 headlined, "El PCE pide una regulación legal de la Agencia EFE" ("The PCE Requests a Legal Regulation of the EFE Agency").

7-38.   "Don't Cry for Me, Argentina!" was the title song for the 1976 musical play, *Evita*, by Lloyd Webber and Tim Rice, on the life of the second wife of the late (1946–1955) Argentine president Juan Domingo Perón. The military governments of the 1970–1980s prohibited the play in Argentina.

7-39.   EFE 1982 Memorial, p. 10.

7-40.   Ibid., p. 11.

7-41.   "Television and Radio," *1983 Britannica Book of the Year* (Chicago: Encyclopaedia Britannica, 1983), p. 655.

NOTES TO CHAPTER 8

8-1.　　The 7 were from: "Confederación Española de Cajas de Ahorro" (CECA = Spanish Confederation of Savings Banks), IBERIA (Spanish national airline), Instituto de Relaciones Agrarias (IRA, Institute of Agrarian Relations), Ministry of Finance, Ministry of Education, and Instituto Nacional de Industria (INI, National Institute of Industry). INI —which owned about 38% of EFE shares— was represented by 2 councilors. Two nongovernment councilors, of course, did not have any power. One of them, Alfonso Sobrado Palomares, was removed from the EFE council in 1984. (Ironically, Sobrado Palomares would replace Ricardo Utrilla as EFE president in 1986). The other private councilor, Carlos Luis Alvarez "Cándido" Alvares, was dismissed during a 1985 controversy at EFE.

8-2.　　The lunch companion, the author, was also greatly impressed by the apparent intimacy existing between the president and a reporter of EFE, despite the differences in their ages and ranks. They employed the intimate Spanish term *tu* rather than more formal *Usted* —both meaning "you" in English. Higueras, a graduate of the journalism college of the Complutense University, Madrid, was hired by EFE in Beijing, China, where she had gone to do postgraduate work in Chinese language and history. (Her personal history had prompted Utrilla to state his relationship with EFE.) His claimed "friendship" with Felipe González is plausible, as both men spent time in France in the early 1970s. Utrilla worked at AFP's Paris headquarters, and the future Spanish premier was active in the exiled PSOE leadership in France.

　　　　As to the intimate term in their address to each other, Utrilla said —in an interview at his Madrid office on 20 December 1985— that he believed in "democracy" in his dealings with his employees, and remarked that the "democratic intimacy" among the EFE personnel had also impressed an editor-in-chief of the Soviet TASS news agency.

8-3.　A page-long typed (double-spaced) biography of Utrilla by the "EFE-Documentation" leaves a 6-year "hole" in his career between 1977 and 1983. Charo de la Rica Gruber was the EFE presidential "chief of staff." The able presidential public relations person De la Rica "clarified the error in journalistic writing style" that created a noninexistent 6-year gap in the Utrilla biography. She explained that Utrilla continued as the director of *Cambio 16*.

8-4.　　*El País*, 31 July 1983; *ABC*, 13 July 1983.

8-5.　　There had been only 9 directors under Anson. Utrilla committed a flippant "error" in saying "it looks to me 12" (*me parece que doce*) in his remarks about the Anson "excesses" in an interview on 23 July 1984 with *Diario 16* (his old paper).

8-6.　　*El País*, 31 July 1983.

8-7.　　*Diario 16*, 16 March 1983.

8-8.　　José Antonio Flaquer was the Madrid correspondent for Barcelona publications. He first worked for the daily *El Noticiero Universal* (*Universal News Bulletin*) and later the magazine *Día 32* (*Day 32*). Anson was accused of having paid Flaquer for the EP subscription and having quartered the Catalán journalist in an office in the EFE locale, complete with a teletype. This way Anson and Flaquer "rifled" (*fusilar*) the EP news items.

8-9.　　EFE 1983 Memorial, p. 22.

8-10.　　The numbers and some names of the participating stations vary among the EFE memorials of 1983, 1984, and 1985, and 3 lists —dated 5, 26, and 29 November 1984— supplied to Utrilla by UPI's Cristóbal Tortosa, also variously called vice president for the Spanish Radio Network and of Marketing Services. Of the U.S. radio stations receiving UPI-EFE service in 1984, some 20 were located in the South and Southwest, 3 in Florida, 3 in Chicago, and a station each in New York City and the Maryland suburbs of Washington.

8-11.　　For example, *La Vanguardia*, 13 June 1984.

8-12.　　The disparaging remarks were made on UPI-EFE radio service to the author during interviews with Anson on 18 December, and Roldán on 16 December 1985.

8-13.　　These conditions are set forth in 4 subparagraphs of Articles 21 and 25 of "Estatutos de la Agencia EFE, S.A.," Madrid: EFE Publicaciones, 1981, pp. 19, 22–23.

8-14.　　*Diario 16*, 23 July 1984.

8-15.   Article 26, EFE 1984 Statutes, p. 21.

8-16.   Mendo's pretention that "his" EFE administrative council was represented more than half by the newspapers was described in chapter 5. Anson repeatedly emphasized his preference for a "privatized" EFE and his "fight to pass to private hands the state's one-third share of EFE stocks and maintain them" there, in the interview of 18 December 1985.

8-17.   *ABC*, 3 March 1984.

8-18.   The former EFE president patterned his denunciation after the famous 1898 open letter by Emile Zola against the French military high command in defense of Alfred Dreyfus, wrongly accused of pro-German espionage. Zola's "J'accuse" (I accuse) letter had turned the tide into an eventual reversal of the Dreyfus sentence.

8-19.   Gossip floated around that Utrilla did not do any work! An EFE reporter told of the cleaning women who worked in the presidential suite. They did not find any trash at all in Utrilla's waste basket; Anson used to fill his several times a day! They gossiped that the new president "just sat in his office, not doing anything." These innocently impressionistic women have to stay anonymous for their job security.

8-20.   José Luis Roldán, interview, 16 December 1985.

8-21.   On these parliamentary exchanges on EFE in 1985, the author was provided with the following papers, typed double-space: Oscar Alzaga Villaamil, "Interpelación, Cortes" 13 March 1985, 13 pp., "Moción Legislativa," 20 March 1985, 10 pp., and "Interpelación, Cortes," 25 September 1985, 10 pp.; Ricardo Utrilla Carlón, "Discurso sobre EFE," in testimony before the congressional committee on public administration, 21 May 1985, 8 pp.

8-22.   *ABC*, 26 September 1985.

8-23.   EFE 1985 Memorial, p. 47.

8-24.   *ABC*, 26 September 1985.

8-25.   *La Vanguardia*, 26 September 1985.

8-26.   *Ya*, 26 September 1985.

8-27.   The "Parkinson's rule" is an appropriate reference to the "Parkinson's Law," satirically set by C. Northcote Parkinson in his book by that title (1957), which states that the amount of work done is in inverse proportion to the number of people employed —thinking similar to that of the law of diminishing returns.

8-28.   Armero letter.

8-29.   De Mier interview. This die-hard Franco loyalist, 70, who limps because of a civil-war wound to his left leg, had just finished writing a book, *La Herencia* on the heritage" that "Franco left for a New Spain."

8-30.   Mendo interview.

8-31.   The company was denominated "Promotora de Informaciones, Sociedad Anónima (PRISA)" (Promoter of News, Inc.) Prisa in Spanish means "haste, hurry," which suggested the group's urgency in the project for a new paper.

8-32.   Cited by Schulte, "Spain," p. 820.

8-33.   Cebrián in PBS program, "Spain Ten Years After."

8-34.   Cebrián interview.

8-35.   "Disposición Derogatoria" (par. 3), "Constitución Española," Madrid: Rivadeneira, S.A., 1978, p. 47.

8-36.   *El Alcázar*'s book reviewer De Mier said in a (taped) interview on 12 November 1985 that King Juan Carlos I had tacitly acquiesced the February 1981 coup plan, then lost his nerve and reneged on his "loyal soldiers." De Mier repeated all the profanities allegedly hurled at the king by rebel Lt. Gen. Jaime Milans del Bosch at his trials and in prison. De Mier said that he "would not care if 'that ——— Juan Carlos found out' about it."

8-37.   On his visit to the *El País* plant on 10 December 1985, the author asked Cebrián why such elaborate electronic physical screening was conducted at the entrance of a newspaper. Cebrián referred to the 30 October 1978 letter bomb. At *ABC*, visitors are "required" to produce a picture ID card (passport from foreigners) which the guards photocopy and hold until the departure of visitors. *Diario 16* did not have any such "security" measures other than a guard's watchful observation. At the EFE headquarters, no one —including EFE management personnel— can enter or exit unless with a electronic gate card or guards' individual opening with notations on a registration book kept under close watch of national police officers.

8-38.   Cited by Maxwell, ed., "Introduction," p. 17.

8-39.   Cebrián interview.

8-40.   *El País'* "society" (*sociedad*) section is not equivalent to U.S. newspapers' "society pages" but is a section dealing with wide-ranging "social issues" of Spain. Weddings, engagements, teas, parties, and other U.S. "society" events are carried in the Spanish newspapers' sections variously entitled, such as *acontecimientos* (happenings), *alta sociedad* (high society), or even *sociedad* (society) in some other Spanish newspapers.

8-41.   Schulte, "Spain," p. 817.

8-42.   The story also gave the 1984–1985 subsidy budgets by concepts as shown below:

YEAR	DIFFUSION	NEWSPRINT	RENOVATION	TOTAL P ($) million
1984	1,260.0	1,320.0	0	2,580.0 ($15.03)
1985	1,148.2	1,112.4	500.0	2,760.6 ($17.16)

(1984-85 % hikes in P and $ amounts do not match because of P/$ ratio changes.)

The newspapers and news-agency subsidy law and its various implementing decrees and resolutions spell out the following bases for actual subsidy amounts for 1985. They change annually.

DIFFUSION (circulation) subsidies given "per copy":
P3.0 (1.9 cents US) —dailies up to 5,000-circulation
P1.1 (0.7 cents) —dailies up to 50,000-circulation
P0.6 (0.4 cents) —dailies of 50,001-circulation or more
P0.4 (0.2 cents) —supplementary for dailies in outlying isles
P12 (7 cents) —overseas circulation at least weekly
NATIONAL PAPER subsidy: P12.6 (7.8 cents US) per kilogram
RENOVATION subsidy: % of investment decided by MCSE yearly

8-43.   Robert G. Picard, "Levels of State Intervention in the Western Press" in *Mass Comm Review*, vol. 11, nos. 1/2, Winter–Spring, 1984, pp. 27–35. Picard listed these 12 categories of state interventions in capitalistic countries: tax advantages, government advertising, postal-rate advantages, education/research grants, transportation rate advantages, grants/subsidies, loans, price regulation, news-agency aid, party aid, ownership regulations, and telecommunication rate advantages. The U.S. and U.K. also have press subsidies and assistance in various forms.

8-44.   *ABC,* 1 February 1985.

8-45.   *El Alcázar,* 1 February 1985.

8-46.   *Ya,* 2 February 1985. The paper's claim that it did not have any state debt was disputed by a reliable source. Porfirio Barroso Asenjo is a lawyer/psychiatrist, who teaches press ethics and law at the journalism department of the Information Sciences Faculty of the Complutense University of Madrid. He also writes occasional columns for the Catholic church paper. Barroso said, in an 11 November 1985 interview, that *Ya* was still not up to date with the state in its payment but that it would be updated by the end of December 1985.

8-47.   *Diario 16* is "freakish" in the sense that its stories are usually short on substance, it uses excessive color to make up for its erratic contents, and does not seem to realize the poor legibility of italic type which it uses for all proper nouns and all direct quotations, perhaps again to compensate for its lack of substance. *El País* has never used color (as of spring 1989) like its U.S. "models," the *Washington Post* and *The New York Times,* though it is in tabloid format, which most Spanish dailies have used for years.

8-48.   The Spanish government "announced" a bill on 4 April 1986 to authorize private television operation. Three nationwide private television networks will be given 10-year licenses. This information comes from the "News Letter" of the Prague-based International Organization of Journalists (IOJ), June 1986, p. 6. The IOJ note said that only 10% of airtime will be permitted for commercials of private television. It will be a subject of contention between the private operators and RTVE.

8-49.   In Spanish —of both Spain and Latin America— there is no distinction between "advertising" and "publicity"; all commercial messages carried in all mass media are called *publicidad*. The term *anuncio* would be a rough Spanish rendition for "advertisement" and is rarely used, except for reference to individual advertising messages. The term *propaganda* is used almost as often as the term *publicidad* for "advertising or advertisement(s)."

8-50.   *Ya*, 17 March 1985.

8-51.   *Cinco Días*, 22 March 1984.

8-52.   Tomás de la Cruz Serna, interview, 15 March 1985. The breakdown of advertising revenues by the 3 sources:

Media	Nielsen-"Ya"	J.W.T.-RTVE	Alas Group
Dailies	20.87 %	28.45 %	30 %
Magazines	12.48	12.07	15
Television	**56.38**	**23.82**	**40**
Radio	7.86	10.07	15
Cinema	0.56	1.02	- *
Outdoors	1.84	3.15	- *
Others	-	23.40	5
TOTAL	101.98	99.99	100

Totals do not add up to 100% because of rounding.
* Alas Group includes 'Cinema' and 'Outdoors' in 'Others.'
- Nielsen-Ya does not have 'Others.'

8-53.   "Lid" for "lead" is a Pidgin translation common in the newsrooms of Spanish-language print and broadcast media everywhere.

8-54.   There is a Central American saying: "Le mordió el gusano vagabundo" (The vagabond bug bit him).

8-55.   *El País* and *Diario 16*, 19 February 1985.

8-56.   EFE 1985 Memorial, p. 12.

8-57.   Ibid., p. 13.

8-58.   Mort Rosenblum, *Coups and Earthquakes* (New York: Harper Colophon Books, 1981.)

8-59.   In 1986, Velasco was separated from EFE, and Miguel Higueras was moved up as EFE executive editor. It had been rumored in the EFE newsroom that Velasco would be sent to Washington, D.C., "the most important news post also for EFE" —Velasco himself had said it. But he was no longer with EFE in 1986 and Víctor Olmos, of EFE exterior relations, was assigned to the U.S. capital post instead. Then, Olmos was called back to Madrid on 11 September 1987 by the new Palomares manangement of EFE. The EFE team sent Higueras to Lisbon.

8-60.   Agencia EFE, *Manual de Estilo*, third, corrected and increased edition, 1981, pp. 115-16. The number of bells for "Flash" has now become 8. The current fourth edition of 1985, called *Manual de Español Urgente*, has no rules on transmission priorities.

8-61.   EFE 1985 Memorial, p. 12.

8-62.   Velasco conversations, 1985.

8-63.   A lengthy interview and observation of ELS on 12 December 1985 revealed this information: Porter, 41, was a philosophy student at the San Francisco State College ("for only a year"); worked for the *San Francisco Examiner* during 1961-1963; and "roved over the globe" to Chile, Mexico, Scandinavia, and England, to settle in Spain with English-born wife.

8-64.   The London weekly magazine *Worldwatch* listed in the masthead of its 9 December 1985 issue, as its correspondents, the ELS's Dwight Porter, plus 2 EFE journalists, Zoilo Martínez de la Vega and Fernando Martínez Laínez.

8-65.   Executive editor Velasco said that, when "put on computer tapes," the information in the EFE databank will be offered on the market for computerized retrieval "at certain fees." He intimated the commercial plan in daily conversations with the author in March 1985.

8-66.   Velasco conversation, 20 December 1985.

8-67.   The 1985 EFE Memorial did not list EFE's Warsaw office, a correspondent's office, dependent certainly on the EFE Vienna bureau. The EFE Warsaw bureau was definitely operating in November and December 1985, when the author visited it. It was run by a Basque-born woman, Gemma Aizpitarte, married to a Polish photographer. It is not clear whether the 1985 Memorial simply missed the Poland office —which often occurs with various EFE documents— or if the Warsaw bureau had been eliminated between the end of 1985 and June 1986, when the 1985 Memorial was prepared and printed.

8-68.   EFE 1984 Memorial, p. 18; 1985 Memorial, p. 19.

8-69.   Olmos interview.

8-70.   On 16–17 December 1985, Víctor Olmos blocked the supply to the author of an "exchanges policy document" he had previously prepared for EFE president Utrilla. Utrilla was willing through his chief of staff (Charo de la Rica) to provide a copy. The ever-secretive Olmos offered a "taped" interview in lieu of the document. The interview did not reveal any new facts; he talked only of the wire-service generalities available to students of international journalism.

8-71.   EFE 1984 Memorial, p. 18.

8-72.   When the "Three EFE Old Guards" showed up at the EFE headquarters on 14 November 1985 for a group interview with the author, an old-timer concierge gave each a copy of the manual, saying, "I kept these for you," obviously trying to ingratiate his old "bosses."

8-73.   EFE 1985 Memorial, p. 18.

8-74.   Ibid., pp. 47, 55.

8-75.   Alfonso Sobrado Palomares, EFE president since 1986, is among the numerous Spaniards who prefer their maternal surnames to paternal in their daily usage. "Sobrado" means "leftover, excessive, superfluous, forward, brazen" in Latin American Spanish at least. "Palomares," which means "dovecot," is more elegant.

8-76.   EFE 1986 Memorial, p. 1.

NOTES TO EPILOGUE

E-1.   Interview, 12 December 1985, with Dwight Porter, editor-in-chief of the EFE English Language Service.

E-2.   Estatutos de EFE, 1984, p. 9. The nominal share value of P1,000 has not changed since the 1939 EFE incorporation, although its dollar value varied from $110 in 1939 to $6.22 in 1985, as the dollar-peseta ratio deteriorated over the 46-year period.

E-3.   EFE 1985 Memorial, p. 59.

E-4.   It is difficult to pin down the exact number of radio stations in Spain. Schulte ("Spain," p. 807) gave "442" as the "[total] number of radio stations." The *Europa Year Book—1985* (p. 827) lists 17 "commercial and independent stations." These 2 figures give an approximate number of "425 public stations" (442 - 17 = 425).

E-5.   Anson interview.

E-6.   In November–December 1985 the author sent out a survey questionnaire to all 13 private general news agencies, 5 major dailies, 13 journalism scholars, 18 political parties, and 2 labor organizations. The survey had a low rate of return: 5, 1, 2, 2, and 1, respectively. With editors of the 3 dailies, the author conducted in-depth interviews, and their views on EFE are presented throughout this book. One of the editors, Anson of *ABC*, had been EFE president (1976–82), and was thus not an objective observer.

E-7.   The 13 private general agencies are: Agencia SEIS, COLPISA, Europa Press, Iberia Press, LID, Logos, Mencheta, Mike Censor, MultiPress, OTR (Off the Record), Radial Press, Reco Press, and Vasco Press. Their preference for Anglicized agency names is noteworthy.

In addition, there were 25 collaborations agencies and 10 photographic agencies. Most of these in all 3 categories were shoe-string operations, except perhaps for Europa Press.

E-8.   Armero interviews, and his letter dated 19 August 1986.

E-9.   Article 19 of "EFE Estatutos," 1984, p. 18. This article on administrative council membership did not change from the earlier statutes of 1981.

E-10.   A cable Utrilla was supposed to have sent, from the Dominican Republic in April 1984, to an EFE manager, urging him to "suppress all reference to the parliamentary control to the [EFE] agency," as the Spanish Congress was debating then the constitutionality of EFE. The alleged cable was reported by the old leading daily of Barcelona, *La Vanguardia*, on 13 June 1984.

E-11.   Boyd-Barrett, *International News Agencies*, p. 34.

E-12.   Ricardo Utrilla, interview, 20 December 1985. This was the author's last day of one-year on-site research at EFE headquarters. Utrilla invited the author to a year-end party for EFE personnel on the Friday before Christmas. The author, with mixed feelings on EFE's future, returned to the United States the next Sunday, 22 December.

E-13.   Ibid.

E-14.   Merrill, et al., *Foreign Press*, p. 37.

E-15.   Boyd-Barrett, *International News Agencies*, pp. 39–40.

E-16.   Charles R. Eisendrath, "France," p. 356. The data on AFP given in nn. E-13, E-14, and E-15 above are admittedly 9 to 30 years old, because of the reticence of AFP executives. Throughout 1986, Jean Burner, international editor-in-chief, and Xavier Baron, *redacteur en chef—France*, responded, with stony silence, to repeated requests from the author for AFP's annual reports or other data. It may have been some kind of AFP policy not to give information to outside inquirers. This question arises, because the author visited AFP Paris headquarters on 5 April 1985, during his European tour of EFE bureaus. Michele Cooper, chief of AFP English language service, a Chicago-born U.S. journalist, spent 2 hours with the author, showing him around the AFP central newsroom and presenting him to the aforementioned AFP editors. Ms. Cooper also failed to respond to the author's written inquiries.

E-17.   Oscar Alzaga Villaamil, letter, 25 August 1987. Deputy Alzaga, president of the Popular Democratic Party (PDP), succeeded in December 1985 in obtaining a concession from the PSOE government to form a committee on EFE, and he was elected to the committee vice chairmanship. Defeated in the June 1986 elections, Alzaga retired from politics, and confided to this author in his letter that the EFE committee had not met a single time in 1-1/2 years.

E-18.   Higueras interview.

E-19.   Mendo interview.

E-20.   Sources for these EFE subscription rates are: *La Tribuna*, EFE contract signed on 11 March 1985; *Opinion*, EFE contract signed on 25 October 1984; Overall EFE rates from Maraña thesis, pp. 566–75.

E-21.   On the 1,600 overseas subscribers for EFE services, there is no single source that can document the number. Schulte cites 1,590, obviously having to depend on EFE sources. Anson counted 1,144 clients abroad in *EFE History and Organization* for 1981. Utrilla never would give any clear information on EFE in his highly "PR-ish" and purposely vague documents. Two documents, one of them undated, given to the author by his "cabinet" in late December 1985 cited 292 Latin American clients for EFE and 57 for ACAN, that add up to mere a 349, a far cry from 1,100–1,600. EFE gave IOJ "about 1,200" as the number of total EFE clients. The conclusion to draw from this confusion is that no number is trustworthy on the number of EFE subscribers. And EFE likes to keep it intentionally "very ambiguous and confusing."

E-22.   The 11 papers were: *La Nación* (Buenos Aires); *Listín Diario* (Santo Domingo); *El Mercurio* (Santiago, Chile); *Presencia (La Paz, Bolivia); El Comercio* (Quito); *La República* (San José, Costa Rica); *El Nuevo Diario* (Managua); *El Universal* and *El Nacional* (Caracas); *El Tiempo* (Bogotá); and *La Estrella de Panamá*. The last 2 were not EFE subscribers.

E-23. LATIN is a regional news agency which the British Reuters helped (financially and administratively) establish in 1971 as a cooperative among 13 member papers from Mexico to Chile. The 2 agencies shared an office in Buenos Aires. Some refer to this as Latin-Reuter (without an "s" at the end). This is a satellite agency like another Reuters subsidiary CANA (Caribbean News Agency) and EFE's ACAN (Central American News Agency). See Michael H. Anderson, "Emerging Patterns of Global News Cooperation," in Jim Richstad and Michael Anderson, eds., *Crisis in International News: Policies and Prospects* (New York, Columbia University Press, 1981), pp. 331–32.

E-24. CIESPAL (International Center for Superior Studies for Latin America) was founded in 1958 by UNESCO as the regional journalism training institution. Participation in CIESPAL programs is highly coveted by Latin professionals.

E-25. Eleazar Díaz Rángel was one-time president of FELAP (Latin American Federation of Journalists), an organization dedicated to search for regional mass communication arrangements "independent of intervention" by multinational, mainly U.S., media systems.

E-26. Fernando Reyes Matta, who has been a prolific writer on of Third World communication "independence" from Western predominance, is director of the Division of Communication Studies of the Instituto Latinoamericano de Estudios Transnacionales (ILET) in Mexico.

E-27. "Royalty Exchange Visits," *Daily Intelligencer/Montgomery County Record* (Pa.), 10 February 1987, p. 2C.

Bibliography

This bibliography is presented in a straight alphabetical order throughout. This is to facilitate the location of information sources, in conjunction with the end-notes in the preceding section.

ABC (Madrid daily), 14 February 1945; 9 December 1946; 26 January & 21 March 1964; 16 January 1966; 1 January 1969; 20 October 1976; 13 July 1983; 3 March & 19 July 1984; 1 February, 11 July, 26 September, & 12 December 1985.

Actualidad Española (Madrid magazine), 23 November 1967.

Agence France-Presse officials (Jean Burner, international editor in chief; Xavier Baron, *redacteur en chef*—France; and Michele Cooper, chief of AFP English language service). Interviews [Paris], 5 April 1985.

Agencia EFE, S.A. "Analisis y Estudios," Control de Publicaciones, November 1985.

————. "Biography" file of Vicente Gallego Castro.

————. "Datos Biográficos de Alejandro Armesto Buz." 20 October 1983.

————. "Delegaciones y Corresponsalías" (4 eds.: 1980, 1981, and March & October 1982).

————. "EFE en Iberoamérica." 1982.

————. "Ejercicio de 1950, Informe." April 1951.

————. *Entre Nosotros.* April 1979.

————. "Estatutos de la Agencia EFE, S.A." Madrid: EFE Publicaciones, 1981 and 1984.

————. *History and Organization.* 1980, 1981, and 1982.

————. *Manual de Español Urgente* (4a edición). Madrid: Ediciones Cátedra, S.A., 1985.

————. *Manual de Estilo* 3d ed. 1981.

————. "Manual de Organización" por Arthur Young, 31 May 1983.

————. "Memoria": 1950; 1962; 1966; 1967; 1971; 1981; 1982; 1983; 1984; and 1985.

————. *1969: Un Año de Desarrollo Constitucional.* Madrid: Agencia EFE, S.A., 1970.

————. "Nota Informativa a la Dirección General de Prensa," 1 February 1946.

————. "Nota para la Subsecretaría de Educación Popular," 6 November 1946.

————. "Resumen, Informe sobre Penetración de las Agencias Internacionales en América Latina," April 1984.

————. "Semblanza Biográfica de Carlos Mendo," 12 February 1976.

"Agenzia ANSA, Relazioni e Bilancio al 31 Dicembre 1984."

El Alcázar (Madrid daily), 12 June & 23 September 1963; 14 January 1969; 6 January 1978; 1 June 1979; 1 February 1985.

Altabella Hernández, José. "Notas para la prehistoria de las agencias de prensa en España," *Estudios de Información.* Enero–Junio 1972 (Nos. 21–22). Madrid: Instituto de la Opinión Pública.

Alzaga Villaamil, Oscar (Spanish congress deputy and president of Partido Demócrata Popular—PDP). "Interpelación en las Cortes," 13 March 1985.

――――. "Interpelación en las Cortes," 25 September 1985.
――――. Letter, 25 August 1987.
――――. "Moción Legislativa," 20 March 1985.
Anderson, Michael. "Emerging Patterns of Global News Cooperation." In Jim Richstad and Michael Anderson, eds., *Crisis in International News: Policies and Prospects*. New York: Columbia University Press, 1981, pp. 317-43.
"AP Fact Sheet #2," AP Corporate Communications, 7 December 1983.
Arias-Salgado de Cubas, Gabriel (Spanish Minister of Information and Tourism 1951–1962). *Textos de Doctrina y Política de la Información*, 3 vols. Madrid: Ministerio de Información y Turismo, 1960.
Armero Alcántara, José Mario. Letter of 19 August 1986.
Arriba (defunct Madrid daily), 24 October 1940; 20 August 1947; 12 June 1963; 22 September & 20 December 1963; 21 March & 8 May 1964; 9 March & 27 October 1965; 5 August 1966; 25 April, 19 July & 25 April 1968.
Aznar Zubigaray, Manuel. (EFE president 1968–1976). *Historia Militar de la Guerra de España*. Madrid: Ediciones Idea, S.A., 1940.
Boletín Oficial del Estado (Spanish State Bulletin). 15 May 1964; 10 May 1982; 3 August 1984.
Bolin, Luis (Franco's press officer 1936). *Spain: The Vital Years*. London: Cassell, 1967.
Boyd-Barrett, Oliver. *The International News Agencies*. Beverly Hills, Calif.: SAGE, 1980.
Bustamante Ramírez, Enrique. *Los Amos de la Información en España*. Madrid: AKAL Editor, 1982.
Cambio 16 (Madrid weekly news magazine), 17 October 1976.
Castro Bobillo, Antonio. *Elementos Básicos para el Análisis de la Censura Cinematográfica Estatal en España desde 1936 hasta Nuestros Días. Unpublished thesis, Facultad de Ciencias de la Información, Universidad Complutense, 1980*.
Cendan Pazos, Fernando. *Historia del Derecho Español de Prensa e Imprenta (1502–1966)*. Madrid: Editora Nacional, 1974.
Cinco Días (Madrid business daily), 19 July 1978; 9 March 1985.
"Constitución Española". Madrid: Rivadeneira, S.A., 1978.
Cortada, James W., ed. *Historical Dictionary of the Spanish Civil War, 1936–1939*. Westport, Conn.: Greenwood, 1982.
Crónica de Un Año de España (18 julio 1968–1918 julio 1969). Madrid: SIE, 1969.
Crozier, Brian. *Franco*. Boston: Little, Brown, 1967.
Delibes, Miguel. *La Censura de Prensa en los Años 40*. Madrid: Ambito Ediciones, S.A., 1985.
Diario de Barcelona (defunct Barcelona daily), 12 March 1964.
Diario 16 (Madrid daily), 20 October & 27 October 1981; 26 December 1982; 16 March & 29 June 1983; 23 July 1984; 16 & 19 February 1985.
Diccionario de la Lengua Española. Madrid: Real Academia Española, 1970.
Dígame (defunct Madrid magazine), 10 September 1940.
Dueñas, Gonzalo. *La Ley de Prensa de Manuel Fraga Iribarne*. Paris: Editorial Ruedo Iberico, 1969.
Editor & Publisher, 21 September 1985.
Eisendrath, Charles R "France" in George Thomas Kurian, ed., *World Press Encyclopedia*, 2 vols. New York: Facts on File, 1982, volume I, pp. 341-360.
Emery, Edwin, and Michael Emery. *The Press and America*. Englewood Cliffs, N.J.: Prentice-Hall, 1984.
Espina, Antonio. *El Cuarto Poder*. Madrid: Aguilar, 1960 (as cited by Schulte, 1968).
Fernández Areal, Manuel. *Libertad de Prensa en España (1938–1971)*. Madrid: Editorial Cuadernos para el Diálogo, S.A., 1968.
Fernández Pombo, Alejandro. "La Agencia Prensa Asociada Fue Fundada en 1909," *Gaceta de la Prensa Española*, 15 November 1964 (as cited by Schulte, 1968).
Foltz, Jr., Charles. *The Masquerade in Spain*. Boston: Houghton Mifflin, 1948.
Gaceta de la Prensa Española (Spanish press journal), 15 September 1968.
Gallo, Max. *Spain under Franco: A History* (translated from French by Jean Stewart). New

York: E. P. Dutton, 1974.

Garriga, Ramón. *La España de Franco*. Vol. 1, *Las Relaciones con Hitler*. Madrid: G. del Toro, Editor, 1976.

———. *La España de Franco*. Vol. 2, *De la División Azul al Triunfo Aliado*. Madrid: G. del Toro, Editor, 1976.

Giménez-Arnau Gran, José Antonio (an EFE founder). *Memorias de Memoria*. Barcelona: Ediciones Destino, 1978.

Gíner Junquera, Juan Antonio. "Journalists, Mass Media, and Public Opinion in Spain, 1938–1982." In Kenneth Maxwell, ed. *The Press and the Rebirth of Iberian Democracy*. Westport, Conn.: Greenwood, 1983, pp. 33-54.

Gómez Aparicio, Pedro (EFE director 1944–1954). "Agencias de Prensa." Madrid: Club de Prensa "Círculo Jaime Balmes," 1955.

———. *Historia del Periodismo Español*, 4 vols. Vol. 2, *De la Revolución de Septiembre al Desastre Colonial*. Madrid: Editora Nacional, 1971.

———. *Historia del Periodismo Español*, 4 vols. Vol. 4, *De la Dictadura a la Guerra Civil*. Madrid: Editora Nacional, 1981.

Gramling, Oliver. *AP—The Story of News*. Port Washington, N.Y.: Kannikat, 1969.

Hayes, Carlton J. H. [U.S.] *Wartime Mission in Spain*. New York: Macmillan, 1945.

Higueras Cleries, Miguel (EFE news director, 1986). *La Agencia EFE y la Información de España al Exterior*. Unpublished graduation thesis, Escuela Oficial de Periodismo. Madrid: Ministry of Culture Central Archive, 1967.

Hills, George. *Franco: The Man and His Nation*. New York: Macmillan, 1967.

Hoare, Samuel. [UK] *Ambassador on Special Mission*. London: Collins, 1946.

Hoja del Lunes de Madrid, 22 October 1979.

Informaciones (defunct Madrid daily), 28 November 1946.

International Organization of Journalists (IOJ). *Handbook of News Agencies in the World*. Prague: IOJ Books Dept., 1986.

———. *News Letter* (Prague). June 1986, no. 11.

Keesing's Contemporary Archives, vol. 31, no. 10, 1985.

Kurian, George Thomas, ed. *World Press Encyclopedia*, 2 vols. New York: Facts on File, 1982.

Lloyd, Alan. *Franco*. Garden City, N.Y.: Doubleday, 1969.

Maraña Marcos, Felipe. *La Información Internacional en España*. 3 vols. Unpublished doctoral thesis, Facultad de Ciencias de la Información, Universidad Complutense, 1984.

Maxwell, Kenneth. "Introduction: The Transition to Democracy in Spain and Portugal." In Kenneth, Maxwell, ed., *The Press and the Rebirth of Iberian Democracy*. Westport, Conn.: Greenwood, 1983, pp. 1-30.

Merrill, John; Carter Bryan; and Marvin Alisky. *The Foreign Press*. Baton Rouge: Louisiana State University Press, 1970.

Ministerio de Información y Turismo (MIT) (Secretaría Técnica). *Gobierno Informa*. Madrid: Editora Nacional, 1964.

———. *Textos Legales: Prensa*. Madrid: Editora Nacional, 1969.

Moliner, María. *Diccionario de Uso del Español*, 2 vols. Madrid: Editorial Gredos, S.A., 1971, vol. 2.

Molinero, César. *La Intervención del Estado en la Prensa*. Madrid: DOPESA, 1971.

Montero-Ríos y Rodríguez, Juan. *De Fabra A EFE*. Unpublished graduation thesis, Escuela Oficial de Periodismo. Madrid: Ministry of Culture Central Archive, 1956.

Mostaza, Bartolomé (Falange press official). "Nota para el Delegado Nacional." 3 May 1950.

Nieto Tamargo, Alfonso. *La Empresa Periodística en España*. Pamplona, Spain: Ediciones Universidad de Navarra, S.A., 1973.

"1986 World Population Data Sheet." Washington, D.C.: Population Reference Bureau, 1986.

1970 Book of the Year of the Encyclopaedia Britannica. Chicago: Encyclopaedia Britannica, 1970.

"Nota Biográfica de Anson," in "Boletín Mensual de Información." Madrid: Dawson y Fry, March 1981.

Nuevo Diario (defunct Madrid daily), 10 October 1969; 30 September 1973.

Oxford English Dictionary, 8 vols. London: Oxford University Press, 1971.

El País (leading Madrid daily), 25 June 1976; 31 May 1979; 24 November 1981; 13 July 1983; 31 January, 14, 16, & 19 February, 12 December 1985.

PBS program, "Spain Ten Years After," as aired by WETA-Channel of Washington, D.C., at various times in March–April 1986.

Picard, Robert G. "Levels of State Intervention in the Western Press," *Mass Comm Review*, vol. 11, nos. 1/2, Winter–Spring 1984.

Pincus, Walter. "CIA Funding Journalistic Network Abroad," the *Washington Post*, 16 January 1976.

Prados y López, Manuel. *Etica y Estética del Periodismo Español*. Madrid: Editorial Espasa-Calpe, 1943.

El Progreso (defunct Madrid daily), 12 March 1964.

Pueblo (defunct Madrid daily), 22 February & 10 April 1967; 13 March 1968; 3 January 1979.

Reuters. *Reuters Holdings PLC, Offer for Sale by Tender*. 1984.

Rodríguez Couceiro, José Antonio (EFE Mexico bureau chief). *Proyección en las Américas de la Agencia EFE*. Unpublished graduation thesis, Escuela Oficial de Periodismo. Madrid: Ministry of Culture Central Archive, 1967.

"Royalty Exchange Visits," *Daily Intelligencer/Montgomery County Record* (Pa.) (an AP Wire), 10 February 1987.

Rubio, José Luis. "Agencia Norteamericana Nos Separa de Hispanoamerica," *Juventud*, 11 December 1953.

Santamaria, Francisco J. *Diccionario General de Americanismos*. 2 vols. Mexico, D.F.: Editorial Pedro Robredo, 1942.

Schulte, Henry F. *The Spanish Press, 1470–1966*. Urbana: University of Illinois Press, 1968.

———. "Spain." In George Thomas Kurian, ed. *World Press Encyclopedia*, 2 vols. New York: Facts on File, 1982, vol 2, pp. 807–820.

Seco, Manuel. *Diccionario de Dudas y Dificultades de la Lengua Española*. Madrid: Aguilar, S.A., de Ediciones, 1965.

Serrano Súñer, Ramón (Spanish Civil-War interior minister and EFE's Godfather) *De la Victoria y la Postguerra: Discursos*. Madrid: Ediciones FE, 1941.

———. *Entre Hendaya y Gibraltar*. Madrid: Ediciones y Publicaciones Españolas, S.A., 1947.

———. *Entre el Silencio y la Propaganda, la Historia Cómo Fue: Memorias*. Barcelona: Editorial Planeta, 1977.

Sotomayor y Ojeda, José. *La Información Nacional de la Agencia EFE*. Unpublished graduation thesis, Escuela Oficial de Periodismo. Madrid: Ministry of Culture Central Archive, 1963.

SP (defunct Madrid weekly news magazine), 10 July 1966.

"Television and Radio," *1983 Britannica Book of the Year*. Chicago: Encyclopaedia Britannica, 1983.

Thomas, Hugh. *The Spanish Civil War*. New York: Harper and Row, 1977.

Utrilla Carlón, Ricardo (EFE president, 1983–86). "ACAN: Una Pequeña Gran Agencia para Centro América." Speech, at the Universidad Internacional Menéndez Pelayo of Santander, Spain, 19 July 1984.

———. "Discurso sobre EFE." Testimony before the Congressional Committee on Public Administration, 21 May 1985.

La Vanguardia (Barcelona daily), 2 September 1978; 13 June 1984; 26 September 1985.

Washington Post, 19 February 1976.

Webber, Lloyd, and Tim Rice. "Don't Cry for Me, Argentina!" Title song for the 1976 musical play, *Evita*.

"World Data," *1989 Britannica Book of the Year*. Chicago: Encyclopaedia Britannica, 1989.

Worldwatch (London weekly), 9 December 1985.

Ya (Madrid Catholic daily), 14 February 1945; 13 April 1948; 12 May 1978; 24 December 1982; 2 February, 17 March, & 26 September 1985.

Interviewees

Accornero, Arrigo, Dr. (ANSA vice director). Rome, 26 April, 1985.

Agence France-Presse officials (Jean Burner, international editor, in chief; Xavier Baron, *redacteur en chef*—France; and Michele Cooper, chief of AFP English language service). Paris, 5 April 1985.

Aizpitarte, Gemma (EFE Warsaw correspondent). Warsaw, 20 and 31, October 1985.

Alberca Alberca, Alberto (EFE Moscow correspondent). Moscow, 23, October 1985.

Aldazabal, Ramón (EFE Moscow bureau interpreter-driver). Moscow, 23 October 1985.

Anson Oliart, Luis María (EFE president 1976–1982 and *ABC*, director). Madrid, 18 December 1985.

Armero Alcántara, José Mario. (owner and president of Spain's biggest private news agency, Europa Press). Madrid, December 1985.

Aznarez Mozaz, Juan Jesús (EFE Havana bureau chief). Interviews, Havana, 19-21 September 1985.

Barroso Asenjo, Porfirio (Spanish journalism-law professor). Madrid, 11 November 1985.

Candanedo Acosta, Rafael (Panamanian EFE reporter). Madrid, November 1985.

Cebrián, Juan Luis (editor, *El País*). Madrid, 10 December 1985.

Covarrubias, Luis F. (Washington director of UPI/EFE radio news, "Nuestras Noticias"). Washington, 22 August 1985.

De la Cruz Serna, Tomás (president, Spain's Alas advertising agency chain). Pamplona, Spain, 15 March 1985.

De la Rica Gruber, Charo (EFE presidential chief of staff). Madrid, 12 December 1985.

Del Corral, Jorge (EFE Rome bureau chief). Rome, 26 and 27 April, 1985.

De Mier, Waldo (EFE subdirector, 1957–1970). Madrid, 12 November, 1985.

García Herrera, Ernesto (EFE Paris bureau chief). Paris, 2 and 3, April 1985.

García Marrder, Alberto (EFE Washington bureau chief). Washington, D.C., 22 August 1985.

Giménez-Arnau Gran, Enrique (EFE's CPA). Madrid, 18 December, 1985.

González, María Luisa (EFE Moscow bureau acting chief). Moscow, 23 October 1985.

González González, José (SEIS agency director). Survey response, of November–December 1985.

Group interview with the EFE "Old Guard" (José Luis García, Gallego; Jesús Martínez Tessier; and Francisco del Valle Arroyo). Madrid EFE headquarters, 14 November 1985.

Higueras Cleries, Miguel (EFE news director, 1986). Madrid, December 1985.

Joannides, Alexandre (Reuters European Media Service manager). London, 17 April 1985.

Martínez Flores, Filadelfo (ACAN-EFE Managua bureau chief). Managua, 11 September 1985.

Mendo Baos, Carlos (EFE director 1965–1969). Madrid, 5 December, 1985.

Mora, Manuel R. (EFE Panama bureau chief and ACAN-EFE director). Panama City, 16 September 1985.

Olmos, Víctor (EFE executive). Madrid, 17 December 1985.

Ortiz, Fabian (EFE London bureau chief). London, 15 April 1985.

Oyrzabal, José Ignacio (Madrid publishing house official). Madrid, 15 November 1985.

Porter, Dwight (EFE English language service editor). Madrid, 12, December 1985.

Poveda Longo, Alberto (secretary of EFE administrative council). Madrid, 6–21 November 1985.

Ramírez, Pedro J. (editor, *Diario 16*). Madrid, 15 October 1985.

Rodríguez, José (EFE Manila bureau chief). Madrid, 2 November, 1985.

Rodríguez Couceiro, José Antonio (EFE Mexico bureau chief). Mexico City, 9 September 1985.

Roldán, José Luis (EFE labor union chief, 1983–1986). Madrid, 16, December 1985.

Royo Masía, Vicente (EFE lawyer). Madrid, November 1985.

RTVE officials (José Luis Rodríguez Fraguas, technical cabinet, chief; Ignacio Lasa Irola, secretary). Madrid, 20 March, 1985.

Rubio, María Luisa (EFE Athens correspondent). Athens, 22 April, 1985.

Serrano Súñer, Ramón (Spanish Civil War interior minister and, EFE's godfather). Madrid, 27 November 1985.

Utrilla Carlón, Ricardo (EFE president, 1983–1986). Madrid, 20, December 1985.

Velasco López, Manuel "Manolo." (EFE executive and managing editor) Conversations during the months of 1985; interview on 17 December 1985.

Index

About the Author

SOON JIN KIM worked in Central America for 14 years (1961–1974) as a foreign correspondent and as a founding foreign-news editor of the Guatemalan daily, *La Nación*. Kim also taught journalism at the University of El Salvador. During this journalistic sojourn in the Isthmus, Kim used the news services of EFE and its subsidiary, ACAN (Agencia Centro Americana de Noticias).

His research interests on international news agencies grew out of this experience, and also from his concern for the Third-World claim for a New World Information and Communication Order (NWICO). His work on EFE was supported by a $20,000 Tinker Foundation grant, which accorded him 1985 residence at EFE's Madrid headquarters and also travels to EFE bureaus in Western and Eastern Europe, the Americas, and the Far East.

Born in Korea and educated in Japan, Kim holds a master's degree in journalism (University of Missouri) and a doctorate in American Studies (University of Maryland). Kim has taught journalism and international communication at Towson State University in Baltimore since 1975.